The New Voice Pedagogy

by
Marilee David

The Scarecrow Press, Inc.
Lanham, Maryland, and London

SCARECROW PRESS, INC.

Published in the United States of America
by Scarecrow Press, Inc.
4720 Boston Way, Lanham, Maryland 20706
www.scarecrowpress.com

4 Pleydell Gardens, Folkestone
Kent CT20 2DN, England

British Library Cataloguing in Publication Information Available

The hardback edition of this book was previously cataloged by the Library of
Congress as follows:

David, Marilee, 1944-
The new voice pedagogy / by Marilee David.
p.   cm.
Includes bibliographical references.
1. Singing—Instruction and study.   2. Singing—Physiological
aspects.   3. Voice—Care and hygiene.   I. Title.
MT820.D245   1995   783'.043'07—dc20   94--30743

ISBN: 0-8108-2943-6 (cloth : alk. paper)

ISBN: 0-8108-4391-9 (paper)

Manufactured in the United States of America.

To all those who sing and teach others to sing because of a love of their art, regardless of the world's recognition of their efforts.

Contents

Illustrations

Acknowledgments

I owe an immense debt of gratitude to libraries and librarians all over the country. I would particularly like to thank the Robert Woodruff Health Sciences Center Library of Emory University in Decatur, Georgia, for access to their reading room and materials; the Dunwoody Branch of the DeKalb County Library System in Atlanta, Georgia, and the library of Armstrong State College in Savannah, Georgia, for helping me to obtain materials through inter-library loan; the libraries which provided those materials; the Music Library of Indiana University at Bloomington, particularly Carol Crowley McCormick, who helped me locate journals available in only two libraries in the U.S.A.; and the music librarian at the State University of New York at Stoneybrook who graciously sent me the information from these journals at no charge. I offer special thanks to my friend, Mr. Keith Nash, who helped me with the intricacies of Emory University's library system.

I would like to thank the publishers and authors who allowed me to reproduce drawings from other publications. The ability to reproduce these drawings was the deciding factor in bringing this book to publication. Thank you also to the employee of Kinko's Copy Center in Sandy Springs, north of Atlanta, who helped me do computer scans on five of the drawings. He patiently taught me to use the equipment so that I could get good pictures easily without undue expense. My thanks to Patricia King, Secretary to the Music Ministry of Dunwoody Baptist Church and to the Dunwoody School for the Arts, who, once again, solved a problem for me -- this time by reproducing an illustration on the graphics program of her computer. I am particularly grateful to Dr. Bill Grist of the otolaryngology department of Emory University who provided me with a still photograph of the larynx from his file of stroboscopic tapes.

I also owe a great deal to the many teachers and coaches who assisted me in building vocal technique and musicianship and who served as models for my own teaching, which is the core of this book. I have been fortunate to find the right person at the right

time. Special acknowledgments go to Dr. Robert Olson, retired
from North Dakota State University in Fargo, and Oren Brown,
retired from The Julliard School in New York City. Mr. Brown
was one of the pioneers who saw the potential benefits in learning
about voice therapy and vocal health. My attendance at his
seminar in 1975 was my first introduction to this remarkable and
fascinating field. Many of the exercises and concepts in this book
originated with Mr. Brown and were taught to me by Dr. Robert
Olson, with whom I studied when I lived and taught in Moorhead,
Minnesota. I have also included Dr. Olson's original vocalises and
concepts. I am also indebted to Ms. Gianna d'Angelo, my teacher
at Indiana University at Bloomington, who polished what all the
others had started. The sections on breathing and placement
include many of the concepts and exercises which she taught me
and which she continues to teach to others.

Like all teachers, I owe a great deal to my students who, over
the years, have proven the effectiveness of teaching in the manner
described in this volume. In many cases, their needs inspired
development or alteration of a particular exercise or concept, once
again proving that necessity is truly the mother of invention.

Finally, I must thank the many friends who offered literally
YEARS of support on this project. I am particularly indebted to
my friends Karen Bryan, Ph.D., and Wayne Bryan. They were
there when the rejections came and there to celebrate when the
contract came. In addition they helped me to select and purchase
my computer and printer and made available to me their computer
for production of musical examples and their laser printer for
printing the final copy of the book. The first copy off the press is
theirs!

Introduction

A musician's artistry and range of expression is determined in part by the quality of the instrument on which he or she performs and the performer's technical abilities on that instrument. Singers are unique among musicians because our instruments are part of our bodies. This, however, poses many problems. Not only are we unable to exchange or alter these instruments, they are hidden so that we cannot even examine them or their workings. And, because they are part of a living organism, our instruments are subject to the same ebb and flow of influences that affect the rest of our bodies.

Over the centuries many have tried to penetrate the mystique of the human voice, first via the laryngoscope and, more recently, using various instruments of measurement and analysis. However, the majority of singers and voice teachers have remained happily uninformed about the workings of the larynx and the vocal tract, preferring to leave that understanding to the medical community and the few voice teachers and voice scientists who choose to do research. With only a general understanding of the anatomy and function of the respiratory and vocal tracts, past generations of teachers taught traditional methods handed down through a long line of teachers and singers. Many of these techniques are wonderfully effective in spite of the users' lack of understanding of the why of such effectiveness. Others are not only ineffective over the long term but potentially damaging to the health and longevity of the voice.

In recent years the education of singers and voice teachers has improved dramatically. It is now virtually impossible for a singer or voice teacher to embark on a career without some college or conservatory training, and many have studied at the graduate level. At the same time, scientific research has given us a more thorough understanding of the structure and function of the respiratory and vocal tracts as they relate to singing. The new generations of singers and voice teachers are more inclined to ask questions and less inclined to accept traditional teaching methods without an understanding of why they are being asked to do certain exercises.

The emergence of voice therapy as a discipline independent of speech therapy has given rise to a new awareness on the part of the human voice for harm. Many voice teachers have developed an interest in vocal health and in working with singers who have sustained laryngeal damage through incorrect singing or faulty use of the speaking voice. Still others are becoming aware of the inadequacy of teaching exercises simply because they have always been taught. We are learning new ways to teach old techniques so that the beauty of the individual voice can be developed to the utmost without compromising its health and longevity.

Out of these various factors a new voice pedagogy is emerging which is based on an understanding of the structure and function of the vocal and respiratory tracts of the human body. This new pedagogy makes use of information from a variety of fields. From laryngology we have learned more about body structures and functions, what the effects of abuse and misuse of those structures do medically and the treatments required to restore health. From voice therapy we first learned what could go wrong with the voice and what should be done to fix it. This knowledge has evolved into a systematic understanding of proper voice use in order to avoid laryngeal damage before it happens. From voice science we have learned to quantify and assess the various functions of the laryngeal and respiratory mechanisms in both normal and disused voices. Most recently, voice science has begun to quantify and verify the activities used by professional singers and to determine why and how singers are able to perform the feats required for artistic achievement.

The goal of the studio voice teacher is, and always has been, to develop the individual student's talent to the fullest. This means providing that student with a technique which will produce a free and beautiful tone and the artistry and poise to express text and music. Many of us work towards this goal using the information gained from the above-mentioned sources. Although the individual methods and exercises may differ from studio to studio, the concepts are basically the same. This book provides one person's overview of this new approach to singing and teaching of singing and the sources of information from which this new approach is derived. Vocal exercises are offered as examples to clarify the ideas presented and to stimulate the reader to reapply or invent his or her own vocalises. The author has attempted to summarize the literature of the related fields and to provide needed information for the studio teacher who may not wish to read the literature of those fields. Teachers and singers who wish to delve deeper into that literature can use the citations in the text and bibliography as guides for further reading.

Chapter 7, "When the Voice Is Sick: Therapy and Dysphonias," is included for two reasons. This information is encountered in nearly every book on voice therapy. Omitting it would significantly reduce the reader's understanding of that field. Only those dysphonias which are attributable to abuse and/or by which singers are affected are included. Thus, information on structural deformities, such as cleft palate and partial or total laryngectomies, is not included. The information in this chapter is also included to increase the teacher's and singer's awareness of the ramification and symptoms of abuse, keeping in mind that only examination by a qualified medical professional can determine the health of the vocal cords.

Just as a voice therapist or laryngologist who is not a trained singer does not try to teach singing techniques to clients or patients who are singers or singing students, so the voice teacher who is not qualified should not try to do voice therapy in the studio. Voice therapists are licensed by the state in which they practice and work closely with the medical community, often in a hospital or clinic setting. The purpose of this book is to enhance the voice teacher's teaching of singing technique to students with healthy voices. Because the author has had experience in retraining the singing techniques of singers who have incurred vocal damage, she is acutely aware of the responsibility involved in such activity. Teachers who wish to work with these singers must have a strong anatomical background and should work with the singer's laryngologist and voice therapist. This is not something to be undertaken lightly.

The fields of voice therapy, laryngology, and voice science use anatomical and technical terms which may be new to some singers and voice teachers. Such terms are italicized for easy identification and study the first time they are used in the text.

Chapter 1

The Larynx: Structure and Functions

Voice is produced by the larynx which is located in the throat.   It sits horizontally across the windpipe or *trachea* so that the opening (*glottis*) extends from back to front.   The top two rings of that trachea, the cricoid and thyroid cartilages, form the framework of the larynx.

The ability to communicate through speech and the written word is one of the more noticeable factors that separates humans from lower animals.   And yet speech is not the primary function of the human larynx.   The larynx is a sphincter, an evolved constrictor-dilator mechanism capable of a variety of functions.   One of its most primitive functions is to seal off the respiratory tract below it so that foreign materials cannot enter the lungs and bronchi (Fried & Miller, 1988, p. 41).   Laryngeal closure also acts as a seal to fix the amount of air in the lungs and thus the position of the chest wall for muscular effort by the arms and shoulders.   It provides adequate intrathoracic pressure for such functions as lifting and throat clearing and abdominal compression to aid in urination, defecation, and childbirth (Aronson, 1985, p. 3;   Fried & Miller, 1988, p. 49).   The release of this pressure causes the involuntary sounds which we sometimes make when lifting or pushing heavy objects or in association with bodily functions.

Speech may be seen as a secondary or as an "overlaid function" for which we use "equipment that was 'designed' for basic biological survival -- breathing, swallowing, chewing and the like"   but which has been adapted for oral communication (Perkins & Kent, 1986, p. 8).   All laryngeal activities necessary for speech and song are borrowed activities.   To produce voiced sounds, the true vocal folds must close just enough to vibrate when air pressure builds to the proper level below them.   For unvoiced consonants the larynx must open to allow "bursts and hisses of noise" (Perkins & Kent, 1986, p. 65).   The same is true of other structures involved in speaking and singing.   The muscles controlling the jaw and the teeth against which many consonants are formed are primarily for chewing.   The tongue which forms those consonants acts as a food carrier as part of the act of swallowing.   And the soft palate separates

1

the nose from the mouth so food will not enter the sinuses and so
breathing can continue during chewing.

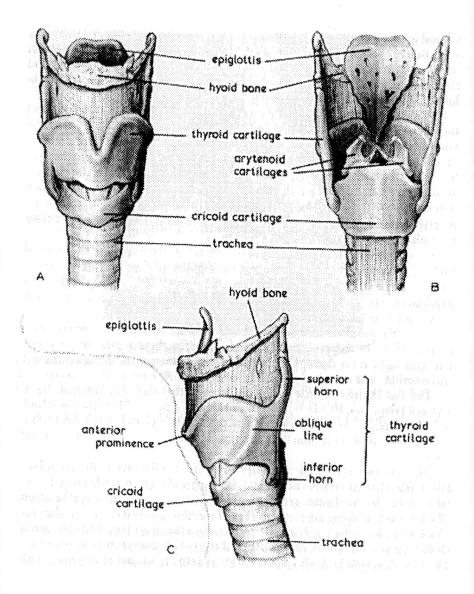

Fig. 1. Cartilages of the larynx
From *Dynamics of the Singing Voice*, Meribeth Bunch, 1982, Fig. 35, p. 56.
Published by Springer-Verlag. Used by permission.

Cartilages of the Larynx

The *thyroid cartilage* is the largest and topmost cartilage of the larynx. It is in two halves or "wings" (laminae) which join in the front (anterior) to form the "Adam's apple" (isthmus) and the thyroid notch. These laminae extend a bit over halfway around the tracheal opening. Each wing has, at its back edge, a superior cornu which extends up and a short inferior cornu which extends down. The thyroid cartilage is more noticeable in men because the larynx is larger and because the angle formed by the laminae is sharper. In men the wings of the thyroid cartilage form a 90° angle, and in women they form a 120° angle. The isthmus of the thyroid cartilage sits at an angle to the horizontal, so that in the adult male it tilts approximately 60° downward and backward (Fried and Miller, 1988, p. 42).

The *cricoid cartilage* is the only tracheal ring that forms a complete circle (Perkins & Kent, 1986, p. 66). It is shaped like a signet ring with the wider portion in the back (posterior). It is positioned so that the thyroid cartilage is above it in the front, with the inferior cornu of the thyroid cartilage extending over the outside and about halfway down the lateral posteriors of the cricoid cartilage. This is because of the widening of the cricoid cartilage in the back. The inferior cornu of the thyroid cartilage articulates with (joins) the cricoid cartilage via synovial joints. Movement of the cricoid cartilage on these joints affects the angle between the isthmus of the thyroid and the anterior aspect of the cricoid cartilage (Fried & Miller, 1988, p. 44).

The two *arytenoid cartilages* are positioned on top of the sides of the widest portion of the cricoid cartilage. In appearance these cartilages resemble extracted canine teeth with the base of each divided into two parts or *processes*: the posterior muscular process and the anterior vocal process to which the true vocal cords are attached. The arytenoid cartilages are capable of two movements. The entire cartilages can slide away from or towards each other on the slope of the cricoid cartilage (Fried and Miller, 1988, p. 46), and their tops can rock towards or away from each other (Perkins & Kent, 1986, p. 69).

The vocal processes of the arytenoid cartilages are extremely important in vocal fold physiology. Because the tip of each vocal process attaches to the posterior end of the membranous vocal folds, their position in large part determines the position, shape, tension and mechanics of those vocal folds and the shape and size of the glottis (Hirano et al., 1985, p. 3). Elastic cartilage is found at the tip of the vocal process extending up to and including the point of the top of the cartilage. Cartilage at the ends of the vocal processes assists in *adduction* (closing) of the vocal folds by bending inwardly and *abduction* (opening) by bending outwardly. The elastic cartilage at the top of the arytenoid appears to cushion the arytenoids and their cover from mechanical damage that might occur when they come into contact (Sato, Hirano, Kurita, & Kiyokawa, 1990, p. 368).

The *corniculate cartilages* (*Cartilages of Santorini*) are two small cartilages situated on the top of the arytenoid cartilages. They are similar in shape to the arytenoids with the top point of each slightly hooked toward the center of the glottis. They provide protection for the arytenoid cartilages (Schneiderman, 1984, p. 59).

External cartilages. The *epiglottis* is attached to the inside of the front (anterosuperior aspect) of the thyroid cartilage. It broadens and extends upwards like a leaf or spade and is able to fold down and seal the trachea to keep food out of the lungs and airways. Within the membrane which slopes down from the top of the epiglottis to the posterior of the larynx are the *cuneiform cartilages* (*Cartilages of Wrisberg*). These are small, rod-shaped elastic cartilages that give support to that membrane (Schneiderman, 1984, p. 59).

The *hyoid bone* is located in the base of the tongue. It forms a broad U with a posterior opening. The ends of the U are considered the greater cornu, and lateral projections on the top of the base of the U are considered lesser cornu (Gray, 1974, pp. 122-123).

The Laryngeal Folds
The larynx appears as a series of five folds of mucous membranes supported by elastic tissues and membranes. Three of these are actually pairs of symmetrical folds on either side of the glottis. One pair, the vocal folds, form the glottis. The other four folds, two paired and two unpaired, are above the level of the glottis (supraglottic). With the epiglottis, the *aryepiglottic folds* make up the entry into the larynx. During reflexive closure of the airway, their side walls collapse at the midline as the epiglottis folds down (Putnam & Shelton, 1985, p. 94). The two unpaired supraglottic folds are the *interarytenoid fold*, which lies posteriorly between the arytenoids and contains the arytenoid muscles, and the *median thyrohyoid fold* containing numerous supporting structures between the thyroid and hyoid cartilages (Fried & Miller, pp. 48-49). The *vestibular folds* or *false vocal cords* are the second set of paired supraglottic folds. These are wedge-shaped and extend into the glottic airway almost like shelves. They extend from the arytenoid cartilages in the back of the larynx to the isthmus of the thyroid cartilage in the front (Fried & Miller, 1988, p. 48). They are involved in sealing the larynx. The *true vocal folds*, the final pair of folds, extend from the vocal processes of the arytenoid cartilages to the inside

of the thyroid cartilages. The space between the vestibular folds and
the true vocal folds is known as the *laryngeal ventrical.*

Suspension of the Larynx

The laryngeal structure is suspended in the neck by ligaments
and membranes. Ligaments, membranes and muscles usually take
their names from the bones and cartilages they connect. Stylohyoid
ligaments attach the lesser horns of the hyoid bone to the styloid
process of the skull. The lateral thyrohyoid ligaments connect the
superior horns of the thyroid cartilage to the greater horns of the
hyoid bone and the thyrohyoid membranes attach the hyoid bone to
the thyroid cartilage (Fried & Miller, 1988, pp. 47-48). The
epiglottis is attached to the hyoid bone by the hyoepiglottic ligament
(Saunders, 1964, p. 76).

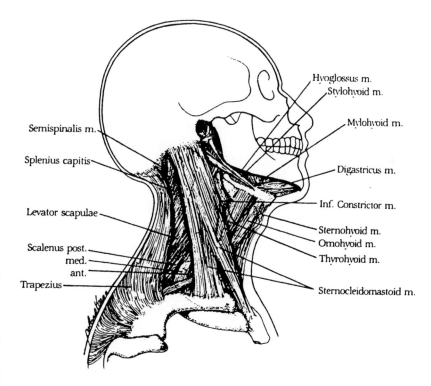

Fig. 2. The extrinsic laryngeal muscles
From *The Larynx: A Multidisciplinary Approach*, Marvin P. Fried (Ed.), 1988,
Fig. 4-11, p. 50. Published by Little, Brown & Company. Used by permission.

Extrinsic Muscles of the Larynx

The extrinsic muscles of the larynx are those which attach it to the body and which are capable of altering its position as a unit. Elevation of the larynx occurs during swallowing and may occur when high pitches are sung. It is caused by contraction of the *suprahyoid muscles*. They include the *stylohyoid, digastric, geniohyoid* and *stylopharyngeus* muscles (Fried & Miller, 1988, p. 49). Contraction of the *thyrohyoid muscle* shortens the distance between the larynx and the hyoid bone and assists in elevation of the larynx. Lowering the elevated larynx is accomplished by the *infrahyoid muscles* which act as antagonists to the suprahyoid group. The infrahyoids include the *omohyoid, sternohyoid* and *sternothyroid* muscles (Fried & Miller, 1988, p. 49; Saunders, 1964, p. 76). Laryngeal position affects the relationships of the laryngeal cartilages and the intrinsic muscles attached to them. Therefore these extrinsic muscles are critical to maintaining a stable laryngeal skeleton to enable the intrinsic muscles, including the vocal cords themselves, to work effectively (Sataloff, 1987a, p. 92).

Intrinsic Muscles of the Larynx

The intrinsic muscles of the larynx are those that are attached at both ends to cartilages of the larynx and that move those cartilages in relationship to each other. They include the *thyroarytenoid muscles*, the *cricothyroid muscles*, the *cricoarytenoid muscles*, and the *arytenoid muscles*. Working in various combinations, the intrinsic muscles are capable of three actions affecting the vocal cords: opening or separating them (abduction), closing or approximating them (adduction) and altering their mass, length and tension. Like all muscles, when the intrinsic muscles are contracted they become shorter and thicker.

The *thyroarytenoid muscles* form the edges of the glottis. They originate on the inside face of the isthmus of the thyroid cartilage, where they are fixed together, and extend across the trachea to the arytenoid cartilages. Each muscle is in two parts.

> The difference in the two parts of the thyroarytenoid depends on where they insert into the arytenoid cartilage. The internal thyroarytenoid inserts into the vocal process, the external part into the muscular process. These external fibers do not participate directly in vocal fold vibration. The affect of their contraction apparently is to shorten and adduct the vocal folds thereby closing the muscular glottis. (Perkins & Kent, 1986, p. 70)

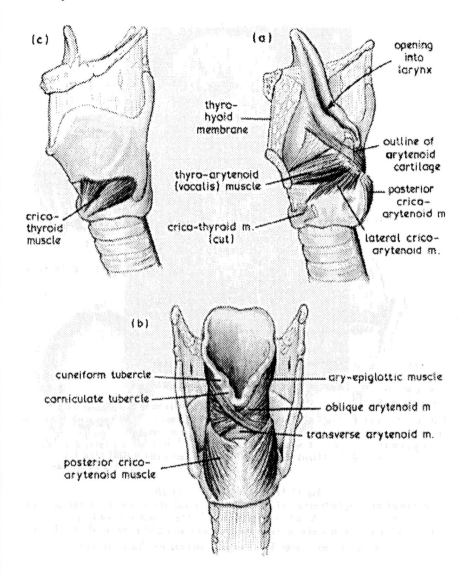

Fig. 3. Intrinsic muscles of the larynx
From *Dynamics of the Singing Voice*, Meribeth Bunch, 1982, Fig. 36, p. 57.
Published by Springer-Verlag. Used by permission.

The *internal thyroarytenoid muscles* which rim the inner edge of the glottis are also known as the *vocalis muscles* or true vocal cords. When the thyroarytenoid muscles contract the vocal fold is adducted (closed), shortened and thickened and the edge is rounded. During

phonation, vibration of the vocalis muscles occurs primarily in the
cover or mucosa with less extensive vibration in the body of the
muscle. Thus, the vocalis muscle appears to function as a base or
body of variable configuration and tension "to shape a vibrating
cover composed of the epithelium and underlying connective tissue
layers" (Cooper, 1988, p. 351). Contraction stiffens the body of
the muscle and reduces its area. Therefóre, the cover and transition
area of the contracted vocalis muscle appear slackened and flexible
(Hirano, 1981, p. 52, 1988, pp. 54-57).

The *cricothyroid muscles* are also in two parts. They connect
the inside of the thyroid cartilage to the outside of the cricoid cartilage. The *anterior* or *vertical* portions extend from the sides of the
thyroid laminae to the sides of the front of the cricoid cartilage.
Contraction of the vertical cricothyroids shortens the distance between the front thyroid and cricoid cartilages. The *oblique* portions
of the cricothyroid muscles connect the tops of the inferior horns of
the thyroid cartilage to the sides of the cricoid arch. They slide the
posterior of the cricoid cartilage back and down. Since the arytenoids are on top of the now lowered posterior of the cricoid cartilage, this increases the distance between the thyroid and arytenoid
cartilages. Both of these actions elongate and thin the vocal folds
and stiffen the mucous membrane that covers them (Cooper, 1988,
p. 340; Hirano et al., 1985, p. 345), thus sharpening the edge of
the vocal fold (Hirano, 1981, p. 52). Since stretching the vocal
cords pulls them to a paramedian position (next to the middle of the
glottis), the cricothyroids can be considered auxiliary adductors or
abductors, depending upon the position of the vocal cords. If the
cords are in the midline position, contraction of the cricothyroids
will tend to pull them apart; if they are in a lateral or intermediate
position, the cricothyroids will assist in adducting them (Saunders,
1964, p. 73).

The *arytenoid muscles* assist in adduction of the vocal cords by
sphincter-like actions which slide the arytenoid cartilages to the midline (Fried & Miller, 1988, p. 52). The *transverse arytenoid muscle*
(*interarytenoid*) is an unpaired muscle which connects the posterior
surfaces of the arytenoid cartilages. It extends horizontally across
the back of the arytenoid cartilages and pulls their middle edges together. The *oblique arytenoid muscles* extend from the muscular
process of one arytenoid to the apex of the other and pull the upper
tips together (Perkins & Kent, 1986, p. 75). By adducting the arytenoid cartilages, these muscles close the posterior part of the larynx
and the membranous vocal fold (Hirano, 1988, p. 56).

There are two pairs of *cricoarytenoid muscles*. The *posterior
cricoarytenoid muscles* connect the muscular processes of the arytenoid cartilages to the outside center of the back of the cricoid carti-

lage. They abduct the vocal cords by pulling the muscular processes of the arytenoids towards the back. This rotation of the arytenoid cartilages swings the vocal processes away from the center of the glottis and towards the sides of the thyroid cartilage. Since the thyroarytenoid muscles are connected to those vocal processes, separation of those processes pulls the thyroarytenoids apart. If, however, the posterior cricoarytenoids contract when adduction is already taking place, such as during inspiration, the arytenoid cartilages will rock posteriorly and lengthen the vocal cords (Fried & Miller, pp. 50 & 52). Action of the posterior cricoarytenoids also thins the vocal folds (Hirano, 1988, pp. 55 & 57).

The *lateral cricoarytenoid muscles* are also attached to the muscular processes of the arytenoid cartilages but extend along the tops of the sides of the cricoid cartilage to points about halfway around that cartilage. Their contraction can adduct the vocal folds by pulling the muscular processes of the arytenoids towards the sides of the thyroid cartilage. This rotates the arytenoids so that the vocal processes with their attached thyroarytenoid muscles swing inwards toward the center of the glottis (Hirano, 1981, p. 52, 1988, pp. 53-55 & 57). This action also thins, stretches and elongates the vocal folds (Hirano, 1988, pp. 53-55). The lateral cricoarytenoid muscles can also cause the arytenoids to slide along the cricoarytenoid articulation to abduct or open the arytenoids and the vocal folds (Fried & Miller, 1988, p. 50).

Thus, the muscles that adduct or close the vocal folds include the vocalis or thyroarytenoid and all three arytenoid muscles. The posterior cricoarytenoids abduct or open them, while the lateral cricoarytenoids **adduct** by rotating the arytenoid cartilages or **abduct** by rocking the arytenoid cartilages. The cricothyroid muscles, by pulling the cords towards the paramedian position, also assist in either action. The folds are elongated and thinned by the cricothyroids and posterior cricoarytenoids (Fry, 1979, p. 64; Hirano, 1988, p. 55; Hirano et al., 1985, p. 345) and shortened and thickened by the vocalis or thyroarytenoid muscles (Hirano, 1988, p. 55).

The Structure of the Vocal Cord
The vocal fold is made up of the thyroarytenoid muscle and the *mucosa* that covers it. The mucosa is similar to that which lines the mouth and pharynx as well as the trachea, the bronchi and the rest of the larynx. The mucosa in turn is made up of *epithelium* and *lamina propria*. The lamina propria can be further subdivided into three layers according to the density and type of its fibers. The top layer, known as *Reineke's space*, is 50 to 100 micrometers thick (Hirano, 1985, p. 339) and is composed of loose, pliable fibers. The second

or intermediate layer is made up of elastic fibers, and the deep layer
is almost exclusively collagenous fibers, i.e., connective tissue.
The intermediate and deep layers together are known as the *vocal
ligament* (Cooper, 1988, p. 332). Thus, the vocalis muscle is
covered with the vocal ligament which is covered by the Reineke's
space which is covered by the epithelium.

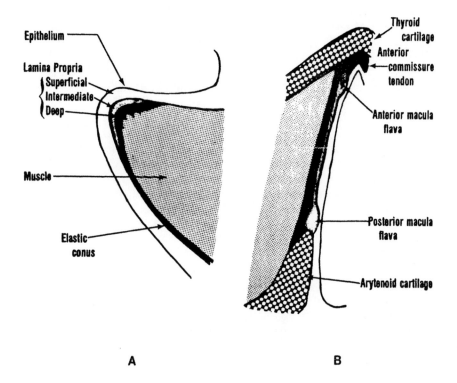

A   B

Fig. 4. "Schematic presentation of the structure of the normal human adult vocal fold. A. Frontal section at the middle of the membranous vocal fold. B.
Horizontal section at the edge of the vocal fold." From "Histological structure
of the vocal fold and its normal and pathological variations," by Minoru Hirano
and Shigejiro Kurita in *Vocal fold histopathology: A symposium*, J. A.
Kirchner (Ed.), Fig. 3-2, p. 20, 1986. Used by permission of authors.

Hirano gives a further description of the composition of these layers.

> From a mechanical point of view, the epithelium may
> be regarded as a thin but stiff capsule whose purpose

is to maintain the shape of the vocal fold. The superficial layer of the lamina propria may be regarded as a mass of soft gelatin. The elastic fibers of the intermediate layer are like soft rubber bands, while the collagenous fibers of the deep layer are like cotton thread. (1981, p. 48)

Mechanically these five layers function as three. The epithelium and Reineke's space function as a cover for the vocal fold. The vocal ligament is a transitory area where the fibers change gradually from fibrous to collagenous. The vocalis muscle is the deepest layer (Hirano, 1988, p. 52).

This five-layer structure is present at the glottal edge of the center portion of the vocal fold. Moving away from the edge to the internal part of the vocal folds there is no ligamentous structure. The lamina propria there has one layer, and the vocal ligament is replaced by a single-layered elastic conus (Hirano & Kurita, 1986, p. 19). At the edge of the vocal cord the fibers of the mucosa and muscle run parallel to the edge (Hirano, 1985, p. 341), but in the lateral portions they are perpendicular to that edge (Hirano and Kurita, p. 20).

The structure also changes as the ends of the vocal cords are approached. At both the anterior and posterior ends the tissue changes gradually from the hard cartilages to which the muscle is attached to the more pliable vocal folds. A mass of collagenous fibers called the *anterior commissure tendon* is located at the anterior end where the vocal fold joins the thyroid cartilage. Immediately behind that is the *anterior macula flava*, "a network of elastic fibers, fibroblasts and stroma" (Hirano, 1988, p. 53). A similar mass called the *posterior macula flava* is located at the posterior end of the vocal fold. Between it and the arytenoid cartilage there is a small transitional area that is more pliable than the cartilage but stiffer than the macula flava. And, of course, the cartilage on the tips of the vocal processes is elastic (see p. 3 under Cartilages of the Larynx). These gradual changes may offer protection for the membranous vocal folds from the mechanical trauma of vibration (Hirano, 1988, p. 53).

While the anterior edge of the vocal fold is clearly defined by the anterior commissure with the isthmus of the thyroid cartilage, the posterior edge is less clearly defined. Anatomists and laryngology and otolaryngology textbooks define the glottis as having two portions, the inter-membranous and the inter-cartilaginous, with the posterior juncture between these two portions defined as the tip of the vocal processes of the arytenoid cartilages. However, some sources prefer to define the posterior end of the vocal fold as the junction with the vocal processes because that is where the actual mucosal fold ends (Hirano, 1985, pp. 340-341). The posterior end of the vocal folds is further defined by changes in the epithelial cover. The vocal processes are covered with pseudostratified ciliated epithelium, i.e., epithelium which is covered with eyelash-like hairs. The muscular portion of the vocal fold is covered with stratified squamous epithelium, which has a scaly or platelike surface. Near the tip of the vocal processes where these two types border each other is a small area of transitional epithelium (Hirano et al., 1985, p. 6).

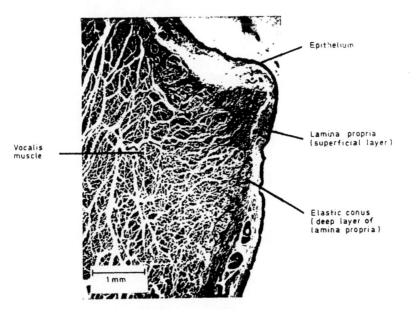

Fig. 5. "Histological structure of the human vocal cord. Frontal section. Note that fibers of the elastic conus go into the vocalis muscle, resulting in tight connection of the elastic conus and the vocalis muscle. Note also that the elastic conus and the superficial layer of the lamina propria are connected loosely with each other." From "Morphological structure of the vocal cord as a vibrator and its variations," Minoru Hirano, *Folia Phoniatrica*, **26**, Fig. 1, p. 90. Used by permission.

Phonation

Phonation is "sound generated by rapid vocal fold movement excited by the exhaled airstream" (Aronson, 1985, p. 3). Since Garcia's invention of the laryngeal mirror in 1841, man has been trying to discover **how** this sound is produced. The 1950 thesis "Étude des phénomènes physiologiques et acoustiques fondamentaux de la voix chantée" ("Study of the physiologic and acoustic fundamentals of the singing voice") by Husson outlined his *neurochronaxic theory of voice production.* Grossly simplified, his theory stated that individual neural impulses cause the vibrations of the vocal cords (Van den Berg, 1958, p. 230). He believed that generation of recurrent laryngeal nerve impulses would produce these vibrations by active contraction of the thyroarytenoid muscles (Husson, 1950 quoted in Sasaki, 1988, p. 64).

Myoelastic-aerodynamic theory. Husson's theory was challenged in 1958 by the publication of the article "Myoelastic-Aerodynamic Theory of Voice Production" by Janwillem Van den Berg. Van den Berg stated that "the vocal folds are actuated by the stream of air delivered by the lungs and trachea" (p. 230) and provided a compilation of the research and data supporting that theory of voice production. The two theories were irreconcilable, and studies in vocal cord innervation and other physiological and physical data eventually disproved Husson's neurochronaxic theory and validated the myoelastic-aerodynamic theory first proposed by Van den Berg.

During inhalation the vocal folds abduct either partially or totally, depending on the speed and volume of inhalation. With the beginning of exhalation the adductor muscles draw the vocal folds close together (approximate), narrowing the glottis. The air flows faster through the narrowed glottal opening, which sucks the folds tighter together. This is due to a law of physics called the *Bernoulli effect* which Vennard defines as "suction produced by the fact that air in motion has less density or pressure than air that is not in motion" (1967, p. 232). Pulling the cords together blocks the airway and increases pressure below the cords (subglottic pressure). When subglottic pressure reaches a point where it can overcome the resistance of the glottis, the vocal folds are blown apart. This release of air causes a decrease in subglottic air pressure which, with the elasticity of the folds and the Bernoulli effect, again brings the folds to the midline (Harrison & Tucker, 1987, p. 136; Prater & Swift, 1984, p. 6). The vocal cords open and close because of air pressure generated below them and their own muscular and elastic properties reacting to that pressure.

The vocal folds open and close gradually beginning at the lower (inferior) portion of the medial (middle) edges and then at the superior portion. This results in "propagation of a mucosal wave upwards over the vocal folds" (Cooper, 1988, p. 351). For production of voiced sounds the folds are adducted at the midline of the glottis but with an "adjustable firmness" so that air from the lungs can blow them apart slightly, and they close again in a regular pattern. For whispered sounds air flows in regular currents between folds that are partly adducted (Putnam & Shelton, 1985, p. 90).

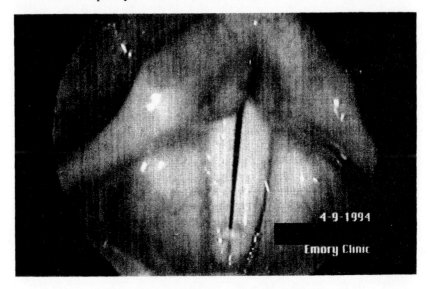

Fig. 6. Cords in partially abducted position
Photograph courtesy of Department of Otolaryngology, Emory University
School of Medicine, Atlanta, Georgia.

Pitch. Pitch is determined by the frequency of vibration of the sound producer. Frequency of vibration is dependent upon the mass, length and tension of the vibrating structures. A longer string sounds a lower pitch; a more tense string sounds a higher pitch; and a heavier string sounds a lower pitch. The length, mass and tension of the vocal folds are controlled by the intrinsic muscles. Unlike violin strings, muscles are tense only when they are contracted, and contraction also shortens them (Perkins & Kent, 1986, p. 71). Lengthening a muscle thins it and stiffens it. Therefore, while lengthening the cords might lower the pitch, that is offset by thyroarytenoid action which thins the cord and increases its internal tension (Sasaki, 1988, p. 64).

The pitch of the tone produced by the larynx is determined by the frequency with which the puffs of air are emitted by opening and closing of the glottis, one cycle. A change in the time that it takes to complete that cycle changes the frequency and thus the pitch. The fundamental frequency of laryngeal tone is increased by shorter folds, stiffer folds and increased subglottal pressure. It is decreased by an increase in the mass of the vocal fold (Hirano, 1981, pp. 63-64).

The sound wave emitted by the glottis is *periodic* because it is caused by **repeated** cycles of motion. As a periodic sound wave it is made up of a fundamental frequency plus a range of harmonics (Fry, 1979, p. 65). Resonance in the cavities above the larynx provides the harmonics, which are multiples of the vibrator's fundamental frequency. Harmonics occur as *partial* or whole number multiples of that frequency (Harrison & Tucker, 1987, p. 136). Some *aperiodicity* or variation between cycles is expected, but when aperiodicity predominates, harmonics are replaced by noise (Harrison and Tucker, p. 136).

While the larynx is the sound source for the complex activities of speaking and singing, we have little or no direct control over the actions of its musculature. By itself it can offer little in the way of communication. It must be powered by breath from the lungs and controlled by impulses from the brain, and its sound, once produced, is modified and formed into words by the resonating structures above the glottis.

Chapter 2

The Basics: Posture and Relaxation, Mouth Position and Breath

Body posture, mouth position and breathing are closely related and have a direct effect on singing. The position in which the head is held directly affects the suspension of the larynx and jaw position. Overall body stance influences breathing, and, sometimes, the method employed for breathing affects posture. Tensions in the neck, jaw or tongue or those affecting posture may be direct causes of voice problems. Therefore, we begin with relaxation and posture.

Posture

There are no quick answers to achieving good posture. Vennard recommends thinking of oneself "as a marionette hanging from strings, one attached to the top of your head and one attached to the top of your breast bone" (1967, p. 19). In his compendium of vocal pedagogy (1947), Fields reports finding 79 fundamental concepts regarding posture related to singing, with 46 of those statements related to physical conditioning and 33 to the maintenance of correct chest position (p. 81). He states that "the forty-six opinions in this group are all insistent that toneless physical exercises should be practiced to cultivate physique, posture and breath capacity" (p. 82). Since posture is affected by muscle tone, it would surely be affected by exercise so long as that exercise leaves the muscles of the head and neck area flexible and free of tension.

The singer's posture must achieve and allow several things. The feet should be squarely placed on the floor with the weight on the balls of the feet. The knees should remain flexible. The back should be straight to allow for costal/abdominal expansion for breathing. The shoulders must be back to allow the upper chest to be held high and open. At the same time, the shoulders should not be tensed and raised but must be kept relaxed with their blades lowered and the arms able to swing freely. The head and neck should be held straight as a continuation of the line begun by the spine. Many singers exhibit neck and shoulder tensions by pushing their

16

heads forward or "turtling." Still others will jam their chins into their necks in a military fashion. The neck, like the arms, must be able to move freely.

Posture is highly individual. Some individuals have an almost military bearing which looks wonderful but produces great tension in the neck and shoulders. Others, in an attempt to achieve good posture, may arch their backs and stick out their derrières, thus creating lower back tensions. It is up to the teacher to take a good look at each student and then work with that student to achieve the best possible posture.

Relaxation

Relaxation techniques are a major factor in voice therapy simply because excessive tensions can have strong negative effects on respiration, phonation and articulation (Murry, 1982b, p. 493). There are many techniques and exercises to relieve muscular tension. Most of those in therapy literature pertain specifically to the throat, neck, shoulders and face and are quite applicable for the voice studio. Techniques which are applicable to the voice studio include the tensing and relaxing of muscles of the neck, shoulders and arms (Boone, 1983; Fisher, 1975; Polow & Kaplan, 1979; and Rubin & Lehrhoff, 1962), head rolls or nods (Boone, 1983; Fisher, 1975; McClosky, 1959; Polow & Kaplan, 1979; and Rubin & Lehrhoff, 1962), progressive relaxation and Froeschels' chewing method (see Chapter 3) (Harrison & Tucker, 1987, p. 142).

Additional relaxation exercises may be found in voice therapy literature (viz., e.g. Fox & Blechman, 1975; Landes, 1977; and Moore, 1971a) as well as in the abundance of "how-to" books available on the subject. Many of the latter are part of a total fitness program. This is also the suggestion of therapist Diane Bless who urges her clients with problems with excessive tension to participate in a regular exercise program such as jogging, racquetball, aerobics or walking. Because such programs reduce overall tension and improve respiratory support, they improve the voice. She refers those clients whose tension is not sufficiently reduced by exercise to a relaxation therapist (Bless, 1983, pp. 24-25).

Alexander Technique. One of the most graphic illustrations of the effects of tension on vocal function is the story of F. M. Alexander. Alexander was a professional Shakespearean actor who developed symptoms of extreme hoarseness and eventually lost his voice completely. Unable to obtain medical help, he watched himself speak in the mirror to discover tensions around his head and neck which were causing his problems. He learned to remove these tensions by realignment of his body posture and developed the

Alexander Technique, a system of posture and relaxation based on body alignment (Barlow, 1973). The Alexander Technique is "a method of showing people how they are mis-using their bodies and how they can prevent such mis-use, whether it be at rest or during activity" (Barlow, p. 172). Removing tensions and pressures provides the necessary reconditioning for the spine to assume its maximum length and for the body to align and balance itself with proper weight distribution (York, 1957, p. 29). The Alexander Technique is known and taught all over the world as a system of relaxation and posture and as a philosophy which teaches "Use affects functioning" (Barlow, p. 7). Since it involves physical manipulation of the body, particularly the neck and spine, it is taught only by specially trained teachers who work with individuals or with selected subjects in small classes.

Laryngeal Massage

Massage of the throat and laryngeal area is also suggested by several authors. Aronson's recommendation is for the clinician to use massage to lower the larynx to a normal resting position (1985, pp. 340-341). McClosky recommends a gentle side-to-side massage of the larynx with thumb and forefinger, making sure that the larynx is "floating" and does not become rigid. "*It should not click!*" (1977, p. 140). Prater and Swift recommend massage of the entire throat area starting with the hyoid bone and proceeding down. The hyoid bone and larynx should be moved together while the subject sustains the vowel [a] (1984, p. 122). They describe their massage technique in great detail in their book.

Laryngeal manipulation is further discussed in the section on constriction in Chapter 3 of this book. However, the author cannot commend these massage techniques to the reader unless he or she is very well trained in the physiology of the neck and vocal tract. Even then care must be taken to avoid injury to this delicate area.

Atmosphere

The atmosphere of the studio and the attitude of the studio teacher towards his or her students is tremendously important. More and more students are selecting teachers based on teacher personality and studio atmosphere as well as on the vocal techniques taught. Without question, the teacher controls the psychological environment of the studio through his or her own body tension, voice and general behavior. While the professional singer must develop the personal strengths and confidence to enable him or her to withstand the rigors and criticisms of the performance world, many are beginning to question the effectiveness of imposing that same atmosphere upon what is supposed to be a learning situation.

One of the best ways to withstand the pressures of performance is to have a reliable vocal technique so that the vocal muscles will function as optimally as possible regardless of outside pressures on the singer. If relaxation will help create this technique, then the atmosphere in which it is learned will be a contributing factor. Just compare the picture of the teacher who one minute tells the student to relax the jaw and the next minute bellows "No! That is not what I want!" with the picture of the restrained teacher gently and patiently urging the student's best efforts with a well-modulated and relaxed tone of voice. Both students will achieve the goal but for very different reasons.

Teachers are also beginning to recognize the necessity of positive reinforcement in all levels of students. This does not mean effusive or unwarranted compliments. It means genuine encouragement that tells the student the teacher recognizes when effort is being made, when hard-earned gains are made or goals are reached. The sincerity and willingness on the part of the teacher to correct errors or offer necessary criticism helps the student to recognize and value the encouragement and compliments which are given. Above all, the teacher must remember that the voice is attached to a body which is also a person with intellect and emotions.

Mouth Position

The lower jaw is attached to the skull by five ligaments. One of these, the *stylo-mandibular*, connects it to the styloid process. The larynx is also attached to the styloid process by the *stylohyoid* ligament. The jaw is depressed or lowered by four muscles which run vertically to or near the hyoid bone: the *diagastric*, the *stylohyoid*, the *geniohyoid* and *mylohyoid*. Any tension in the lower jaw is communicated to the larynx via its proximity and by these muscles. Keeping the jaw relaxed and loose helps to maintain a passive, low laryngeal position. Such a position helps to improve phonation (Shipp, 1979, p. 47).

Physical manipulation of the jaw can aid in relaxing the muscles which control it. Brodnitz suggests shaking the jaw from side to side while keeping the mouth slightly open and producing a neutral voice sound (1961, p. 161). McClosky goes farther and suggests moving the jaw up and down with the hands and then from side to side with the hands (1977, pp. 139-141). Some help by the muscles of the jaw is usually necessary when first trying the McClosky exercises. The student should select a moderate and comfortable speed; as the jaw relaxes it can be moved more quickly. It must not be forced or jerked but should be moved in smooth even

motions, first up and down and then side to side. After some practice the jaw will relax enough for the hands to do the work.

Voice therapists favor an open mouth position for reducing vocal
cord hyperfunction because it "promotes more natural size-mass
adjustments and more optimum approximation of the vocal folds"
(Boone, 1983, p. 16). Opening the mouth also improves oral resonance which makes the voice sound louder, often improving problems with pitch, volume and quality (p.16). The resonators, including the mouth cavity, enhance the partials of laryngeal sound with
frequencies which are close to the formants produced by those resonators and suppress those partials which are farther away. Opening the mouth raises its formant frequencies. Thus, this is one way
to enhance the partials of the voice source, especially when singing
at higher pitch frequencies (Sundberg, 1985, pp. 203-204).

Once the jaw is relaxed, the next problem is to keep it that way
while opening the mouth. Most voice teachers follow Boone's advice to have clients face a mirror to observe their mouth position.
Facing the mirror they can also be assisted in identifying tightness
around the lips or in the jaw or excessive movement in neck muscles
(1983, p. 162). A hand laid gently against the cheek or lightly on
the chin will also alert the singer if the mouth starts to close. This is
particularly helpful for students who must practice without a mirror.

Additional exercises facilitating a relaxed, dropped jaw include
falling and rising five-note scales on the syllable "yah." The singer
should move quickly through the [j] so that the jaw drops in a single
motion. A similar pattern uses the syllable "Bwah-ah" repeated on
alternate notes of a descending five-note scale. "Thah" repeated on
each note of the descending scale allows the tongue and jaw to open
as a unit.

Ya ya ya ya ya   Bla- ahBla- ah Blah

TM Joint

The joint which attaches the upper and lower jaws is called the
temporomandibular -- temporo for the temporal bone of the skull
and mandibular for the mandible or lower jaw bone. Temporomandibular (TM) joint problems are serious for anyone, but for
singers they are particularly troublesome because of the multiple
openings and closings of the mouth. TMJ problems can cause
spasms radiating from the joint to the neck, the eustachian tubes and

the ear (Von Leden, 1978, p. 175). Because they create muscle tensions in the head and neck which in turn are communicated directly to the larynx, other symptoms of TMJ problems may include decreased range of the voice, vocal fatigue and change in the quality or focus of the voice. Such problems are often accompanied by excessive tongue tension, especially tongue retraction (Sataloff, 1981, p. 257, 1987a, p. 98).

Just as malocclusion demands the attention of a dentist and/or orthodontist, TMJ problems, especially in singers, are best treated by a qualified professional. Temporomandibular joint problems were first recognized in 1934 by otolaryngologist James B. Costen. He believed that a "closed bite" was responsible for this syndrome, and treatment to open the bite became the province of the dental profession. Since then a variety of theories about the etiology of and treatments for TMJ problems have been tried by the dental profession.

Dentists and doctors now recognize that TM joint function is the result of muscle action as well as dentition. The position of the joint is largely determined by the skeletal muscles until the teeth make contact with food and with each other. Then the shape and position of the teeth becomes a factor. In addition, action of the TM joint is influenced by sensory messages to the central nervous system from the "oral mucosa, the mucogingival tissues, the muscular structures of the mouth, the periodontal ligaments and the capsular and articulatory ligaments of the TM joints" (Bell, 1979, p. 12). For this reason, Bell suggests that a diagnosis must be carefully made by a dentist who specializes in locating sources of pain as well as masticatory problems. He also suggests that, although such a dentist is the best person to diagnose the problem, he or she may not be the best to treat it. "Some TM disorders are associated with conditions that are not responsive to dental treatment measures: management of these conditions should be done by an appropriate medical practitioner or by a cooperative interdisciplinary item" (Bell, 1990, p. 12).

Many singers, in their eagerness to open their mouths, allow the lower jaw to pull forward. This too creates tension, particularly at the TM joint. The effect can be demonstrated by folding a piece of paper in half so the edges meet. Keeping the "hinge" of the folded paper in place, pull the lower half down and notice the angle it makes with the upper half. Although the two edges meet exactly when the paper is closed, the lower edge angles back slightly from the upper one when it is opened. In order to keep the edges exactly in line, the fold of the paper (representing the TM joint) must be pulled forward. The same is true of the lower jaw; if it is kept relaxed it will open to a position slightly behind the upper jaw. At first it may be helpful for the singer to think of this position as a feeling of overbite, but eventually it will seem that the jaw falls away smoothly. The lower jaw should not be jammed back into the throat but must be kept as relaxed as possible. It should also be pointed out that, unlike the paper, the upper jaw of a closed mouth is usually slightly in front of the lower jaw. Few people, even those who have had orthodontia, have teeth which meet exactly in the front.

Breathing

> The lungs are elastic, spongy structures that continuously attempt to shrink. They are prevented from doing so as they are surrounded by the subatmospheric pleural pressure. . . . When they are filled with air, they attempt to expel this air with a force that is determined by the amount of air contained in them. This means that the lungs exert an entirely passive expiratory force that increases with the amount of air inhaled. (Leanderson & Sundberg, 1988, p. 3)

Physiology of Respiration
The organs of respiration include the lungs, bronchial tree and the thorax.

Inspiration. The lungs themselves have no voluntary muscles, so the work of expanding and contracting them is done by the chest wall. The chest wall is made up of the rib cage or thorax and the diaphragm-abdomen. The rib cage, which encircles the lungs, is made up of the ribs, the sternum to which the ribs are anchored in the front, the dorsal region of the spine to which they are anchored in the back and the muscles connecting and covering all of these parts. The floor of the chest is formed by the diaphragm. The lining of the chest wall (*parietal pleura*) and the outer covering of the lungs (*visceral pleura*) are connected by a thin liquid so that when the chest wall is expanded the lungs expand. Such expansion reduces the air pressure within the lungs until it is less than the atmosphere outside of the body. This allows air to be drawn in through the nose or mouth until the air pressure inside the chest is equal with the outside pressure (Putnam & Shelton, 1985, pp. 84-86).

The chest can be expanded in three directions: vertically via the diaphragm and sideways (transversely) and front to back (anteroposteriorly) using the inspiratory muscles.

Inspiratory muscles. The muscles associated with inspiration are those that run (1) from the head, neck and shoulders to the ribs; (2) between the ribs (inward) and (3) the back muscles that run from the cervical and thoracic vertebrae to the ribs (Schneiderman, 1984,

p. 47). The primary muscles of inspiration include the *external intercostals,* the *levatores costarum* and the *diaphragm.* The *external intercostals* are eleven muscles which extend from the lower border of each of the top eleven ribs to the upper border of the rib below. They lift and expand the rib cage. The *levatores costarum* are twelve small muscles that connect the vertebrae to the rib immediately below it. The *diaphragm* is a single, "arched musculo-tendinous partition" which divides the thoracic and abdominal cavities. When the diaphragm contracts during inspiration it flattens or drops and thus enlarges the chest cavity by displacing the contents of the abdomen (viscera). Because these viscera will not yield completely, the central tendon of the diaphragm becomes a fixed point from which the muscular fibers act to elevate the lower ribs and expand the lower part of the thoracic cavity (Gray, 1974, p. 355).

Additional muscles act to stabilize the upper ribs and clavicle (collarbone). These include the *serratus posterior superior,* the *sternocleidomastoids,* and the *scalenus anterior, medius and posterior (scalenus group).* Other muscles which may assist in forceful inspiration by raising the ribs include the *pectoralis major* and *minor* and the *serratus anterior.*

Expansion of the lower ribs enlarges the chest laterally (sideways) and anteroposteriorly (front to back). The upper ribs are hinged in such a fashion that they are able to move forward somewhat when they are raised, but greater expansion is provided by raising the lower ribs (Perkins & Kent, 1986, p. 23).

Expiration. During normal inspiration the lungs begin to empty as soon as they are filled with air. This is accomplished partly by the natural recoil forces of the lungs which pulls the diaphragm into the rib cage (Leanderson & Sundberg, 1988, p. 3) and partly by natural recoil of the muscles of the thorax and abdominal wall to their pre-contracted state (Case, 1984, p. 114). During forceful expiration the diaphragm is pushed upward by contraction of the powerful abdominal muscles against the abdominal contents which were displaced by contraction of the diaphragm during inspiration (Guyton, 1976, p. 517). This is aided by the abdominal muscles and the internal intercostals which compress and lower the rib cage. All of these factors diminish the size of the chest cavity and thus force out the expiratory reserve volume (Case, 1984, p. 114).

Expiratory muscles. The muscles associated with expiration include those that extend from the pelvis up to the sternum or ribs, from the vertebrae upwards to the ribs, between the ribs (outward) and from the sternum (Schneiderman, 1984, p. 47). Thus the muscles of expiration include the *external oblique, internal oblique* and *transverse abdominus* that form the lateral abdominal walls and the *rectus abdominus,* a pair of muscles that form the front of the

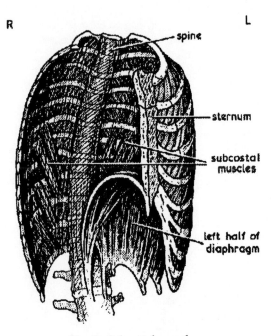

Fig. 7, Subcostal muscles
From *Dynamics of the Singing Voice*, Meribeth Bunch, 1982, Fig. 29, p. 47.
Published by Springer-Verlag. Used by permission.

abdominal wall. These muscles function like a corset to compress
the viscera (Perkins & Kent, 1986, p. 32). They are assisted by the
internal intercostals. These are eleven small muscles extending from
the inner surface of each rib to the upper border of the rib below,
encompassing the area from the sternum to the vertebral column.
They lower the rib cage and decrease its volume (Gray, 1974, p.
350).

The *total lung volume* in an adult male is about seven liters.
Tidal volume is the air that moves in and out of the lungs during
normal, resting respiration. It is about 600 cubic centimeters in a
young male. The *inspiratory reserve volume* is the maximum
amount of air that can be taken into the lung (Darby, 1981, p. 6;
Schneiderman, 1984, p. 49). It equals about 3,000 cc in the adult
male (Darby, p. 6). The maximum amount of air that can be
breathed out with effort is called the *expiratory reserve volume* and
equals 1,200 cc. The *residual volume* is the small amount of air
that remains in the lungs after maximum exhalation (Darby, 1981, p.
6; Schneiderman, 1984, p. 50), about two liters in an adult male
(Leanderson & Sundberg, 1988, p. 5). The difference between the

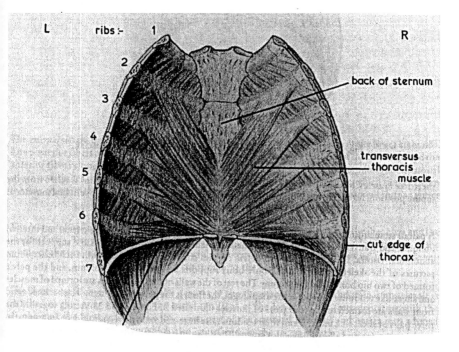

Fig. 8, Transversus thoracis (sternocostalis) muscles
From *Dynamics of the Singing Voice*, Meribeth Bunch, 1982, Fig. 30, p. 46
Published by Springer-Verlag. Used by permission.

the total lung volume and the residual volume is the *vital capacity*. It represents what is available for phonation and to sustain life. In the adult male it amounts to about five liters (Leanderson & Sundberg, 1988, p. 5).

Types of Respiration
Four different types of respiration may be described according to the part of the thorax that provides the most muscular activity: "abdominal, costo-abdominal, costal and clavicular" (Tarasco, 1984, p. 224).
When air is added to a tire or balloon its walls expand. Likewise the walls of the chest must expand for air to be added to the lungs. In clavicular breathing the shoulders are raised to increase the size of the chest. In costal breathing the lower ribs are purposefully pushed out. For diaphragmatic-abdominal breathing the person pushes out the waist and the area immediately below it to allow the diaphragm to drop. Thus, it becomes a question of how and where the necessary chest cavity expansion can be achieved.

Singers have traditionally avoided clavicular breathing. The correctness of this choice is reinforced by voice therapists who indicate such breathing spreads tension to the throat, elicits constriction and is "inefficient in terms of vital capacity" (Perkins, 1971, p. 522). Murry also indicates that it is inefficient and generally interferes with exhalation, making it harder to control and a "strain or struggle" (1982a, p. 481; 1982b, p. 494). Cooper found 86% of his functionally misphonic patients and 89% of his organically dysphonic patients had upper chest or clavicular breathing (1973, p. 28).

Both therapists and laryngologists favor a breathing method that includes use of the diaphragm. Tarasco prefers costo-abdominal breathing for voice professionals because of the increased volume of air available. He finds reserve expiratory volume more readily available to the person who has taken a diaphragmatic breath (1984, p. 224). Isshiki considers diaphragmatic breathing critically important in treating various dysphonias as well as in singing pedagogy. Such deep breathing relaxes muscle contraction which facilitates smooth and coordinated phonation (1989, p. 6). Aronson cites greater lung volume available to the diaphragmatic breather (1985, p. 336). Kleinsasser warns against holding the abdomen in so as to appear slim while speaking and singing, especially after laryngeal surgery, because the muscle tension involved is damaging to health (1979, p. 36). Brodnitz (1962, p. 475), Damsté and Lerman (1975, pp. 65-66) and Wilner and Sataloff (1987, p. 314) also prefer diaphragmatic breathing. Thus, the methods of choice appear to be abdominal or costo-abdominal.

Whether the teacher chooses to teach rib cage expansion alone, abdominal expansion or a combination of the two, the student learning a new method of breathing must learn to control the correct muscles. A full-length mirror and the student's hands are the best tools available. After the teacher has described and demonstrated the correct way to take in the breath, the student can observe himself or herself in the mirror and monitor his or her progress. Even more effective is the use of the student's hands. For rib cage expansion one hand can be placed on the sides of the rib cage. For abdominal expansion the hand is placed at the front of the student's waist. In both methods the student is told to push that hand out. The other hand can be placed where the collarbone meets the sternum to make the student aware of unwanted upward movement there. The muscles for abdominal breathing can also be found by a sharply forced bark of the breath on "Hah." Again, the hand can be a helpful monitor.

Although some rib cage expansion is inevitable with diaphragm contraction, this can be increased by suggesting the student think of inflating an inner-tube or balloon around the waist. To facilitate learning this coordination, the student should place one hand on the side of the rib cage and one in front at the waist.

Voice therapists, like voice teachers, may ask the client to lie on his or her back on the floor to get the feeling of diaphragmatic breathing. Both Boone (1983) and Cooper (1973, 1977 and 1983) have the client begin with relaxed, even breathing in this supine position then have him or her do the same in a standing position. Cooper has clients place one hand on the chest and the other on the stomach and breathe through the nostrils with the lips closed as if they were going to sleep.   He follows this with open-mouth breathing (1983, p. 78).   Boone uses this technique only with singers, actors and lecturers.

Controlling the Exhaled Air
Singing requires a prolonged and steady flow of breath. Not only must the student learn to take in the full capacity of air with every breath, he or she must also learn to control the speed and manner of exhalation. Thus prolonged hissing, humming or vocalized vowels are common exercises in the voice studio. After taking a deep breath the student prolongs the [s] sound as long as possible without tension. This is followed by the hum and then by an [a] or [o] vowel. It may be necessary for the student to place one hand at the waist or on the ribs and one where the clavicle and sternum meet to ensure that all control of exhaled air is done by the abdominal and/or thoracic muscles.

It should be emphasized that a **steady** rate of expiration is important. This is particularly important for initiating the sound. The student must be careful not to force a "gust" of air out at the beginning but should start the air flow gradually and continue evenly. To keep the flow of air even the student is told he or she should neither hold the breath back nor push it out. Similarly, all vocalizing should be done at a medium volume -- neither very softly (which would be similar to holding the breath back and could cause constriction) nor very loudly which would increase the subglottal pressure (Wyke, 1980, p. 46).

Once the student is able to coordinate the inhale and exhale using the breathing method the teacher prefers, he or she may enjoy counting mentally during the exhale. The teacher must emphasize this is not a competition and that the student is merely "keeping track" of his or her own rate of expiration.

This type of exercise is also used by voice therapists to improve economy of expiration. Boone recommends an even phonation on [a] or a similar open vowel for as long as possible without change of quality (1983, p. 175). He increases expiratory control by increasing the duration of phonation. He begins by taking a baseline measure of the time the client can prolong a sound then setting a timer for a slightly longer duration (2 seconds) and asking the client to phonate until a signal attached to the timer appears. This is repeated until they reach the longest duration the patient can comfortably prolong the sound without an increase in tension. Boone finds that such practice increases the client's expiratory reserve volume.

Brodnitz also recommends beginning with the voiceless [a] sound. If the person is unable to maintain it longer than 10-15 seconds he suggests using in its place an [f] or [s] sound. He indicates that this is best performed standing with arms raised to a horizontal position at deep inspiration and slowly lowered during expiration. "The exercise should not be performed more than three times in a row because, if done in excess, it might become a strain on the heart" (1961, p. 196). He then uses vowels "ah, oh, ih, uh" sung with crescendo-decrescendo from pianissimo to forte and back.

Murry uses a similar exercise but with instructions to the client to inhale only a comfortable amount of air and to move only the abdomen and lower thorax when taking in the breath. Exhaling is done first on [h] beginning with ten seconds and then on [s] and [z] beginning with 15 seconds. Each phoneme is increased by two seconds every day (1982b, p. 494). Murry also uses what he calls "Interrupted Vocalization" in which the client inhales in the same manner as above then exhales a short [h] sound for two seconds. When this sound is steady it is followed by an [a]. The sounds can then be combined for two or three [ha]s per breath. The same exercise is repeated for the [i] and [u] vowels and with [s] and [z] using the vowels [a], [i] and [u] (1982b, pp. 494-495). Note that Yanagihara, Koike and Von Leden established 20-25 seconds as normal maximum phoneme duration in adults (1966).

Fox and Blechman (1975, p. 59) and Polow and Kaplan recommend beginning with a hum at a comfortable pitch followed by vowels. The client is instructed to inhale deeply and to repeat [a] every three seconds. They watch that exhalation is controlled with the abdominal muscles rather than with the throat or shoulders (1979, p. 56). Rubin and Lehrhoff have the client begin with a deep breath followed by a steady hiss, then a quick breath followed by longer hissing. The client then tries different lengths of phrases with quick intakes of breath. The same pattern is followed on an [a] vowel with the tone supported with a firm, inward push of the abdominal muscles. Their final exercise is a whispered "'ah-ay'" running the sounds together as long as possible on one breath (1962, p. 158).

Rather staying on one pitch or using standard exercise patterns, the singer may use a "wandering hum." After taking a full breath he or she hums at a steady rate and "wanders" or slides up and down, directly or in a circular fashion, through the comfortable parts of the singing range. The same thing is then done on an [a] or [o] vowel. This is an exercise in vocalization, not singing. Though done primarily to facilitate breath control, it has the added advantage of freeing the student from self-imposed restrictions or attitudes he or she may have assigned to particular notes or parts of the voice. Eventually the student will be able to wander about the entire range of his or her voice like one wanders through a large empty room.

Brown has students practice inhaling and exhaling while walking. They vary the number of steps taken during the inhale as well as during the exhale to learn to take both quick and long breaths and to be prepared to sing phrases of different lengths.

This is similar to the "take a walk exercise" which was developed by Eugene Conley. The client is asked to take in a slow breath for five steps and then let it out as a hum for the next five. There should be no observable break between the fifth and sixth step. After this pattern is well established, the patient is instructed to inhale in the same way and then count the next five steps, one word per step (Boone, 1988, p. 22).

Support

Phonation is caused by movement of air across the cords. To overcome the resistance of the closed cords, there must be a build-up of air pressure below the glottis. Subglottal pressure is controlled by a combination of passive recoil forces of the lungs and thorax and active muscular forces. If the pressure generated by the recoil forces is too high for the intended phonation, it can be reduced only by contracting the muscles of inhalation. As lung volume decreases, the need for such contraction will be diminished until the lung volume is reached which is appropriate for such recoil pressure. At this point the muscles of exhalation will begin to function to compensate for increasing compression of the rib cage and prevent inhalation from taking place (Leanderson & Sundberg, 1988, p. 4).

Breath support is a term used by singers and teachers alike, often without a real knowledge of its meaning. Sataloff, O'Connor and Heuer consider support to be the power source of the voice. "It generates the force vector that propels expired air between the vocal cords." They see it as a function primarily of the thorax and abdominal musculature (1984, p. 236). Damsté considers support the "inspiratory 'rein' during phonatory exhalation." For him it is the indirect control of the voice's resonance that most professional speakers and singers claim, whether it is in the abdomen, sides or back. He believes that even the back of the neck may exert a powerful control over the quality of the voice (1987, p. 122).

Because of the natural recoil forces of the lungs and thoracic wall, some kind of muscular force must be exerted to prevent the air from going out just as fast as it comes in -- support. Since the air flow needs to be up and out of the lungs and chest cavity, pressure below the lungs and diaphragm or at the lower edge of those organs would logically be the most productive. Too often the singer learns to fill the lungs completely but fails to learn to use the same muscles to control the outward flow of the breath or, worse yet, allows the upper chest to fall during or at the start of the phrase. Such downward pressure opposes gravity and pulls the shoulders and neck forward which alters the posture negatively. Depressing the upper ribs in this manner lowers the entire rib cage so the singer will have to raise the rib cage for the next breath or the space available in the chest cavity and lungs will be limited.

The most efficient possibilities for muscular control of exhalation can be summed up in two different abdominal positions: the abdomen out position and the abdominal tuck. In the first of these, the singer, following inspiration, pulls or tucks the lower abdominal wall inward. In this position the rib cage wall is elevated and expanded compared to the relaxed rib cage wall at the same lung volume. Because it is highly domed, the diaphragm is actually more arched than in its relaxed state (Hixon & Hoffman, 1979, p. 9).

As its name implies, the abdomen out position requires the singer to push continually against the abdominal wall to keep it expanded. There are many variations on this technique involving the position of the abdominal and thoracic walls. Most common is with the rib cage raised or expanded all the way around (Hixon & Hoffman, 1979, p. 10). Variations include pushing against only the front of the abdominal wall or focusing efforts on the back at waist level. With this "belly-out method" the diaphragm is flattened out (Leanderson & Sundberg, 1988, p. 11).

Each position has its advantages and disadvantages. The "tuck" position has the advantages that the rib cage wall expiratory muscles are in position for rapid and forceful expiration while the diaphragm is in position for fast and forceful inspiration. However this inspiratory tension on the diaphragm may be counter-productive to overall expiration (Hixon & Hoffman, 1979, p. 9).

The abdomen out position offers the same rib cage expansion advantage as the tuck position. It also has the advantage of not distending the diaphragm enough to create inspiratory tensions on the rib cage so that all of the respiratory system is working toward expiration (Hixon & Hoffman, 1979, p. 10). The disadvantage of this position is that it both denies and fails to take advantage of the role of passive elastic recoil of the muscles (Lavorato & McFarlane, 1983, p. 56). Sataloff warns singers that distending the abdomen to breathe is dangerous because it forces the singer's muscular effort downward and outward. The singer may exert considerable effort in this way without achieving breath support (1987a, p. 93).

Excessive breath pressure. Some singers, after expanding the abdominal wall for inhalation, pull the abdominal wall in sharply *as the sound is initiated*, especially for higher pitches. In addition to the obvious disadvantage of forcing out a large quantity of the breath with the initiation of sound, this method, used over a period of time, may create so much breath pressure that the laryngeal muscles cease to function properly.

Singers with excessive breath pressure are easily identified. They will be unable to sing an even scale, and some notes will be harsh and pinched and others breathy and faint. These singers are often unable to sing a normal phrase in one breath. Excessive breath pressure was identified as a hyperfunction by Froeschels when he first compiled his list (see Chapter 7) but eliminated when he revised it in 1943.

In speech loudness and pitch are interdependent so that increasing subglottal pressure to increase loudness also raises fundamental frequency (Murry, 1982a, p. 480). However, a singer needs to be able to control these factors so that subglottal pressure regulates loudness and laryngeal muscles regulate pitch (Sundberg, 1990, p. 109). The singer with excessive breath pressure uses subglottal pressure to raise the pitch as well as to increase the loudness (Leanderson & Sundberg, 1988, pp. 6-7). Thus, the high notes become increasingly difficult to produce. Because of the excessive breath pressure, the registration will probably be in heavy mechanism (see Chapter 4) or a mix with the balance toward heavy mechanism. It is important to remember that in upper register the cords are thinned and stretched so there is less mass to vibrate. Thus, a *smaller* amount of air is required.

The remedy for excessive breath pressure is to regain the balance of pressure required for optimal laryngeal function. Either the "abdomen out" or "tuck" position discussed previously will help with this. Balancing the registers by finding the upper register, and blending it if appropriate, is nearly always necessary, particularly with female voices (see Chapter 4). It would be a mistake to say that male voices never fall victim to excessive breath pressure or even that they are less likely to develop the problem. However, it does seem that the male voice can withstand high subglottal pressures better than female voices and that tenors and sopranos are more prone to this problem than their lower-voiced counterparts -- perhaps because of the greater frequency of and their greater concern with high notes.

Part of finding the upper register is to ask the singer to sing a short pattern like the following in the upper medium range after taking only a small breath.

ah - - - - - -

It is sometimes necessary to have the singer with excessive breath pressure blow out air before phonation or start without taking a breath and then to take very small breaths for succeeding patterns (Olson).

Staccato. Staccato singing requires an amazing and unconscious coordination of the breath. Studies show that the vocal folds must open the glottis to create the silent segments which separate the notes. To do this without wasting air, subglottal pressure must be reduced to nothing during these intervals. This means that the singer has to change the subglottal pressure from whatever is required from the first pitch down to zero and back up to whatever is required for the next pitch. If these adjustments are not made, the singing will be out of tune (Sundberg, 1990, p. 109).

Can this be taught? Not directly, perhaps, but there is a right way to do staccato. Rather than feeling that each pitch must be pounded with the breath, the singer should follow a full intake of breath with a slight bounce in the midriff area. One way to learn this is to do light, silent "ha-ha's" somewhat like panting. Staccato offers an opportunity to catch breaths, but it is better controlled if the only breath taken is at the beginning of the phrase or passage.

Chapter 3

The Sound: Method of Attack, Constriction and Tone Quality

Regardless of what other gifts the singer may exhibit, the sound or tone quality of the voice is the first thing the listener hears. While the innate quality of each voice is dictated by the person's natural endowments, the amount of tension or degree of relaxation present in the muscles of the throat and neck seriously affect the sound. That tension or relaxation is affected significantly by phonation practices including the method of attack.

Method of Attack

A great deal of time is spent in the voice studio working on the manner in which the tone is attacked or begun. That method of attack determines many things including the quality of the tone and its placement. How the tone is attacked is in turn determined by factors such as the energy used and the timing of the flow of breath related to the initiation of sound. Aronson describes three kinds of attack common to both speech and singing.

> 1. The hard, glottal, or stopped attack. Voice is produced by first adducting the vocal folds to the midline, building up infraglottal pressure, and then initiating the vowel. The explosive sound that results is called the *glottal stop* or glottal coup.

> 2. The even or static attack. The vocal folds are nearly approximated as exhalation begins. Voice onset is smooth and instantaneous.

> 3. The breathy attack. The vocal folds are abducted [opened] as exhalation begins and adducted [closed] after exhalation has begun. The effect is a moment of breathiness heard just prior to voicing. (1985, p. 36)

Activity of the adductor muscles of the larynx is different for each of the three types of attack. The vocalis and lateral cricoarytenoid muscles show greater prephonatory activity for the hard attack than for either the static or breathy attacks. This activity is even greater than that shown during normal phonation. During both the static and breathy attacks their activity, as well as that of the cricothyroid muscles, increases gradually and reaches maximum level around the onset of voice (Hirano, 1988, pp. 66 & 68). In addition, the forceful adduction of the folds for the glottal attack causes colliding of the arytenoid cartilages, which can cause injury to their delicate mucosal cover.

When working with muscular coordination, it is sometimes easiest to balance one extreme by asking for the other. The extremes of attack are, of course, the glottal attack and the breathy attack. Thus, the fastest way to rid a student of a glottal attack is to ask that student for a breathy attack. Since the goal of singing is normally the static or even attack, the teacher may wish to explain to that student the necessity of getting rid of the glottal attack's constant assault on the cords and to assure the student that he or she will not be left indefinitely with the breathy attack. The breathy attack is easily achieved by having the student begin the vowel sound with an aspirate [h]. This can be adapted to any vocalise, although five-note ascending or descending scales and slides are the easiest.

Vennard describes the imaginary [h] as similar to the aspirate [h] in that it is employed to create a flow of breath before the tone starts. This allows the cords to begin vibration with the Bernoulli effect (Vennard, 1967, p. 44). Here the singer merely thinks the [h] before the vowel.

The aspirate [h] is the method most commonly used by therapists to eliminate the glottal stop. It is recommended by Boone (1983), Case (1984), Fisher (1975), Mowrer and Case (1982), Prater and Swift (1984), Polow and Kaplan (1979) and others. McFarlane uses the [h] sound before vowel-initiated words so that words such as "'eat apples and oranges'" come out "'*heat happles hand horanges*'" (1988, p. 430). He later lightens the [h] to a slight breathiness. Drudge and Philips use [h] followed by vowel sounds such as [a], [ɔ], [æ], [u] and [i]. They also explain and demonstrate the hard glottal attack so the client is able to identify it in the clinician's speech (1976, pp. 407-408). With his patients who have had laryngeal surgery, Kleinsasser uses unvoiced consonants in combinations such as "hoo, hooa, hip," and "hello" (1979, p. 35).

Perkins uses combinations of [hmeI], [hmaI], and [hmɔI] in treatment of the glottal attack. The initial [h] provides a breathy attack, and the [m] provides a "vocal posture" with the correct oral and nasal balance. He uses the [e], [a], and [ɔ] to sample the high,

low, front and back vowels and combines them with brilliance of the
[I] (1971, p. 529). Perkins also suggests that a laugh can help shift
the breathy attack to the even attack (p. 530).

Susan Gray uses a prolonged [h] flowing smoothly into a vowel
sound with her therapy clients. The clinician models the exercise for
imitation by the patient. The same procedure is then used with an
[m]. Again following cues given by the clinician, the patient gradually shortens and then eliminates the initial [h] and [m]. This is
followed by short phrases spoken slowly without undue emphasis
on the [h] or [m] cue sounds. Gray also combines the [h] and [m]
with vowels to produce "[hma, hmo]," etc. Eventually the [h] and
[m] sounds are eliminated.

Vennard used the yawn-sigh as the basis of much of his teaching. Although his use of it was for relaxation of the throat and
placement, it is also useful in elimination of the glottal attack. To
create a mood of relaxation, the student should imagine himself or
herself sitting in an easy chair where he or she stretches and says
"'ah-h-h-h, what a day!'" The student simulates a yawn which is
followed by a vocal sigh into the vowel. The attack must be with an
imaginary [h] and should not be at a definite pitch. To facilitate a
clear, light tone, it must begin in the upper part of the range so that it
can be produced with head voice or near falsetto. For some students
it may be necessary to use the temporary measure of beginning with
the falsetto tone and letting it break on the downward slide. Those
with especially tight throats may produce a breathy tone, but the goal
is a clear, light tone (1967, p. 211).

The yawn-sigh technique is also used by Boone for eliminating
glottal strokes in his therapy clients. After the patient has been instructed in the physiology of the yawn, Boone has him or her yawn
and then exhale with light phonation. The client is next instructed to
follow the yawn with a word beginning with [h] or with an open
vowel. The clinician then demonstrates the sigh which would follow the yawn, prolonged and easy with the mouth open, and the
same sigh done after a normal, quick inhalation. Once the client
learns to do a relaxed sigh, it is followed with words which begin
with [h] such as "hah." Blending the phonation is sometimes difficult initially, but it is vital in learning to eliminate the glottal attack.
Once the client is able to do the yawn-sigh easily, he or she should
be able to attain the relaxation it provides by just thinking of the
yawn-sigh (Boone, 1983, pp. 180-181).

Polow and Kaplan have the client yawn into the tone while
reading a list of words. Once able to do this, the client should add a
sigh before the word (1979, p. 86). Fisher uses a yawn followed
by a prolonged and easy "ah" (1975, p. 66). Gray has the client
yawn and then produce vowel sounds on the exhaled sigh. She also

has them yawn and silently articulate counting on exhalation. This is gradually evolved into breathy voice then into full voice (1983, p. 16). Fox and Blechman suggest a yawn followed by whispered words which are initiated with the [h] sound such as "hate, hot, hit, her and how." The words are then repeated using voice (1975, p. 53).

It may be preferable to use only the sigh with singers with lighter voices. This is easiest done by imitation, with the teacher beginning with a normal unvoiced sigh which is imitated by the student. This is followed by a quietly voiced sigh at a natural pitch preceded by an aspirate [h], again imitated from the teacher's model. The teacher then starts the sigh at a pitch in the upper middle of the student's range, again using the aspirate [h]. The voiced sigh is then "sung" by briefly sustaining the top note. And finally, the last step is duplicated with the teacher giving roughly the same initial pitch on the piano rather than having the student imitate the teacher's voice. A return to the initial unvoiced sigh may be necessary if the student uses a glottal attack on any of these steps. Most students do very well until they hear the pitch of the piano; for some reason they suddenly revert to their old habits and begin to "sing."

Fisher (1975), McClosky (1977), and Moore (1971b) use phonated sighs with their therapy clients. Fisher follows this with a "glide-down sigh" in which the client begins phonation on a fairly high note and glides down to a fairly low pitch during the sigh. McClosky follows with a slide interrupted by [m] then reopened (Hay-may-mee-mo-moo) (pp. 143-144).

A light slide on a hum is also easily adapted. Imitation again is useful, this time of an inflected rising hum as if asking a question "Um-hm?" and falling as if answering "Hmm" (Brown). This should be followed by the falling hum opening to an [a]. Only the teacher's imagination limits the possibilities so long as [h] and [m] are employed at the beginning of phonation followed by open vowels such as [a], [o] and [ɔ]. This is similar to techniques used by Polow and Kaplan (1979), Fisher (1975) and Kleinsasser (1979) as therapy to eliminate glottal attacks. Polow and Kaplan (1979) suggest humming and adding a vowel. Fisher (1975) uses humming up and down the scale and words which begin with [m] or [n] (p. 72). Kleinsasser uses combinations with voiced consonants such as "mo, mo, mo, ma, ma, ma, no, no, no, na, na, na, me, me, me, my, my, my, moo, moo, moo" and longer words which begin with m (1979, p. 35).

It is relatively easy to move a student from a breathy attack to a static attack. Whether the breathy attack has been learned to compensate for the glottal attack or is a habit resulting from other factors, the student must first be made aware that the goal is for the sound and the breath to begin simultaneously. A student who has always begun vowels with a glottal stroke will require several weeks or even months of vocalizing with the aspirate [h] to break the glottal habit. The singer who has adopted an aspirate [h] to compensate for glottals can be lead through the imaginary [h] or, in some cases, simply told to abandon the [h] altogether. Some can then move easily to the static attack, while others will need the imaginary [h]. If the student returns to the hard attack, it will be necessary to backtrack to either the aspirate or imaginary [h]. The student is ready when he or she no longer uses glottals on words beginning with vowels when they appear in songs.

Those whose breathy tone is a result of poor breath coordination must be taught to start the flow of breath and tone together without the use of a glottal stroke. This may be a conceptual problem. The teacher should provide a brief explanation and demonstration of each of the three types of attack, beginning with a comparison of glottal and breathy as opposites. The teacher should then explain that the static attack is the most desirable, demonstrate it and have the student try it.

However, the breathy tone is more often a matter of preparedness and timing. Teachers preferring the abdomen out method of breath support described in the previous chapter should teach these students to wait for a moment after completing the inhale of breath before beginning the sound. This may be practiced using the hiss, the wandering hum and the wandering vowel also suggested in that chapter.

The tuck method of breath support suggested in Chapter 2 is quite helpful in coordinating the static attack. Once the singer completes the inhale, he or she "tucks" or tightens muscles of the pelvic girdle **before** initiating the sound. The lower abdominal muscles, which are tightened in that split second following the intake of breath, help coordinate the flow of air with the sound.

Ending the Phrase
The manner in which the sound is extinguished at the end of the phrase is often overlooked. The tone should be released by stopping the flow of breath. It is only necessary to close the mouth as required to pronounce the final word. The throat should never be closed.

To facilitate this habit, the student should be encouraged, when vocalizing, to avoid closing the mouth between repetitions of the same pattern. It is also helpful if the student learns to breathe in with the mouth in the shape of the vowel to be sung. Doing this on repetitions of vocalises on the same vowel will help to discourage any kind of closure at the end of the preceding pattern. Even if the phoneme which follows the breath begins with a consonant, the breath should be taken through the shape of the vowel which follows rather than through a neutral shape, so that the consonant can be opened quickly to form the vowel.

Constriction and Tone Quality

Constriction is probably the most common problem seen in the voice studio. It appears in many forms, often as a cause or symptom of other problems. Some forms, such as the retracted tongue, are immediately recognizable for what they are; others are more evasive. The healthy singer who sounds fine one day and terrible the next with no predictability or the one who is nearly unable to speak after twenty minutes of practice may both be examples of some form of constriction. Worse yet, some voices are so deceptive that only the singer is aware of the constriction, and he or she may be so accustomed to the sensations associated with it as to be unaware there is a problem until age and/or bad habits finally take their toll.

The speaking voice may also exhibit symptoms of constriction: the harsh, raspy voice; the high-pitched, pinched voice; the voice that tires quickly or the speaker who is forever clearing the throat are all examples of constriction. Perkins defines constriction as "any vocal tract adjustment, given a positioning of the cords for vibration, that weakens the Bernoulli effect" (1971, p. 521). He considers it a separate entity because it can increase or decrease independently of other facets of vocal production. This means that an increase in pitch or in breath pressure will not necessarily coincide with an increase in constriction and vice versa (Perkins, 1983, p. 277).

Constriction can exist independently, but it usually interacts with other elements. It seldom exists in one part of the vocal tract alone, for the extra effort required to overcome the constriction in one part of the tract will spread it to another.

> Constricted vocal production cannot exist without vocal effort, but effort can, and should, be exerted without constriction. Some degree of effort is required for any form of vocalization, so effort is necessarily ubiquitous, but constriction is not. The mark of the poorly produced voice is inability to differentiate the two, to regulate effort independently. (Perkins, 1971, pp. 519-520).

Simply stated, constriction is tightness in any part of the throat, mouth or pharynx. Tension in the extrinsic muscles of the larynx, the tongue and the pharyngeal muscles raises or lowers the larynx from the resting position and contracts or closes a part of the vocal tract.

The Elevated Larynx

Singers elevate their larynges under a variety of circumstances. Some find a relaxed laryngeal position only when not singing; others move their larynges up and down with the pitch, much like climbing stairs. Either way, the cause is hypercontraction of the extrinsic laryngeal muscles. This may also indicate hypercontraction of the intrinsic muscles of the larynx (Aronson, 1985, p. 311).

Elevation of the larynx shortens the vocal tract (the distance from the vocal folds to the lips of the mouth). The shorter vocal tract gives the resonators higher formant frequencies and thus accentuates higher overtones. A high laryngeal position also stiffens the tissues of the vocal folds themselves. This increases their fundamental frequency and alters their vibratory patterns so that their acoustic energy is changed (Shipp, 1987, p. 218). The result of all of this is a "tight," strident or harsh sound usually associated with constriction. Elevating the larynx also changes the position of the cricopharyngeus muscle so that it now pulls the cricoid cartilage backwards. This stretches the vocal ligaments and causes the tone to be shrill and high (Damsté, 1987, p. 124).

A diaphragmatic breath will lower the larynx at least temporarily. The diaphragm's contraction exerts a downward pull on the bronchial tree which pulls the front of the cricoid cartilage down. This gives resistance to any upward pull on the cricoid or thyroid cartilages by extrinsic muscles. It also shortens the vocal folds, which reduces shrillness. The downward pull is greatest at the point of full inspiration (Damsté, 1987, p. 124).

The yawn-sigh discussed in the previous section will also lower the larynx. For this purpose, Kleinsasser has patients who are recovered from laryngeal surgery make loud yawning sounds on phonemes such as "haa, hoo, hee" while they hold the larynx as low as possible and the mouth and throat as open as possible (1979, p. 34).

The singer who raises and lowers the larynx with the pitch must first be told that this is unnecessary. Although few students require a complex explanation of the workings of the larynx, a basic understanding of where it is and how it works will often drastically alter their approach to singing. Many believe pitch change is caused by the larynx moving up and down like a ladder. Even more have absolutely no idea of the position of the larynx at all. The explanation can be as simple as telling the student that the larynx extends across the windpipe from front to back and that the vocal cords are stretched longer and thinner for high notes and kept shorter and

thicker for low notes. While most pitch change is due to this longitudinal stiffening of the vocal cords, a slight rise in laryngeal position may be necessary for some singers. Shipp points out that "for
many singers and most non-singers a vertical stiffening element
supplements this longitudinal force" (1987, p. 219).

Olson uses an exercise with female students for balancing registers (see Chapter 4) which helps to promote a relaxed laryngeal
posture in both men and women. The student is asked to sing as
quietly as possible three ascending and descending notes in the
lower middle of the range (f-g-a) on the [a] or [o] vowel while
keeping the larynx in the at-rest position. The pattern is then repeated at the half-step moving down over an interval of a fourth (to
c). When the student is able to produce a relaxed, quiet sound on
these three notes, he or she is asked to increase the pattern to five
notes up and down. The perimeters remain c and c.

[o] - - - -   [o] - - - - - - -

It must be stressed that the soft volume is to be found through relaxation rather than by tightening the throat or closing the mouth. If
necessary, the student can be directed to blow a little breath through
the tone to relax the throat. This is a **temporary** measure which
must be abandoned as soon as the student is able to produce a quiet
voice without constricting the throat. Students can, if they wish,
follow Polow and Kaplan's suggestion to track the rise and fall of
the larynx with a finger (1979, p. 60). The goal is for the student to
be able to change pitches without significant change in laryngeal
position.

After the student is comfortable with this exercise, it can be extended up to an interval of a ninth either by sliding or singing individual notes. Women must allow the sound to grow naturally
louder and more intense as the pitch raises, and men should allow
themselves to go into a light head voice or falsetto around middle c.

The complement to this exercise is a descending slide on [a] or
[ɔ] for women and [o] or [u] for men. To stay within a pitch range
where the student can sing in a totally relaxed manner, the perimeters should remain middle c and the c above for women and an octave lower for men. This is similar to the sigh described above.
Once again, the aspirate [h] should be used to assist the student to
achieve the desired relaxation. Once this relaxation is achieved, the
aspirate [h] should be dropped in favor of the static attack. This is

also similar to a technique used by Kleinsasser to facilitate a relaxed voice production following surgery for removal of nodules and contact pachydermia. He asks patients to do soft, voiced sighing that allows the patient to feel openness in the throat.

Brown uses octave arpeggios on [o] in a down-up-down pattern which are very effective for keeping the throat relaxed. The student is asked to keep the mouth open slightly more than the normal [o] and to allow the tongue to loll out of the mouth.

He also suggests that the student "think down" on the top note, in some cases having him or her point towards the floor with one hand simultaneously with the top pitch.

Olson uses the light laugh suggested by Perkins to begin a descending octave slide on [a] produced in the upper middle of the singer's range. Its counterpart replaces the laugh with a short sob. Practice with these techniques should be followed with the slide on the [a] alone.

Brown also uses a rapid scale with thirds above each note on the ascent and before each note on the descent.

Vennard states that use of the vowel [o] places the larynx lower than [a] and that [u] places it lower yet (1967, p. 134). Thus, Brown asks women to begin on [u] and then open to [o] and [a] as necessary for higher pitches. Men begin with [o] and change to [u].

Olson uses the following exercise to enable the student to experience low laryngeal position at the beginning of the exercise and, hopefully, to maintain it as he or she moves higher. He begins with the [æ] vowel to keep the tone up and out of the throat.

The student is instructed to make the dotted notes the most important and to just touch the sixteenth notes. Both men and women should change to [o] in the middle of the range. Before moving into the higher pitches, the pattern should be smoothed out into triplets and the vowel changed to [a] for women and [u] for men. Some male students will get a better head voice sound and still maintain a low laryngeal position if they keep the [o]. This exercise reflects Boone's suggestion to lower the pitch as one treatment for reduction of stridency (1983, p. 115). It is important to add at this point that the larynx should be **left** in its low position and not forced or pressed down (Punt, 1967, p. 55).

Harsh or Strident Tone Quality

The elevated larynx is often accompanied by constriction of the pharynx or upper throat. Tight pharyngeal constriction causes the pharyngeal surface to become taut. The tighter mucosal surfaces combined with decreased pharyngeal size accentuates the higher frequencies of the strident voice (Boone, 1983, p. 225). Boone defines the term *stridency* as the "unpleasant, shrill, metallic-sounding voice that appears to be related to hypertonicity of the pharyngeal constrictors, resulting in a decrease of both the length and the width of the pharynx" (1983, p. 225). Prater and Swift add elevation of the larynx to elements causing stridency. They describe this voice as having "sharp-sounding, carnival barker-like resonance" (1984, p. 231).

Therapy for stridency is focused on relaxation of the pharynx. This also allows a raised larynx to drop into a lower position. Once the extrinsic muscles are relaxed, all other factors being in effect, the intrinsic muscles of the larynx can function. They operate unconsciously rather than directly, so that to activate them we have only to think of speaking or singing. "In a healthy throat, if the outer muscles are relaxed, the inner ones will take care of themselves" (McClosky, 1977, p. 139).

Vennard's yawn-sigh technique described earlier is most useful for relaxation of the pharynx. Wilner and Sataloff use yawn-sigh techniques to relax the muscles of the pharynx and the back of the tongue. Because it is so often accompanied by upper chest breathing, they eliminate the yawn phase early in the process. They also have the patient use a mirror to observe the muscles of the tongue and pharynx as the palate is lifted and the pharynx expanded (1987, p. 316).

To relax the entire laryngopharyngeal area, Oren Brown uses an exercise which combines humming with chewing. He has the student slide through the pitches of a five-note scale in the sequence down, up, down while humming and chewing. The exercise is done throughout the middle of the student's range. He or she begins in the key of E and moves down by half-steps to the key of G or the lowest key possible without straining, begins again in E and moves up to Bb or the highest key possible without straining.

[hm]- - - - - - - - - - -

Both Batza (1977) and Kleinsasser (1979) use the hum. Kleinsasser has patients hum lightly while sliding up and down the scale (p. 35). Batza uses a sustained hum because it provides relaxation to the velum or soft palate. This relaxation "seems to spread to the laryngeal muscles and often produces dramatic, beneficial results" (1977, p. 17).

The student with extreme constriction will also benefit from open-mouth chewing. He or she should vocalize on assorted vowels while moving through random pitches. The results, a series of nonsense syllables, should be pleasantly free and carry over into other vocalizing. Both this technique and Brown's humming and chewing are based on Froeschels' *chewing therapy.*

Chewing therapy. In 1943 Emil Froeschels pioneered the development of what he called chewing therapy. Because the old Egyptians used the same hieroglyphic picture-sign for speaking and eating, Froeschels postulated that speech in man had first developed out of noises made when eating (Brodnitz, 1961, p. 144). Thus, a return to that primitive function would remove the tensions associated with speaking and facilitate better speech habits.

Froeschels first asked the patient to chew in the usual manner, with the lips closed but without anything in the mouth. He or she was to observe the tongue, which should move continually during chewing. The client was then asked to "chew 'like a savage'" (Froeschels, 1943, cited in Brodnitz, 1961, p. 153) with the mouth open and with extensive movement of the lips and tongue. He or she should next add random voice sounds to the chewing. Froeschels had the patient chew with voice for a few seconds twenty times a day for the first few days. After that he or she should follow the "voiced 'nonsense' chewing" with a half-minute of reading several times daily (Froeschels, 1943, cited in Brodnitz, 1961, p. 153).

Froeschels believed that chewing would "at the very beginning remove all the debris that habit and training had put upon the natural function" (Froeschels, 1952, cited in Boone, 1983, p. 129). Therefore, the purpose of chewing is to improve all aspects of voice at once rather than breaking them down into various elements (Boone, 1983). Because it causes better vocal fold approximation and size-mass adjustments, chewing allows the clinician to work on the voice as a whole rather than on individual facets such as pitch or quality. The chewing must be of the primitive kind with the tongue moving freely. "If the chewing is done correctly, that is, with vigorous movements of the lips and the tongue, a great variety of sounds escape the mouth" (Froeschels, 1943, cited in Brodnitz, 1961, p. 153).

Froeschels' method has been popular with a variety of therapists who have modified it for their own use. Landes has the client chew sugarless bubble gum while humming a soft, steady, comfortable, tuneless tone. Eventually the client is asked to stop chewing while continuing to hum on the same breath (1977, p. 133). Wyatt has clients chew a small piece of bread while phonating and instructs them to practice for a few minutes every hour using either chewing gum or bread. In the second therapy session she has clients chew without the use of food (1977, pp. 281-284). Kleinsasser starts patients on chewing therapy with a bolus of chewing gum or bread crusts. He then asks them to do voiced chewing on syllables "mnyan, mnyen, mnyen, mnyin" while keeping a continuous flow of tone (1979, pp. 34-35).

Polow and Kaplan (1979) have the client pretend he or she is going to eat a stack of four or five crackers, first chewing in a relaxed manner with the mouth open and then with the mouth closed. Closed-mouth chewing is facilitated with use of the [m] sound (p. 57). McFarlane uses humming and chewing to achieve an oral-nasal tone focus and to relax the muscles of the larynx (1988, p. 434).

Digital maneuvering. Tracking the location of the larynx with the fingers to know when the larynx rises more than a bit beyond a non-phonating position is one thing; moving it manually is quite another. Few other than the laryngologist know the anatomy well enough to attempt to maneuver the larynx down from a high position without the possibility of inflicting damage, especially on a tense student.

Douglas Stanley pulled his voice students' larynges down from the hyoid bone by inserting his fingers in the space between the thyroid cartilage and the hyoid bone. He later stated, "I have encountered a shockingly large number of voice students who have been seriously hurt through the incorrect use of the manipulations I have described -- some of them were so badly injured that the training of their voices thereafter was impossible" (Stanley, 1957, p. 359). This statement was not offered in the context of retracting his previous directions on laryngeal manipulation but rather in an attempt to clarify them and to stress the need for being correctly trained in his methods before attempting to use them. It should, however, serve as a word of warning to those contemplating digital manipulation of the larynx.

The voice therapy literature contains occasional references to massage of, pressure on or manipulation of the larynx. Polow and Kaplan use the pressure of the therapist's finger against the client's thyroid cartilage while the client phonates to lower the speaking pitch (1979, p. 60). Aronson, a laryngologist, writing, presumably, for other laryngologists, offers a detailed discussion of the use of laryngeal maneuvering to determine the amount of musculoskeletal tension present and to lower the thyroid cartilage as a means of improving the voice (1985, pp. 340-341). Reference was made in Chapter 2 of this book to the massage techniques suggested by McClosky. The fact that digital manipulation of the larynx is found in only a few sources, two of which were written by laryngologists, should serve as a warning to any teacher or student contemplating pulling down a high larynx or holding the larynx in place to keep it from rising. It is just too dangerous. Far better to suffer the frustration of slow progress than that of a ruined voice.

Breathy Tone as a Therapeutic Tool

While production of a breathy tone in singing is normally associated with popular music sung with electronic amplification, a breathy tone can be used as a temporary measure to reduce muscular tension. In a breathy tone the vocal folds never approximate completely, which eliminates any possibility of their striking each other, and the closed phase of the vibratory cycle is shortened (Gray, 1983, p. 15). Breathy tone is, therefore, helpful for reducing laryngeal tension and, as indicated above, eliminating glottal attack. Since the cords come together with less force and for a shorter period of time for breathy tone, there is also less wear and tear on the arytenoid cartilages (Moore, 1971b, p. 563).

Telling a student to produce a quiet, breathy tone can be used as an added direction with virtually any vocalise in the middle of the student's range. The quiet three- and five-note scales used by Olson and the complementary descending slide on [a] or [o] would be particularly applicable. The relaxation gained by singing with a breathy tone should be carried over into other exercises but not the breathy tone itself. The student should be told to stop blowing air through the tone as soon as he or she is able to produce a tone without laryngeal tension.

It may be helpful for students who experience a great deal of throat tension to interrupt their normal practice with a recapitulation of one or both of these exercises or to switch to a breathy tone for a few minutes to regain the relaxation which it produces. This reflects Reeds' suggestion for therapy patients whose vocation requires a great deal of talking to shift to a breathy voice at the first sign of discomfort while speaking (Reed, 1983, p. 94).

There is one disadvantage to using a breathy voice. *Edema* or swelling has been seen in professional speakers who had the habit of speaking with the incompletely closed glottis of the breathy voice. This edema can be explained as an attempt by the body to compensate for the "chink" or empty space between the cords. This is one risk in advising people to whisper when the cords are inflamed. They can "easily acquire a habit of speaking loudly with a breathy voice, while being convinced that in doing so they are sparing their voice" (Damsté 1987, p. 133).

Phonemes to promote breathy tone.   Fairbanks (1940) lists words that are "proharsh" and "probreathy." According to these lists, the vowels [ʊ], [u] and [o] are probreathy, and [æ], [a] and [ɛ] are proharsh. [I] and [i] are considered not harsh, and the diphthongs [ɛI] and [ɔI] are not breathy (p.177). What therapists call the probreathy vowels, i.e., those used to reduce harsh tone quality, are those which are formed high in the back of the mouth. The proharsh ones are those formed low. [Æ] is the lowest of the forward vowels and [a] is the lowest of the back vowels. [E] and [ɔ] are only slightly higher in front and back, respectively (Bernthal & Bankson, 1981, p. 14).

Examples of proharsh words include "ell, as, brag, odd, rob, and awe" (Fairbanks, 1940, p. 177). Examples of probreathy words are "hook, foot, toot, coop, post, and choke" (Fairbanks, 1940, p. 181). Probreathy sentences include many words which begin with the unvoiced consonants [hw], [t], [f], [k], [h], [s], [ʃ] and [p]. Proharsh sentences usually include many words which begin with vowels and with the voiced consonants [j], [l], [b] and [r]. Examples include the following probreathy sentences:

> "Who took the folks to the coast?"
> "So Hope's pooch hooked the soup."
> "Show Stu who took the two suits."
> (Fairbanks, 1940, p. 180).

Proharsh sentences include:

> "Elves are always odd, Al argued."
> "George added a large bag of eggs."
> "Lord Egbert objected to every law."
> (Fairbanks, 1940, pp. 176-177)

Using these concepts it is possible to construct vocalises which will aid the student in achieving a relaxed and less harsh phonation with vowels alone or combined with a voiceless consonant such as [h] to preclude any possibility of glottal stroke. It is better to vocalize a student who has a harsh tone on [o] or [u] rather than on [a], [æ] or [ɛ]. Examples would be downward slides on [hʊ] (Brown) and slides or stepwise patterns using the voiceless consonants [hw], [t], [f], [s] or [p] to limit the harsh quality of the vowel [a]. [K] is best avoided because of the tight adduction required (see The Breathy Voice).

[hʊ] ------   [hʊ] --------------   whoa! ----

Tongue Position
One of the major causes of constriction is the position of the tongue. The retracted tongue fills up the pharyngeal cavity, which

requires more effort on the part of the speaker or singer to get the sound out and gives a swallowed or throaty sound. This tongue position usually exerts downward pressure on the hyoid bone, which in turn presses the larynx down below resting position. In speech the tongue also may be held too far forward which creates what Boone calls the "baby-talk voice" (1983, p. 116). This tongue position creates a tone which lacks resonance and sometimes interferes with articulation. Excessive elevation of the back of the tongue is associated with tension and is often seen in professional voice users who are experiencing voice problems (Wilner and Sataloff, 1987, p. 315).

While a too-forward tongue position would seem to be relatively rare in the voice studio, singers will sometimes develop tension from keeping the tongue directly behind the lower teeth. Having that singer vocalize on an [a] vowel while moving the tip of the tongue around inside the mouth frees these tensions without moving the tongue or the tone into the throat.

Retracted tongues are a common problem and seem to be associated with the singer's desire to achieve a particular sound quality and tonal placement that is too low. The sound produced is often called the *Knödel*, the German word for dumpling, because it sounds as if the singer had a dumpling filling up the throat. This is one time when a tape recording of the student can be quite helpful. Because of the low tonal focus and because the tongue position blocks direct release of the sound out of the mouth, what the student hears through the eustachian tubes that connect the throat to the inner ear is usually quite different from the sound that actually reaches the listener. A tape recording will show the singer that the tone is not at all what he or she was attempting to produce. If the student is able to produce some sounds with the tongue in a forward position, it is helpful to tape those too so he or she can hear the contrast.

Unfortunately, the retracted tongue can be a rather difficult problem to overcome, even when one is fully aware of it. The simplest thing to do is to have the student put the tip of the tongue outside the mouth while vocalizing on the [a] vowel. Brown asks students to allow the tip of the tongue to loll over the lower lip on [o] as well. Fisher suggests the client try to keep the whole tongue slightly forward in the mouth. For this purpose she gives a *vowel fronting exercise* in which the client repeats the forward vowels [i], [I], [e] and [ɛ] ten times, while maintaining a smile and trying to get the tongue nearer the front of the mouth (1975, p. 122). Damsté indicates that sticking out the tongue elevates the hyoid-larynx complex (1987, p. 124), so that sticking out the tongue should indeed raise the larynx that has been depressed by pressure of the base of the tongue against the hyoid bone.

Singers with retroflex tongue positions often drop the base of the tongue before dropping the jaw (see Fisher, 1975, p. 121). This creates a little pocket in the throat against which the singer opens the mouth. The McClosky up-and-down jaw exercises described in Chapter 2 can be slowed down with special attention paid to moving the entire jaw as a unit. The student should watch the movement of the jaw in the mirror. After a few seconds the student should drop the hands and continue moving the jaw alone. This movement can be slowed further so that with each drop of the jaw the student phonates [a] at a comfortable pitch level. The teacher may wish to set a duple rhythm (close - open/[a]). The student should next try a slide at a medium pitch on the same vowel. The rhythm here becomes triple (close - open - [a] slide).

Use of the [l] consonant with various vowels is a tradition in the voice studio and the choral warm-up that exists somewhat routinely apart from its original intent. As Campbell (1980, p. 22) points out, tongue tension and jaw tension are often connected. Use of the [l] combined with open vowels such as [a] with the tongue moving independently of the jaw will free the tongue from the jaw. In addition, exercises such as "guy-lie" and "blah" discussed in Chapter 2 under Mouth Position will help release tensions originating at the base of the tongue and affecting release of the jaw. Also effective are patterns using front consonants such as [v] and [f] and tongue-tip alveolar consonants such as [t] or [d] with the vowel [a]. These should begin on middle c for men and an octave higher for women and be repeated at descending half-steps.

La pada pa la pa da pa la   Ta la ta fa ta

This is similar to Polow and Kaplan's use of frontal sounds [p], [b], [t], [d], [f] and [v] (1979, p. 63) and Boone's use of tongue-tip alveolar consonants [t], [d], [s] and [z]. Boone also recommends frontal consonants [w], [hw], [p], [b], [f], [v], [θ], [ð] and [l] (1983, pp. 116-117). Both use the following vowels alone or combined with consonants listed above: [i], [I] and [e]. Boone adds [ɛ] and [æ].

Changing the tonal focus or placement is also very important with singers with this tongue position. Certainly the retracted tongue and depressed laryngeal position which accompanies it will impede any efforts on the part of the singer to achieve a high tonal focus. Making the student aware of the desirability of a focus that is

forward, up in the head or forward and up will no doubt help the
student conquer the tongue problems (see Chapter 4). This approach will have to be combined with exercises that move the tongue
forward, either by allowing the tip of the tongue to protrude from
the mouth or by the use of frontal vowels such as [i] and [æ].
Boone uses forward or mask placement as a solution to retroflex
tongues. To attain this placement he uses high front vowels and
front-of-the-mouth consonants and a "place-the-vowel approach"
(1983, pp. 227-228).

Removing constriction will often dramatically affect the tone
produced. For example, after releasing the retroflex tongue, it is
quite normal to discover that downward pressure on the strap
muscles has also lowered the soft palate so that the tone is nasal or
remains caught in the throat. The newly freed tone may also appear
fuzzy and unfocused, especially in those who have sung with a particularly constricted, strident sound. Campbell cautions that an unfocused sound is normal in singers who have incurred damage and
that attempting to focus the sound too soon will create new bad
habits. "The reeducation process includes relaxing the muscles involved in hypofunction, allowing them sufficient time and practice
to function free from old tension and retraining them to function in a
healthy manner" (1980, p. 22). Even if the teacher does not encourage breathy quality, he or she must be willing to accept it temporarily when it occurs as a normal consequence of the elimination of
constriction.

The Breathy Voice

A certain amount of breathiness is considered normal in the tone
of young singers. Of course, if there is any question about a medical basis of the problem, the student should be seen by a doctor.
Those who show an exceptional amount of breathiness when they
sing but whose speaking voices are normal may be blowing extra air
through the tone. Some students sing with a breathy tone to create a
particular "style" or tone quality they find desirable. Others may
have misunderstood an earlier instruction or may have the misguided
idea that such singing is "safer" for their voices. The problem may
be solved by simply explaining to them that this tone quality is not
appropriate for the literature being studied and/or that the sung tone
does not come out of the mouth in great gushes of air. Polow and
Kaplan's suggestion of positioning the hands on the throat and in
front of the mouth to monitor breath related to phonation (1979, p.
71) is effective for those who habitually blow air through the tone.
Some work on breath control and attack may also be necessary.

Breathing practice can be adapted for students to reduce breathiness in the tone. Here the student should release the breath first on a

voiced sound then on an unvoiced sound. Examples would include
beginning with [z] and moving to [s] or repeating [b] and gradually
changing to [p]. Polow and Kaplan use this technique with their
clients moving from [b] to [p], [g] to [k], [d] to [t] and [z] to [s] in
the following manner:

> b-b-b-b-p
> b-b-b-p-p
> b-b-p-p-p
> b-p-p-p-p
> p-p-p-p-p (1979, p. 70)

If these suggestions are not effective and medical examination
indicates that voice training is appropriate at this time, the teacher
may use some techniques to improve glottal closure. Murphy uses a
sharp glottal attack to increase tension or degree of contraction of the
laryngeal muscles (1964, p. 63). The use of velar stops [k] and [g]
preceding vowels can replace the glottal stop suggested by Murphy.
This can be combined with a vowel for a five- or eight-note downward slide, kah or gah. These consonants can also be used alone on
every note or combined with other consonants to produce patterns
such as "guy-lie-guy-lie-guy" (Olson) or "ka-key-ka-key-ka" on
rising and falling three- and five-note patterns.

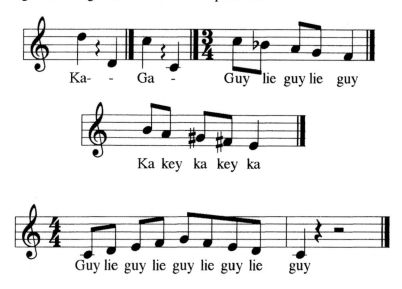

Voiced consonants [b], [t], [d] or [z] can be substituted for the [k]
or [g] as the tone improves.

Again, the choice of vowel is important. Negus indicates that the vowel [a] gives a narrow glottis with straight sides. The vowel [i], however, brings the membranous portions of the vocal cords together for their entire length (1931, p. 429). Therefore, the vowel [i] may require less effort and provide a clearer tone for singers with incomplete closure. This can be done alone or with appropriate consonants such as [g], [k], [b], [d], and [z]. Almost any pattern can be used, although vowel modification towards [a] in the upper range of the female voice is a must.

Starting with the [i] vowel and changing to other vowels such as [a] causes a carryover in improved closure. Again, many exercises can be adapted.

Volume or Intensity

After tone quality, the most noticeable aspect of the voice is the volume or intensity. Singers with too little volume can only be heard in the most intimate recital situations, and those who are only capable of volumes greater than mezzo-forte may miss some of the subtleties of interpretation that make a performance more than adequate. While physiology limits the individual voice's potential for loud singing and, in some cases, for singing quietly, understanding how volume of the voice is varied may help the singer gain better control of this aspect of singing. It may also help him or her prevent abuse of the voice through the incorrect use of volume parameters.

Although there is some confusion over the meanings of the terms volume and intensity, they refer to the same vocal parameters.

Intensity is the acoustical correlate of loudness and, as such, refers to the "magnitude of sound expressed in power or pressure" (Harrison & Tucker, 1987, p. 136). Intensity of sound is a specific decibel level, and loudness or volume is the way a person perceives the sound level (Case, 1984, p. 26).

Volume is increased by increasing subglottic pressure (Harrison & Tucker, 1987, p. 137; Putnam & Shelton, 1985, p. 96). However, subglottic pressure is determined by both air flow and the amount of resistance which meets that air (Hirano, 1988, p. 63). The vocal folds must exert greater pressure to keep from being blown apart by the increased air pressure, and when they are finally blown apart it is with greater force and more energy. This creates a sound wave of larger amplitude, which is perceived as louder (Putnam & Shelton, 1985, p. 96).

The activity of the laryngeal muscles as it relates to volume varies with the register employed. The singer's vocalis muscle shows the greatest increase in activity for increased loudness in the modal or low register regardless of the pitch. There is also some increase in the activity of the lateral cricoarytenoid and interarytenoid muscles. The cricothyroid muscles show less activity as intensity increases, probably to maintain the fundamental frequency against the increased air pressure (Hirano, 1988, p. 63).

In the falsetto register it appears that increased loudness is due solely to increased breath pressure (Isshiki, 1989, p. 18; Hirano, 1988, p. 64). There appears to be no significant contribution by any of the laryngeal muscles in increasing or decreasing intensity in this register, possibly because of the "chink" at the posterior end of the larynx. Again, activity of the cricothyroid muscle shows an inverse variance with increase in intensity in order to maintain the fundamental frequency (Hirano, 1988, p. 64).

Scherer and colleagues reported an experiment on the effects of prolonged loud reading on the vocal cords. They used two female subjects with no history of vocal problems, one trained in speaking and one untrained. The two subjects were asked to read a specified text at a pitch one octave above their lowest pitch available, nearly as loud as possible for 15 minutes (fatigue task). This was contrasted with a diagnostic task of seven prolonged [a] vowels at a comfortable loudness at the same pitch. Thus, the pattern was diagnostic/fatigue/diagnostic, etc. ending with a diagnostic when the speaker became vocally fatigued. The trained speaker was able to read significantly more fatigue episodes without feeling any changes in her voice. Laryngeal examination following the experiment indicated vocal cord edemas in both subjects.   Both were recovered the following day. The untrained speaker stopped because of vocal fatigue before any significant acoustic changes were noted. The trained

speaker first went through a brief period of warm-up followed by changes in perturbation which followed an expected pattern (Scherer et al., 1985).
Although excessive loudness does not necessarily lead to vocal cord pathologies, it is a factor in their continuance. As early as 1960, Von Leden and Moore demonstrated that an increase in loudness also increased the force with which the cords approximated each other. The greater force of glottal closure increased the trauma of vocal abuse, which causes contact ulcers (Von Leden & Moore, 1960, p. 746). Shelton considers excessive volume particularly harmful if it is produced by increasing laryngeal tension alone rather than by increasing the breath flow and allowing laryngeal muscles to make the appropriate adjustments to accommodate it (1985, p. 277). Nearly every program of voice therapy requires the participant to avoid excessive loudness so that rehabilitation can take place (viz. e.g., Boone, 1980, p. 36; Cooper, 1973, p. 128; and Murry, 1982a, p. 484). On the other hand, Landes also warns that speaking softly and with great emotional intensity can cause laryngeal abuse (1977, p.125).
There are several conclusions which can be drawn from the preceding information. First, it is obvious from the Scherer experiment that prolonged loud singing, even for a trained singer, will affect the cords adversely, if only temporarily. Second, singers must be taught to increase volume by using more breath rather than by exerting greater laryngeal pressure. Third, because it is controlled by breath pressure only, prolonged loud singing would appear to be safer in falsetto than in heavy or mixed registers. However, singing loudly in falsetto usually pushes the voice into a mixed registration. And finally, singing loudly is particularly dangerous when the voice is already affected by fatigue or a cold or when the breath is reduced by pulmonary congestion, abdominal distress or other factors.

Vibrato
The vibrato is a rather elusive part of the singer's tone quality. There are those teachers and singers who claim to be able to alter the vibrato through specific exercises and those who believe it is totally beyond the singer's and teacher's control. Research indicates that the origin of the vibrato is in the brain stem where the superior laryngeal nerve is controlled. Motor control oscillators are inhibited and disinhibited in transmitting pulsed motor signals along that nerve to the cricothyroid muscles. This fluctuation causes minute contraction and relaxation of these muscles which varies the stiffness of the vocal folds and causes the slight variation of pitch we hear as vibrato. "The singer has no conscious control over vibrato

rate, but can control a wide range of vibrato frequency extent" (Shipp, Sundberg & Haglund, 1985, p. 117). Variations in vibrato frequency are principally determined by the cricothyroid muscle. "EMG recordings from the CT [cricothyroid muscle] show a rhythmic pulsing of muscle contraction and relaxation in synchrony with vibrato frequency modulation" (Shipp, Sundberg & Haglund, 1985, p. 116). Variations in intensity are caused by sympathetic vibrations within the vocal tract and by movements of the jaw or tongue. When the vibrato is too wide, too fast or too slow it becomes noticeable. Such problems are usually caused by tension in or lack of control of the extrinsic laryngeal and pharyngeal muscles. "We hypothesize that the more skilled singers are able to confine the oscillating motor signals to the superior laryngeal nerve innervating the cricothyroid muscles and minimize the transmission of motor pulses along pathways to extralaryngeal muscle groups" (Shipp, Sundberg & Haglund, 1985, p. 116).

It is apparent from the above that problems with the vibrato are symptoms of other errors in technique. As such it is better altered by the indirect means of finding and fixing the underlying problem. The causes of a too-fast vibrato may include some type of constriction in the vocal tract or a tonal placement that is being forced. Factors which may cause the vibrato to be too slow include a low or throaty tonal focus, improper use of registers or vocal cords which are swollen by a physical problem such as allergy or pre-menstrual syndrome.

Chapter 4

Various Approaches: Registration, Placement and Resonance Extremes

The title of this chapter reflects the fact that the areas covered in it are ones on which teachers and singers often place a great deal of emphasis. Some consider balancing the registers their ultimate goal while others see achieving high tonal placement as a solution; still others prefer to find a tone with a nasal ring to it. Rather than viewing each of these facets separately, the reader is asked to approach the different areas covered in this chapter as representing parts of an overall program of healthy voice production and as solutions to the varied problems found in the voice studio.

Pitch and Registration

Registration

Among teachers, researchers and clinicians who deal with the voice there is a wide divergence of terminology used in regard to registration. "Morner, Fransesson and Fant (1964) published a paper in which they listed 107 different names which have been used to identify one register or another" (Hollein, 1974, p. 125). Before attempting any discussion on registration it is necessary to come to an understanding of what a register is and to sort out the various names given to the registers.

Voice scientists see registration primarily as acoustic events. Independently and with various other researchers, voice scientist Harry Hollein has written many articles on registration. His definition of a voice register, which appears as follows or in some variation in nearly every article, was one of the first.

> A voice register is a series or range of consecutive phonated frequencies of nearly identical voice quality; they are totally *laryngeal* events and there is little or no overlap in fundamental frequency between adjacent registers; . . . Secondly, we propose that three major vocal registers of laryngeal origin have been so defined and described; they are the pulse, modal

and loft registers. (Hollein, Gould, & Johnson,
1974, p. 188)

Hollein, Gould and Johnson also postulated the existence of what
they called "singers' registers" which originate in the vocal tract
above the larynx (Hollein, 1974, p. 80; Hollein, 1977, p. 80;
Hollein, Gould % Johnson, 1974, p. 188).
    Voice scientist Ingo Titze suggests there are two types of register
transition, *periodicity* and *timbre*. Below a certain pitch the ear can
detect the individual pulses of the waveform, while in the registers
above that pitch the tone is heard as continuous. Thus, the transition
from glottal pulse or fry to chest or modal register is one of periodicity. The transition from modal or chest register to loft or falsetto
in both male and female is a timbre transition. It is characterized by
a quality change due to the changes in glottal closure which cause
the gain or loss of high-frequency sound energy at the glottis (Titze,
1988, pp. 183-184).
    More recent definitions of registers provided by people from
various areas of voice working together reflect a broader view. The
first combines the concepts of laryngeal and singers' registers so
that registers are "defined here as patterns of interaction between the
vocal folds and resonators" (Welch, Sergeant & MacCurtain, 1988,
p. 151). Sataloff, Spiegel, Carroll, Darby and Rulnik expand
Hollein's list of registers to include "vocal fry, chest, middle, head
and falsetto." And state that "an overlap of frequencies [pitches]
among registers occurs routinely" (1987, p. 309).
    While it may appear that these definitions cannot be reconciled,
both Hollein and his colleagues and Sataloff and his colleagues accept fry or pulse register, modal or chest register and falsetto. These
commonalties provide a starting point for an investigation into how
these registers are produced.
    Pulse register or *vocal fry* sounds like short pops of tone and
has the lowest range of fundamental frequency and the most complex wave length composition (Hollein, 1974, p. 126; Hollein,
Gould & Johnson, 1974, pp. 189-190). It is also called *creek* and
strohbass (Hollein, 1974, p. 126). The fold lengths are short and
thick and do not change with frequency changes. The closed phase
of vibration is longer (Hollein, 1974, p. 135; Hollein, Gould &
Johnson, 1974, pp. 190 & 192). Because vocal fry can be produced with very relaxed folds and a minimum of subglottal pressure, phonation in the fry or pulse register is used by some clinicians to relax hyperfunctional voice production. The folds become
very compliant and the effects of any masses that may be present,
such as nodules, are minimized. After a few moments of phonation
in this mode or register, the voice is "almost always . . . clearer"

(McFarlane, 1988, p. 42). Pulse register can also be produced under conditions of extreme tension, such as when the speaker constantly uses a pitch at or near the bottom of the pitch range (Case,
1984, p. 33).

Modal register encompasses the pitches most men and women
use for speaking, the majority of the range in the lower male singing
voices and at least the lowest tones in the higher male and all female
voices (Hollein, 1974, p. 126). Because its vibrations are felt in the
area where the sternum joins the clavicle and because it is effective
only at low pitches, it is also called *chest voice* or *low register*. The
fold lengths vary as a function of frequency level from as short as
pulse register to as long as loft register. The folds become thinner
as the frequency level is raised. In this register subglottic air pressure increases and decreases radically with corresponding changes
in frequency. Fold stiffness shows similar variation with changes in
frequencies (Hollein, 1974, p. 137; Hollein, 1977, p. 90 Hollein,
Gould & Johnson, 1974, pp. 190 & 192). On lower pitches the
folds are soft with a large amplitude of vibration. Raising the pitch
increases the firmness of the folds and decreases their amplitude of
vibration (Damsté, 1987, p. 129).

Phonation in chest register begins on the underside of the cords
and moves to the top like a wave, with the lower surfaces beginning
to close while the top is opening. This phase lag between the upper
and lower edges is seen by Isshiki as an indication that the Bernoulli
effect is greater in chest register than in falsetto (1989, p. 11).

Falsetto or *loft register* has the highest fundamental frequency
and simplest wave composition. Here the vocal ligaments are
stretched to their full length for all pitches, the glottal area is reduced
and subglottic air pressure is low (Hollein, 1974, pp. 126 & 138;
Hollein, 1977, pp. 90 & 93; Hollein, Gould & Johnson, 1974 p.
192). The tension of the vocal folds obliterates their upper and
lower lips so that only the tight phonating edges remain; it stabilizes
the anterior and posterior portions of the membranous glottis
(Daniloff, Schuckers & Feth, 1980, cited in Case, 1984, p. 34);
and it greatly reduces the mobility of the mucosa that covers the
cords (Isshiki, 1989, p. 28). Only the outside of the middle of the
vocal folds vibrates (Daniloff, Schuckers & Feth, 1980 cited in
Case, 1984, p. 34). The shorter area of vibration and increased
stiffness reduce the amplitude of the cords (Hirano, 1981, p. 64).
In falsetto the closed phase is virtually nonexistent (Hollein, 1974,
p. 138; Hollein, Gould & Johnson, 1974, p. 192; Shanks &
Duguay, 1984, p. 250). Since the folds do not adduct completely,
there is less interruption to the flow of air and a smoother pressure
wave. The flute-like character of the voice is because the smoother
pressure wave generates only one or two harmonic overtones

(Damsté, 1987, p. 122). With the mobility of the mucosa reduced, the phase lag is no longer noted and adduction is due mainly to elasticity of the cords (Isshiki, 1989, p. 11).

Muscular activity. "Vocal register is basically regulated by the ratio of the vocalis and cricothyroid activities" (Hirano, 1988, p. 59). There is greater vocalis activity in the lower, heavier registers than in the lighter upper registers (p. 58).

BASIC REGISTER AGENT

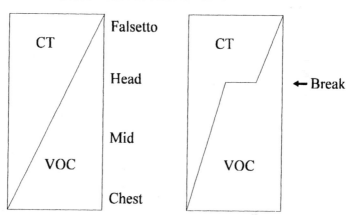

Fig. 9. Basic register agent
From "Vocal mechanisms in singing: Laryngological and phoniatric aspect," Minoru Hirano, 1988, *Journal of Voice*, **2**, pp. 51-69. Used by permission.

Registration is also affected by other factors such as resonance above and below the glottis and activities by other muscles (p. 60).

The four schematic drawings provided by Hirano and Kakita (1985, p. 43) show the cross-sectional structure of the body and cover of the vocal cords during four different kinds of sound production: soft phonation at low pitch levels, heavy voice at medium pitch levels, heavy or modal register and light register or falsetto. For production of modal register (c) the vocalis muscle contracts little more than the cricothyroid. (It will be remembered that the cricothyroid is responsible for stretching or elongating the vocal bands.) In falsetto (d) the vocalis muscle is not active or only slightly active, but the cricothyroid muscle is very contracted. Between those two extremes lies the loud voice at medium pitch levels (b) which shows the vocalis muscle much more contracted than the cricothyroid. This causes the body of the folds to be stiff but with a flexible cover. For soft phonation at low pitches (a) nei-ther muscle

60   The New Voice Pedagogy

is particularly active, and both the body and cover of the vocal folds
remain flexible (1985, p. 42).

Fig. 10. Four typical laryngeal adjustments in physiological condition which
are determined mainly by combinations of different activities of the cricothyroid
and the vocalis muscles. Plus and minus signs indicate relative degrees of contraction of the vocalis and cricothyroid muscles. Kb = degree of elasticity of
body; Kc = degree of elastsicity of the cover. From "Morphological structure of
the vocal cord as a vibrator and its variations," Minoru Hirano, 1974, *Folia
Phoniatrica*, **26**, pp. 89-94. Used by permission.

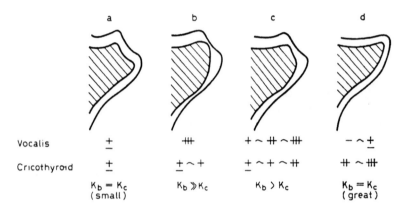

An increase in fundamental frequency in modal register increases the activities of the cricothyroid, lateral cricoarytenoid and
vocalis muscles (Hirano, 1988, p. 60). The cricothyroid stretches
and tenses the vocal fold which raises the fundamental frequency directly (p. 61). In falsetto the cricothyroid muscle does not always
contribute to control of fundamental frequency, nor do the activities
of the lateral cricoarytenoid and vocalis muscles always relate positively to fundamental frequency in this register (p. 61). Fundamental frequency is raised somewhat by the reduced length of the glottis
and by the reduced mobility of the mucosa (Hirano, 1981, pp. 63-
64).

Damsté and Lerman describe the mid-register as a mixture of the
chest and falsetto registers. This mixture is created by moderate
contraction of the cricothyroid muscles, which stretch the vocal
cords, and of the vocalis muscle, which shortens the cords. This
results in a partially stretched vocal ligament with a greater surface
of vibration than in falsetto. The folds are firmer than in chest register and less taut and stretched than in falsetto (1975, p. 20). This
particular muscular coordination is what is used by singers to create
the middle and head registers cited by Sataloff, Spiegel, Carroll,

Darby and Rulnik. The ability to use that coordination to change from one register to another is discussed in a following section on Register Transition.

In 1974, Hollein and Hollein, Gould and Johnson cited "'flute'" or "'whistle'" register as one of the other registers possible in some individuals (Hollein, 1974, p. 127; Hollein, Gould & Johnson, 1974, pp. 188-189). Flute or whistle register lies at the topmost part of the upper register and is the result of damping of the glottis so that only a small anterior part is open and able to vibrate. This damping occurs when air pressure is low and the internal fibers of the thyroarytenoid muscle are very contracted (Negus, 1931, p. 426). In a recent study of the whistle register in the female voice, Walker discovered a significant change in air flow between loft and whistle registers in all subjects investigated. Three of four subjects showed significant reduction in mean flow rate of air (MFR) in whistle register as compared with head register. The fourth, whose MFR for both registers was the lowest of all subjects, showed a slight increase in MFR in whistle register. Analysis of sound pressure levels showed those levels to be much greater in head register than whistle register for **all** four subjects (1988, pp. 144-145). His study also showed that the number of harmonics evident in whistle register was less than the number in falsetto or loft register (p. 147).

Within this book the following names are used to describe the various registers. *Fry* or *pulse register* is the lowest possible register available. It is heard as a series of pops and is acceptable (marginally!) in singing only when used by basses to reach their lowest notes in choral music. *Low* or *chest register* refers to what Hollein calls the modal register. *Upper register* in women's voices and *falsetto* in men's voices refer to Hollein's loft register. *Head voice* is used to refer to those pitches of the male voice which combine the muscular activities of low and falsetto registers in varying combinations so that the lower pitches exhibit more characteristics of low register and only slight influence of the falsetto. As the pitch raises the falsetto becomes more prominent while the influence of low register decreases. The same effect occurs in the female voice in the *middle register* or transition area. Because it covers a much shorter span of pitches in the female voice, the middle register is not always considered a separate register. *Whistle* or *flute register* refers to pitches produced at the uppermost pitches with the glottis dampened so that only the forward part opens. Although flute or whistle is most often used by coloratura sopranos, experience teaches that other voices, including male voices, are capable of it or a similar action (see Vennard 1967, pp. 67-68).

Improper Registration

In 1967 Vennard wrote of the "unused register." "Most beginners tend to sing either all heavy or all light. If they are conscious at all of the other register, they are schizophrenic about it" (p. 73). He considered the unused register for men the falsetto and for women the low or chest register. Women who usually speak in chest register and contraltos who have sung in nothing else were considered exceptions (p. 76).

Trends in voice usage in popular music and in the media often influence singers, particularly young students. At this time this author finds female voices who have carried the low, or a mix of high and low, to what they consider the top of their singing range an all too frequent problem. Occasionally they will know that there is a light heady quality available to them, but they either do not care for the sound themselves or have been discouraged in its use by others who thought it too soft, too breathy or too something else. Again quoting Vennard, "*forcing the female chest voice upward is dangerous if not actually malpractice.* . . . Hyperfunction . . . eventually leads to hypofunction (Froeschels), resulting in the loss of the upper tones of the voice, especially creating difficulty in bridging over into the light upper voice" (1967, p. 76). It is essential that all female singers be taught to find and vocalize in their upper register and through the transition area. Popular, musical theater and country singers will find that warming up this way will help prevent or reduce damage caused by using largely low register throughout their range and will give them more choices of tonal colors and thus a broader range of interpretation.

The exclusive use of the falsetto mechanism by the adult male with a normally developed larynx and the use of a male pitch by a female with a normal larynx are discussed as voice disorders in Chapter 7. Boone specifically names using an inappropriate register as one of the causes of misuse (1980, p. 37). In such cases, changing the register in which the client speaks is the resolution of the problem.

Finding the upper register of the female voice. Although Hirano and Kakita show that muscular activity and vocal fold stiffness is different with soft phonation at a low pitch than with falsetto, Olson's quiet vocalise described in the previous chapter is useful for finding and strengthening the upper register of women's voices at low pitches. This is perhaps because there is so little muscular activity at all with this type of phonation that it allows the voice accustomed to a great deal of activity of the vocalis muscle (i.e., the chest voice) at these pitches to relax enough for the cricothyroid muscle to become active at the appropriate time for the introduction of upper register. The woman should do this exercise on an [o] vowel.

[o] - - - -   [o] - - - - - - - -

The goal here is not a breathy quality but rather a light, effortless sound. After the student is comfortable with the exercise, she should extend it to an interval of a ninth either by sliding or by singing individual notes. Still starting with a quiet sound, the woman must **allow** the volume to grow naturally louder and more intense as the pitch rises. It is essential that the lower notes always be produced in the half voice or "little voice." It may be helpful at first to tell the student to expect some voice skips or breaks and to suggest that the tone does not have to be "beautiful."

Brown uses inflections in the speaking voice to help female students find their upper register. The student is asked to imitate the teacher in a rising "hm?" and an answering, descending "hm." The descending "hm" can also be elicited by the suggestion of imitating a sound of delight. The teacher can make it more fun for the student by suggestions such as "Think of chocolate cake," or "Think of inheriting a million dollars." Brown also has the student slide up and down as much as a fourth saying syllables such as "heigh-ho," "ahso," and "so slow" which use open vowels and bilabial or lingualalveolar consonants. His goal is to get the singer to speak lightly and freely at a pitch in the upper middle of her range (approximately c# or d an octave above middle c for mezzos and contraltos and the e above for sopranos). Once the student has slid up into the light head or upper register, she is asked to speak to the teacher at that pitch while maintaining relaxation. It is helpful if the teacher gives pitch cues appropriate to the student and then joins in the conversation at the higher pitch. To further facilitate a relaxed laryngeal posture sentences beginning with [o] and [u] vowels may be used. Once the relaxation is achieved the student can say virtually anything from reciting license plates seen out the window to what she had for breakfast. A key sentence such as "Oh my what a lovely day!" can be used to return to the optimum relaxation at any point. In addition, the student can be worked gradually into singing by sighing down the first two words ("O-o-o-oh mah-ah-ah-y") then singing them on a five-note descending slide followed by a sung slide on the same vowel only.

oh   my   ma - ah -

This is similar to exercises used in voice therapy for finding a higher optimum speaking pitch. Many therapists use a rising or questioning inflection for such purposes.

McFarlane uses "uh-hum" as if indicating yes because it automatically triggers a higher pitch. This "uh-hum" can be sustained and combined with words and phrases introduced at the higher level (1988, p. 430).

Cooper begins with "um-hum" using a rising inflection as though agreeing with someone. Next the client adds numbers after the "um-hum" on the same pitch: "um-hum one, um-hum two to ten" (1973, p. 80). The "um-hum" is next changed to "nim-nim" and then to "me-me" with numbers one through ten attached at the end of each. The next step is to carry over the new pitch and focus into phrases. Cooper accomplishes this by having the client say "'me-me one, how are you?' 'me-me two, I am fine.' 'me-me three, who said that?'" and so on. The client is then asked to eliminate the number so only the key word and phrase remain. The sentences become longer, and eventually the key words are eliminated (1973, pp. 74-81).

Moore uses vowels such as "oh" and "ah" spoken as though asking questions as well as actual spoken questions as drills for raising the speaking pitch (1971b, p. 563). Polow and Kaplan have the client read the following words with an upward inflection:

oh   how
why   now
when   again
which   today
what   please (1979, p. 17)

The client is then asked to prolong the final sound in each word on the upper pitch. He or she should next attempt to produce various vowels at that upper pitch. When this is achieved, nonsense syllables, words and sentences should be used.

Wilner and Sataloff indicate that singers who have sung with bad habits for many years may find it easier to change their techniques through speech than through singing exercises, perhaps because speech has less ego association for them. The new, correct

techniques can be carried into singing by extending the vowels of
speech and then converting them to singing. Although most speech
pathologists do not work directly with the singing voice, skills
learned through speech usually carry over into singing (1987, p.
314).

Finding the low register. Many sopranos have never tried to
sing below middle c, and, when they are vocalized there on open
vowels, they find the chest register quite easily. Still others will
have sung along with the popular singers on the radio but will not
consider the voice they used to be appropriate to use in front of their
teacher. Asking them if they do sing with the radio and if they could
demonstrate their "radio voice" will usually elicit a strong chest register which can be integrated into their overall technique. Exercises
of limited range beginning on a low pitch may work well for some
women.

Guy   lie   guy   lie   guy

Here the [g] helps assure approximation of the cords while guarding
against the use of a glottal stroke. The student should begin around
a below middle c and move up by half steps only two or three times,
allowing the top notes to grow lighter each time.

One usually associates an unused low register with the female
voice, but some male singers also fail to use that register. Brodnitz
describes one type of what he calls "pseudotenors." These are
countertenors who have the normal vocal cords of an adult male and
who sing in extremely high ranges for long periods of time. They
specialize in singing music which was originally written for castrati
sopranos and altos. Such prolonged use of the normal male voice
"will invariably destroy the singing voice" (1983, p. 72).

While they do not sing as high as the countertenors described by
Brodnitz, some male ballad singers who sing consistently in the
range of the female alto (above the f below middle c) use falsetto to
the point that their low range nearly disappears. The loss of the low
register seldom motivates such a singer to seek help. The motivat-
ing factor is usually the damage done by singing continuously with
the cords not adducting and/or with the constriction of straining to
maintain the high tessitura. These singers will benefit from relaxation exercises to reduce constriction and lower laryngeal position
and from breath training to increase breath pressure and allow the
low register to emerge. The singer must be assured constantly that

finding the low register for low notes and allowing it to mix in for *at least* the middle range at medium volume and louder will not ruin his "style." Many of these men have quite literally been using only half of their voices, both in terms of register and volume. Therefore, some will be so delighted with the new register and subsequent increase in power of their voices that they may tend to overuse the low register to the point of creating new problems. Like any change in registration, this must be carefully monitored.

Finding whistle or flute register. Brown uses a very high-pitched slide with the lips pursed in a tight [u] to locate the flute or whistle register. If necessary, the singer can use the hands to hold the cheeks in a pucker. If the student raises the larynx, the exercise should be stopped until the sound can be produced without extrinsic muscle tension. Whistle register especially cannot be forced but must be found through relaxation.

Register Change

The areas where the voice must change registers are often called breaks because the untrained voice appears to break into a new type of production. The break is a sudden gap in sound which occurs when the thyroarytenoid muscles suddenly decrease their activity and the cricothyroid muscles suddenly begin to function (Brewer, 1985, p. 358). A skillful transition of this muscular activity is one of the marks of the trained singer. Vennard (1967) contains a complete discussion on the different schools of thought about registration and resulting change in register (see pp. 66-78).

The cause of a noticeable shift in registers is almost always excessive use of one register, usually the lower. In most cases locating and strengthening the falsetto or upper register will help to blend the registers. The men discussed above who have developed their falsetto to the point where they sing nearly like light sopranos are exceptions and should be treated as indicated.

Brown's scale with thirds described in Chapter IV can help both male and female students to find and blend upper register or falsetto. The use of the [u] vowel for men not only assures a low laryngeal position but provides the necessary mouth and resonance adjustments for falsetto production. Mixing some falsetto into the lower tones of male voices assures upper notes will not be strained. Women can either mix the registers for the lower notes so as to make the transition out of chest gradual or, if they prefer and the sound is substantial enough, can sing all notes above middle c in upper register. Maintaining a closed [u] into the upper pitches facilitates falsetto in the male voice and whistle tone or flute register in the female voice. When the singer first attempts it he or she will feel a bump or change in the sound. Repeating the exercise on a more open vowel ([a] for women, [ɔ] for men) will usually show the student the benefits of easier, and perhaps more, top notes due to finding the new register.

To find and blend low register, Brown has women begin on the [a] vowel around a below middle c and slide up an octave once while carrying chest register as far as it will go comfortably. He then has her slide down many times on many different pitches beginning in the upper register and allowing the voice to mix the low in naturally as it drops in pitch. He uses the same technique on [o] with the male voice beginning in a high falsetto to give ease to the upper notes. In this way he hopes to find what the voice can do by itself if freed substantially. This is similar to Cooper's use of a long descending slide and a long ascending slide on [o] vowels for correcting severe dysphonias (1973, p. 85).

Again, use of Olson's quiet three- and five-note exercise can be used to help the male voice blend registers. Still starting with the quiet sound, the man should slide up and down a ninth. They should easily find themselves going in and out of falsetto somewhere above middle c.

The Use of Falsetto

Much less breath pressure is required for falsetto than for low register due to relaxation of the thyroarytenoid muscles and the fact that the vocal folds do not have to be blown apart (Van Riper & Irwin, 1958, p. 228). Therefore, falsetto can be isolated and used as a means of reducing breath pressure and hyperfunctional approximation of the vocal folds. Because falsetto requires relaxation of the extrinsic pharyngeal and laryngeal musculature and intrinsic thyroarytenoid muscles, it also aids the singer in reduction of constriction. Most men can easily find falsetto on request or by working up gradually on an [u] vowel. A light falsetto sigh or slide may provide the relaxation that will carry over into vocalization in head voice.

Singing in the Wrong Range

When we think of someone singing at the wrong pitch level, we immediately think of the soprano or tenor obviously straining to reach the high notes. The singer who overuses the low part of the voice is far more common. Although the practice of "belting out a tune" in the low register is most popular with those who perform popular and country music, choral singers are often guilty of similar practices. There are few true basses and contraltos in high school or even college choirs, so baritones and tenors, mezzo-sopranos and sopranos become basses and altos, often merely because they can read music. The practice becomes even more deadly when the singer tries to use "good production" by keeping the larynx down and ends up pushing it down with a retracted tongue or by jamming the chin into the neck.

While therapy literature contains many references to the problems caused by speaking too low, there are few references to the effects of singing too low. Shelton tells of two such individuals. One, a prepubertal boy, belted out pop tunes in a low voice during an amateur program. "We don't know what happened to the lad's voice, but a young woman singer whom we saw as a patient and who used a style similar to that of the boy developed vocal nodules" (1985, p. 275).

In the female voice the effect of singing too low or "pushing" the sound on the lower notes can be anywhere from a throaty low sound and pinched upper notes with a bad break to all of the effects of severe hypofunction. The male voice seems to survive the effects better, although it will develop a somewhat "gravelly" sound and, eventually, a consistent wobble.

Boone also indicates that using an inappropriate pitch level adversely affects the voice. "Speaking or singing at an inappropriate pitch level requires excessive force and contraction of the intrinsic muscles of the larynx, leading to vocal fatigue or the hoarseness related to a tired mechanism" (Boone, 1983, p. 6). Cooper (1973, p. 18) and Shapiro (1973, p. 329) consider singing at a wrong pitch a cause of voice disorders. Shapiro and Brodnitz consider attempting to sing beyond the singer's true range a cause of register divergence. Although the high and low notes remain reliable a "hole" develops in the middle register (Brodnitz, 1962, p. 460; Shapiro, 1973, p. 329). Coleman warns that the singer, particularly an untrained one, who consistently uses pitch extremes is putting the vocal mechanism in a state of maximum stress for extended time periods. Such usage can lead to vocal pathology (1980, p.19).

Singing at excessively high pitches can also cause adverse effects. Even those voices which do have very high notes must be aware of what is required at upper extremes of pitch. Lengthening the vocal folds two or three millimeters requires little effort, but the voice's highest tones require a length which can, if used excessively, injure the inner elastic tissues of the vocal folds. "We should not permit excessive effort to extend the natural upper range of the voice. Neither should we permit excessive use even of those high tones which come relatively easy" (Proctor, 1980a, p. 18).

Voice Classification
Many teachers and students are overly eager to classify voices. The student is told he or she is such-and-such a voice and proceeds to sing literature for and to attempt to sound like that voice without regard for comfort or for the health of the instrument. Certainly

voice classification can be helpful, but it must not be so rigid as to preclude making exceptions for the singer's well-being. Van Deinse, Frateur and Keizer offer general criteria which can be used for classifying voices: "(1) judgment of the timbre, (2) measurement of the range of the singing voice, or tessitura, (3) assessment of the pitch of the speaking voice and (4) assessment of the pitch of the change of register" (1974, p. 429).

Singing the correct literature is very important, especially for young singers. Extremes of pitch should be used as little as possible, and the difficulty of the music as well as the pitch range must be considered. The young singer who wishes to make a career of singing must be particularly careful to limit himself or herself to songs and roles appropriate to his or her state of maturity and natural voice.

> Otherwise, although there may be little immediate evidence of injury, gradually a thickened epithelium over the delicate vocal fold edges and scarring in the traumatized subepithelial tissues will inexorably take their toll. Such injury may be reversible in the earliest stages; but after a year or two of vocal abuse, the vocal folds will be permanently damaged. **This is the sort of injury which is usually totally undetectable on examination of the larynx.** [emphasis added] The damage is to the structures which make up the physiological components of the vocal mechanism and could only be surely identified by measurements which cannot be undertaken in the living larynx. (Proctor, 1980b, p. 129)

Although literature in the studio may be selected that fits the singer's voice, there are times, such as assigning choral parts or opera roles, when it is necessary to use voice classification as a guideline. It is unfortunate that many times this classification is based on group needs and a singer's ability to produce a specific quality in a given range without thought for long-term effects on that singer's voice. Hopefully, the singer and/or the teacher will recognize when error is made, and, hopefully, the situation will be such that the error can be corrected.

It should also be kept in mind that voice classifications are sometimes temporary things. This is particularly true of young singers who have just begun voice lessons and with any singer who has recently changed teachers and/or techniques. Changes in technique often alter the range, weight, timbre or shape of the voice. At such times it is important that the singer be free from categorization so as to allow his or her perception of the voice to change as the voice changes.

Tone Focus or Placement

Definition. Cooper defines tone focus as "the emphasis or placement of resonance in one or more positions of the throat/pharynx" (1973, p. 21). He lists the three major areas of resonance as the "laryngopharynx (lower throat resonance), the oropharynx (middle throat/mouth area), and the nasopharynx (upper throat/nose area)" (1973, p. 21) and states that all voices will have laryngopharyngeal resonance since the sound originates in the larynx which is located in that area (p. 21).

Tone placement or focus is an issue on which singers and voice teachers are sharply divided, not into two or three groups but into many. There are those who teach placement, forward or high in the head almost to the exclusion of other factors. There are those who teach it in combination with other factors, again forward, up in the head or on the cords themselves. And there are those who ignore the whole idea and use other means to achieve whatever sense of placement the student acquires. For each of these attitudes there are at least as many variations in how they go about it and what they hope to achieve.

Voice therapists, when speaking directly of tone focus or placement, have one very definite idea: low or laryngopharyngeal placement is a **major** cause of voice disorders. Cooper states that "Most patients with voice disorders incur vocal misuse by emphasizing/stressing laryngopharyngeal resonance which results in pharyngeal and laryngeal tensions" (1973, p. 21). Perkins indicates that of the two dimensions of vocal abuse, constriction and vertical focus, vertical focus is the most important. "When optimally high, all other dimensions are maximally flexible; one can use the voice in any mode with any pitch, loudness, or breathiness, and even use it with constriction and still preserve vocal hygiene" (Perkins, 1979, p. 114). The goal of voice therapists is to lift the focus from the throat so that the tones go either straight up towards the top of the head or curve forward towards the mask or facial area around the bridge of the nose and upper cheeks

To paraphrase a former student, the head isn't hollow; the tone can't go up there. Placement is where the singer feels the vibrations created by singing and the adjustments that he or she must make in the vocal tract for those vibrations to be felt in the desired place. Thus, placement is traditionally taught by imagery. Voice teachers and singers have known the advantages of imagery in teaching placement and made use of it for centuries.

For high placement the student may be told to pretend he or she has a pipe or string drawing the sound off the top of the head, to imagine a hollow head which is filling with sound or to think of floating the tone. Such high placement usually includes a high soft palate, so the student is often directed to lift the soft palate, to think of the sound going up with the palate or to think of an inside smile or of an arch.

When teaching high placement, it is important to use exercises that go from top to bottom and from bottom to top. In this way the singer can learn to maintain the proper placement at the end of descending passages and to anticipate that needed for high pitches that follow lower ones. All patterns are repeated at the half step. The descending pattern should begin in the key of A for high voices and G for low and move down. The ascending ones should begin in the keys of C or B and move upward, to the key of F for the second and the highest comfortable key (F and A perhaps) for the third.

Additional exercises may be constructed that consist of ascending and descending scales, slides and arpeggio patterns. They should be kept fairly simple when the concept of placement is first introduced. Keeping the tone flowing from note to note with a slight portamento will help the student to find and maintain the desired placement.

The above exercise is for advanced students who have learned to place the tone correctly on simple patterns. The student must be careful that the tone does not fall back into the throat on the initial descending slide of a fifth or the octave jump will be strained and out of tune.

Forward placement may be gained by "thinking forward" or by "placing" the sound on the lips, the teeth or the tip of the nose. The sound can also be focused on an object, such as a pencil, held slightly in front of the mouth or on a point in the room, perhaps on the opposite wall.

Here the [i] and [æ] vowels should be used. It is nearly impossible to sing the [æ] vowel with a low tonal focus.

The [i] vowel is equally effective for achieving forward placement but may require some explanation. Here the student can be told to concentrate on where the sides of the tongue touch the insides of the upper teeth and to attempt to feel the tone there.

It is **not** necessary for the student to smile or otherwise grimace to form an [i] vowel. The tongue position combined with the other vocal tract adjustments which are achieved by thinking the vowel will suffice to form it.

Those seeking high tonal focus may find they have to accept a forward placement as a transition from a low back placement. The vowel [ʊ] as it appears in the words "hook" and "would" will assist. The student must keep the lips slightly pinched.

These two concepts of forward placement and high placement can be combined to create a high, forward placement. Then the student is asked to think of the tone as arching from the soft palate forward toward the forehead and out. Imagery might include telling the student to think of an elephant's trunk. When working with professional voice users, Lavorato and McFarlane strive for high and forward placement. They emphasize lip, cheek and nose vibrations with the use of the [n] and [m] and *labio-dental* (lip and teeth), *bilabial* (both lips) or *lingua-alveolar* (tongue-alveolar ridge) sensations through [t], [d], [f], [v], [p] or [b]. They work towards focusing the tone in these areas with nonsense syllables such as "[ma]" and "[tu]" and with simple words such as "[tIm], [fIn], [vIm] (1983, p. 57)." To facilitate high and forward focus, they also have the patient blow gently and phonate [hu] through puckered lips. The feeling of a voiced breathstream passing through the small lip opening helps to focus the tone. They also use humming, musical scales and simple songs for placing the voice in the mask: such activities are particularly valuable for singers. They teach these techniques plus chanting or singing ascending and descending musical scales on [mi mi. . .] as warm-ups (1983, p. 57).

The overall idea of buoyancy of the sound is used even by teachers who profess they do not teach placement. Their goal may be to get the sound "up" with no particular location in mind, and imagery is modified appropriately. They talk of tones that float or ride on a column of air and often use visual cues, such as a raised hand with the fingers appearing to float in the air, to symbolize this feeling. The opposite, the upturned palm with fingers curved up, symbolizes the logy, heavy tone placed low in the throat.

Here voice therapists borrow from singing and also use imagery. Cooper suggests a variety of images. "One patient visualizes talking through the top of his head; another sees the tone as being placed a short distance in front of the mouth; still another thinks of the sound as hitting the hard palate or upper teeth" (1973, p. 79). The therapist must confirm that the pitch and tone focus produced by the imagery is correct.

Placement in the Nose and Sinuses

Some singers prefer mask placement, sometimes with some nasal resonance in the sound. Vocalizing is done on "me," "ming," "nu" or various other syllables using [m] or [n]. Their goal is to achieve mask placement and carry the nasal resonance produced by the lowering of the velum for the [m] or [n] into the vowels that follow. It should be stressed that, although this is quite different from forward or high placement with a high palate, it achieves a tonal focus which is out of the laryngopharyngeal area and thus healthy.

Cooper stresses the need for nasopharyngeal resonance. To achieve this he uses the vowel [i] in combination with consonants or alone: "e-e," "me-me," "ne-ne," or "he-he." He next combines the vowel or syllable with a number, such as "e one, e two" or "Me one, me two," then with a word, then a phrase, and finally sentences and paragraphs. The goals are to "place" the sound in the mask and to incorporate this correct tone focus into the client's everyday speech (1973, p. 83).

McFarlane uses the [m] and [n] sounds to stress vibrating the tone in the area of the nose and cheekbones and direct attention away from the throat and neck area. This reduces muscle tension in that area (1988, p. 427).

Boone uses "me" and "one," each produced by the clinician in an exaggerated manner so as to produce vibration on the bridge of the nose and in the sinuses. The client is then asked to produce the same sounds and to confirm the vibrations in his or her sinuses. His use of the nasal consonants is not for nasal resonance but to give the voice a higher vocal tract focus. Once the client has achieved this feeling, a few more words can be added such as "*man, mean,* many, *went.*" If there is improvement at this point the clinician will introduce other words such as "*baby, beach, take*" emphasizing the maintenance of mask area resonance. The successful placement of random words is followed by a discussion between client and therapist about the similarity of this imagery to that used by the singing teacher "(we cannot really 'place' the voice anywhere), knowing that when the singer has the imagery of putting his or her voice somewhere there are often audible measurable effects" (1983, p. 167).

Placement is a concept which can operate independently of many other factors in voice production. While a high tonal focus may prevent the onset of constriction, achieving the high focus will not remove pre-existing constriction. In fact, "existing constriction precludes achieving a sharp focus" (Perkins, 1983, p. 279). Although freeing the throat from constriction will often cause a rise in placement, a relaxed, open throat does not guarantee high placement if it is a goal outside the student's experience or if the student has other intentions. Therefore, a teacher desiring to change a student's placement must explain to the student what the goals are. Once this is done, the concept of placement can be "grafted on" to exercises used for other purposes or taught separately by means of exercises appropriate for the desired end.

Placement and Registration

A great many aspects of singing are inter-related. Sometimes fixing one problem will solve or improve another problem. Thus, it is that placement and registration seem to be interdependent. Perkins uses falsetto to facilitate high placement. He has the client begin in falsetto and slide down while counting softly as he or she crosses into chest or low register. A smooth register transition indicates high placement. The goal is for the client to keep that placement in the speaking voice (1977, pp. 187-188). Here again therapy has borrowed from the voice studio. Falsetto often seems to be placed higher than the rest of the man's voice. Having him begin downward slides and scales in the falsetto with the instruction to try to "keep the sound in the same place" will often facilitate correct placement throughout the range. Conversely, such placement will often smooth out the register transition and allow the man to sing a few more top notes in his head voice before going into falsetto.

Women may also find a higher placement more easily on high notes. They too can then "keep the sound in the same place" as they move down the scale. Again, keeping the tone up in the head, forward or forward and up will usually help to smooth out the register transition around middle c and the notes above.

Covering

Covering is another very controversial subject among singers and teachers. Hertegard, Gauffin and Sundberg define covering as "an elevation of the soft palate, a lowering and forward tilting of the larynx. Also a widening of the supraglottal tract as well as of the hypopharynx and laryngeal ventricles. . ." (1990, p. 221).

Covering includes the modification or darkening of vowels. It is used most often by male voices in the area of register change. The vowels [e] and [i] are modified or reshaped towards [ö] and [ü]. Van Deinse, Frateur and Keizer indicate that the following changes take place when covering is used during change of register: the larynx is lowered and the laryngopharynx is widened, the cricothyroid muscle contracts (which causes the cords to stretch, tense and elongate), the thyroid cartilage slips forward and the vocal cords are elongated (1974, p. 431). The longer vocal folds apparently prevent a sudden drop into heavy or low register on descending passages and help bring in the lighter registration on ascending passages.

Hertegard, Gauffin and Sundberg used eleven professionally trained male singers for their study on covered and open singing. Seven subjects showed an elevated velum; six showed anteposterior widening of the hypopharynx only; and four showed general pharyngeal widening. Because the methods used did not provide for easy observation of the larynx, data could only be collected from five of the eleven subjects. Only two showed forward tilting of the larynx and one widening of the laryngeal ventricle, but other data

obtained corroborate previous studies that the larynx tilts forward
and the laryngeal ventricle is widened. Their panel of listeners no-
ticed a clear perceptual difference between the qualities of open and
covered singing (1990, pp. 220-230). Acoustically, covering was
found to be associated with a lowered frequency for the first formant
due to the widening of the pharynx and lengthening of the vocal tract
(p. 227).

In 1962 Brodnitz warned against **excessive** covering because
of the muscular tension required in the pharynx. He reported that
spirometric curves showed changing from open to covered singing
on the same note required an increase of over 20% in air (pp. 444-
445). However, Hertegard, Gauffin and Sundberg's study indicated that a covered voice is healthier because it involves mechanisms which prevent vocal strain, a cause of nodules and polyp
formation. They concluded that covered singing would be preferable for open vowels such as [a] and [æ] sung at high pitches to
avoid the strain of hyperfunction. Used near the passaggio it is
probably desirable in terms of vocal hygiene because it shares characteristics with "flow phonation" (1990, p. 229).

These conclusions support Shipp's speculation that if laryngeal
elevation facilitates vocal fold adduction, such as in swallowing,
lowering the larynx would decrease adductory force. Thus, for
singers who hyperadduct the folds and produce a "'pressed'" or
"'tight'" phonation, covering would inhibit potentially abusive practices which, if used chronically, could cause problems (1987, p.
219).

The more dissimilar the resonating frequencies of the tracheal
tube and those of the vocal folds, the more stable is the vibration of
the vocal folds. Shipp also indicated that lowering the larynx shortened the tracheal tube and reduced the volume. Both of these factors
raise subglottal resonant frequency, which would provide more laryngeal stability (1987, p. 219).

There is a fine line between raising the palate for high tonal
placement and stretching the pharyngeal area excessively, between
keeping the larynx in a relaxed low position and pressing it down
below resting position. One school of voice production favors
depth of sound and a large throat and replaces focus or ring with
volume. Singers following this approach keep the larynx pushed
down and strive for maintaining a covered tone all of the time. Their
problems begin with the tension necessary to keep the throat large.
In addition, this practice is often accompanied by the retracted
tongue (discussed in the previous chapter). This plus the pharyngeal tension involved will often transfer the focus of the tone to the
throat or laryngopharynx. Because of all of these factors, a tremen-
dous amount of force is required to produce enough volume to gain

a sound with an edge. For a negatively biased but thorough discussion of this concept see Vennard, 1967, pp. 155-156.

Resonance Extremes

One of the major factors in identifying an English-speaking person's origins is the amount of nasal resonance in his or her speech. Americans from the Midwest speak with more nasality than Londoners; people from Des Moines exhibit less nasality than those from Peoria. Beyond these variants are the extremes, the voices with too little or no nasal resonance (*hyponasality*) and too much nasal resonance (*hypernasality*).

Resonance defined. Prater and Swift define resonance as "the acoustic phenomenon by which a vibrating structure (sound source) excites the air in an air-filled chamber, which in turn causes the chamber walls to vibrate similarly" (1984, p. 18). While the vibrations of the sound source may be relatively weak, the amount of resonance which these vibrations can excite depends upon the degree to which the size, shape and resiliency of the resonator(s) are acoustically tuned to that source (Prater & Swift, 1984, p. 19). The pharyngeal, oral and nasal cavities provide resonance for sound produced in the larynx. These cavities are made up of a mixture of hard and soft surfaces, all of which are somewhat flexible in size, tension and tuning. Changes can be made in the firmness and tension of these surfaces, in the coupling together of these cavities and in the transmission between them. Shanks suggests that resonance changes are due to the following: "1) changes in the wall separating two cavities; 2) a direct opening connecting two cavities; or 3) the opening between the cavity and the atmosphere outside the body" (Shanks, 1983, p. 40). Therefore, resonance in the mouth or oral cavity depends on the amount of space in the mouth, the amount and type of tissues in the mouth and the openings at the front and back of the mouth (Shanks, 1983, p. 40). Resonance in the pharynx depends upon the amount of space in the throat, the mass of any structures in the throat and the size of the opening from the throat to the mouth (p. 41). Here again the position of the tongue is important because it divides the mouth and pharynx into two sections. Moving it backwards and forwards affects the length of the individual sections, and, in its highest position, the tongue forms a tube which couples those two sections together. Moving the tongue up and down affects the length of that tube (Fry, 1979, p. 76). Thus the retracted tongue, which shortens that tube, may cause a guttural voice quality (Shanks, 1983, p. 41). Nasal resonance depends upon the degree of openness between the nose and throat and the openness or congestion in the nose.

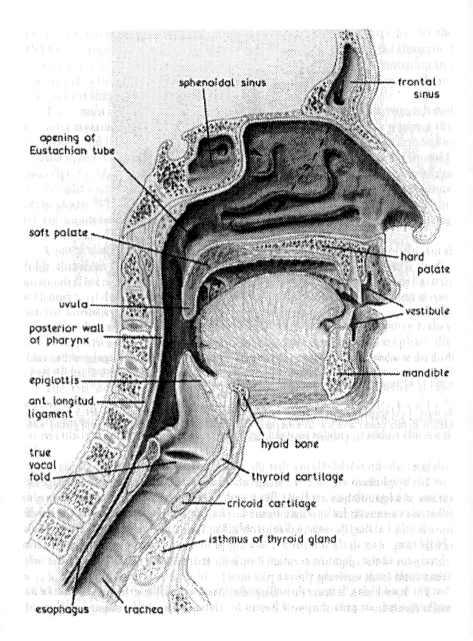

Fig. 12. Midline section of head and neckshowing structure of the left half.
From *Dynamics of the Singing voice*, Meribeth Bunch, 1982, Fig. 33, p. 53.
Published by Springer-Verlag. Used by permission.

Resonance structures. The pharynx or throat can be subdivided into three regions: the lowest part, where the trachea and esophagus open, is called the *laryngopharynx* or *hypopharynx*; the middle part which opens into the mouth is called the *oropharynx* or *mesopharynx*; and the top part which leads directly into the nose and sinuses is called the *nasopharynx* or *epipharynx* (Putnam & Shelton, 1985, p. 97).

The *velum* or *soft palate* separates the nasal cavities from the mouth. It is composed of the paired *palatal tensor muscles* and the *palatal levator muscles* which originate on the base of the skull, the *palatoglossus muscles* which originate on the tongue and the *palatopharyngeus muscles* which originate in the pharyngeal walls. The *musculus uvulae* are paired intrinsic muscles within the soft palate. The *uvula* which extends down from the soft palate is a "vestigial nublin of connective and glandular tissue" (Putnam & Shelton, 1985, p. 99). Two folds of tissue extend down from the soft palate on either side. These are the *anterior* and *posterior pillars of fauces.* The *palatine tonsils* lie between these two folds (Aronson, 1985, p. 206).

When the velum is in its lowest position, the nasal and oral cavities are directly connected. In its highest position the nasal cavities are completely sealed off from the mouth and throat. The ability to close off the nose from the mouth by raising the velum, *velopharyngeal closure*, exists for two primary reasons: 1) to seal off the nasal passages from the mouth and produce a partial vacuum to assist in compression and swallowing of food and 2) to open the *eustachian tube* (the tube which connects the inner ear to the throat) during swallowing and thus ventilate the inner ear (Aronson, 1985, p. 199).

With the velum in a lowered position the sound goes directly from the larynx into the nose. Even when the musculature of the palate is relaxed or thin (due to congenital causes), frequencies above 1200 Hz. are absorbed by the palate, and the sound is perceived as excessively nasal and lackluster (Damsté, 1987, p. 125). Firm muscular contraction lifts the velum up and slightly back (Case, 1984, p. 9) which closes the nasal passages off from the pharynx completely. In this position all of the sound goes directly out through the mouth. In between these two extremes are the various gradations of nasopharyngeal resonance that give each voice its unique resonance characteristics.

Definitions. Nasal resonance extremes are usually defined in terms of perceived sound. Vowel production in spoken English has primarily oral resonance with only a slight amount of nasal resonance. Only three sounds in the English language should have predominantly nasal resonance: [m], [n] and [ŋ]. *Denasality* is a lack of nasal resonance in these three phonemes. Since it results in substitution of [b], [d] and [g] for the nasal phonemes, denasality could be characterized as an articulatory substitution disorder. However, the normal speaker gives some nasal resonance to vowels too, so they are also affected by denasality, much like when a normal speaker suffers from a head cold (Boone, 1983, p. 209). The causes of denasality are overclosure of the velum or obstruction between the oral and nasal cavities due to some type of tissue growth (adenoids or additive lesions).

"*Hypernasality* is an excessively undesirable amount of perceived nasal cavity resonance during the phonation of vowels" (Boone, 1983, p. 209). In *assimilative nasality* vowels appear excessively nasal only when adjacent to the three nasal consonants [m], [n] and [ŋ] (p. 209). *Nasal air emission* is the "abnormal flow of air from the nares [the nose] during the production of high-pressure consonants" (Aronson, 1985, p. 204). This abnormal air flow, also known as *nasal snort*, is heard as friction noise (p. 204). *Grimacing* is a compensatory action which the speaker makes in an attempt to occlude or close off the nose to impede the flow of nasal air (p. 204).

Consonants are grouped according to the amount and location of closure(s) of the vocal tract required before or during their production and the manner in which the air flows past those points during that production. Isshiki describes *plosive* consonants as those produced by "closing the vocal tract, at both the velopharynx and each articulation site, building up air pressure, and then releasing that compressed air slowly" (1989, p. 17). Sometimes called *stop plosives*, these include [p], [b], [d], [t], [g] and [k] (Appelman, 1967, pp. 254-255, 258). *Fricative* consonants require closure of the nasopharynx, a narrow stricture at the articulation site and strong air flow directed to that stricture. The sound produced is the result of the turbulence generated by that air (Isshiki, 1989, p. 17). Fricatives include [v], [f], [ð], [θ], [z], [s], [ʒ] and [ʃ] (Appelman, pp. 254-255, 258). The *affricates* [tʃ] and [dʒ] are stop plosives followed by continuant fricatives (Appelman, p. 258). *Nasal* consonants [m], [n] and [ŋ] are produced in a manner similar to plosives, but the velum or soft palate is lowered so that the nasal and oropharyngeal cavities are combined (Isshiki, 1989, p. 17).

Hypernasal speakers with a loss of air pressure in the oral cavity may misarticulate some consonants which require a great amount of intraoral air pressure (Aronson, 1985, p. 200; Prater and Swift, 1984, p. 232). These include those consonants requiring the most intraoral air pressure for their production: the fricatives, stop plosives and affricates. Although such speakers may also exhibit additional misarticulations in the form of phonemic substitution errors, velopharyngeal insufficiency is usually characterized by substitution of pharyngeal fricatives for oral fricatives and glottal stops for oral stops or by errors of omission (Prater & Swift, 1984, p. 233). Shanks considers nasal emission as loss of air rather than loss of sound and focuses on the force of exhalation and articulation as a voluntary control factor almost independent of resonance (1983, p. 44).

Hypernasality
There are two schools of thought among singers regarding nasal resonance. Proponents of the first school favor some nasal resonance on the vowel sounds, and those of the second school use a hyponasal sound on all sounds other than [m], [n] or [ŋ]. Each side has supporting evidence for its own position, which suggests this may be a matter of taste.

Excessive nasality indicates inadequate velopharyngeal closure, so the student with an excessively nasal tone must be taught to improve this closure. In some cases this will also involve changing the tongue position and/or the tonal focus. Regardless, reducing excessive nasality must begin with an understanding of what excessive nasality means and an awareness of palate function.

Few people are really kinesthetically aware enough to feel the palate itself move. Most will instead feel the result of its not moving as a "lid" or "cover" on something or as sung tone that "hits against" the roof of the mouth or "gets stuck back there." Having the student use a hand mirror or stand in front of a wall mirror with the mouth open and chin slightly elevated allows the student to watch the uvula rise as he or she inhales (Fisher, 1975, p. 104). While they may never really feel the muscular action of the palate rising, most students will feel the air hit the lifted palate or an open sensation in the back of the mouth. This helps them become aware of where to lift to raise the palate. Polow and Kaplan (1979) have the client look into the mirror to observe a yawn and then try to achieve the same raised uvula of the yawn while phonating [a] (p. 104).

It is also helpful to teach the student to discriminate between nasal and nonnasal sounds. The student should first produce a nasal sound and then contrast it with the same sound produced in an open manner. Curiously, the more nasal the student's own natural sound is, the more difficult it usually is for him or her to produce a sound that is purposefully nasal. Most students can imitate the sounds of children taunting "nya nya-nya nya nya." It is relatively simple to take the [njæ] and work from there to a single note sustained on a nasal [æ] and then [ã] with or without the [n]. Once the student has produced the nasal sound and **recognized** it as such, he or she must sustain the [a] vowel while raising the soft palate to produce an open sound. Much of this work must be done with the student imitating sounds modeled by the teacher. It is important at this point to discuss with the student the differences between nasal and nonnasal resonance. Changes should be felt in the sound, in the placement of the sound and in the shape of the articulators, particularly the palate. Questions such as the following may be used to direct the student's attention appropriately. "Did you feel something change? What?" "Where did it move, forward or back, up or down?" "Did you feel something besides the tone move? What?" "How did it move?"

This is similar to techniques used by several therapists. Fisher uses [n] to [a] and a purposefully nasal [ã] to an oral [a] (1975, p. 104). Thurman contrasts open, fronted vowels with the same vowels produced with excessive nasality (1977, p. 251). Polow and Kaplan teach the patient to discriminate between hypernasal and oral sounds by sound. They have the client contrast prolonged [m] or [n] sounds with different vowels that follow noticing the difference in feeling between the two sounds. They then have the client repeat the following five times while holding the nostrils pinched so no air can escape: "sah, say, see, saw, so, sue" (1979, p. 98). When the nostrils are pinched, nasality can be immediately detected as vibrations under the fingers (Polow & Kaplan, 1979, p. 98) and as a change in sound (Fairbanks, 1940, p. 174). Fisher improves the client's ability to discriminate between nasal and nonnasal voice. She also teaches the client to feel when the velum is closed and to use that sensation to control its function (1975, p. 104). Boone suggests training hypernasal therapy clients to hear the difference between nasal and nonnasal sounds (1983, p. 221), and Murphy found that combining this training with other approaches worked well with a 22-year-old male with mixed nasality (1964, pp. 56-57).

The [ŋ] pulls the palate down and the tongue up. Release of this sound to an open vowel in exercises such as "hung-ah" or "ming-ah" usually places the palate very high. Such exercises used in the middle range may be useful in the voice studio for improving muscle function in the velopharyngeal area and to allow the singer to experience the contrast in positions of the soft palate. The student should go directly to the [ŋ] rather than sustaining the vowel.

Ming- ah - -   Hung ah-   -

A shift in tonal focus will also affect excessive nasality. Singers who prefer a forward focus will find a change in the quality of the vowel from nasal to nonnasal will shift the tonal focus from back to front. They will find helpful Polow and Kaplan's suggestion to shift speech activity consciously from the back of the mouth to the front (1979, p. 103). Boone also suggests placing the focus in the mask of the face as one treatment for hypernasality (1983, p. 221). Those who prefer a high placement focused in the top of the head will feel both the tone and the palate go back and up. Either result may be affected by imagery and suggestions made by the teacher.

Observation and experience indicate that excessive nasality may occur more frequently in singers who sing with little mouth opening. These singers may find increasing the mouth opening an effective complement to their efforts to control the palate. Changing the mouth opening would fit number three on Shanks' list of ways to change resonance which was cited earlier in this section (1983, p. 40). Prater and Swift (1984, p. 236), Shanks (1983, p. 46), Boone, (1983, p. 22), Polow and Kaplan (1979, p. 101), Fisher (1975, p. 104), Moore (1971b, p. 568) and Adler (1960, p. 301) advocate opening the mouth as treatment for hypernasality. Murphy found asking for a more open mouth effective in dealing with the 22-year-old male with mixed nasality (1964, pp. 56-57). This reinforces Van Riper and Irwin's belief that keeping the front of the mouth closed may cause a speaker to compensate by placing the tongue in positions that close off the normal opening from the pharynx into the mouth and force the sound out of the nose (1958, p. 246). Opening the mouth lowers the tongue which will help to raise the velum slightly and block some of the air going through the nose (Polow & Kaplan, 1979, p. 101).

Tongue position, which was discussed in Chapter 3, has a definite effect on resonance. For articulating certain sounds the tongue must temporarily move to extreme positions at the front or back of the mouth, but when it remains fixed in either position, the resonance characteristics of the voice are changed noticeably (Prater & Swift, 1984, pp. 240-241). Persons who are "tongue-tied," that is whose tongues are congenitally attached to the floor of the mouth, may display reduced oral resonance. In contrast, those who have a reduced tongue mass due to congenital or surgical factors will often have a hollow quality to the sound because of too much oral resonance (Shanks, 1983, p. 40).

Prater and Swift consider both too-forward and retracted tongue positions predisposing factors for resonance disorders. Boone finds both retraction and arching of the tongue predisposing factors to hypernasality and to denasality (1983, p. 8). Van Riper and Irwin believe this is because the retracted tongue fills up the opening from the pharynx into the mouth so that opening becomes smaller than the opening from the pharynx into the nasopharynx (1958, p. 24). This also reflects Shanks' view that changing the way in which the pharyngeal, oral and nasal cavities are coupled together causes resonance changes (1983, p. 40).

The effects of the retracted tongue on nasality extend beyond its filling the oropharyngeal area. **When the retracted tongue is finally moved out of the throat, the sound often remains nasal.** Although lowering the dorsum of the tongue from an unnaturally high position may cause the velum to rise, pushing the base of the tongue to an unnaturally low position, particularly over a long period of time, appears to pull the velum down. Perhaps it is the lowered focus of the tone associated with the retracted tongue that causes this. After moving the tongue position forward, changing the focus forward or straight up helps to counter the problem, but it may be necessary to do extensive work on recognition of nasal and nonnasal sound and sensation for the student to learn to control the palate.

Articulation.

> Articulation in a broad sense means the whole process by which the glottal sound is changed into speech sound through the dynamic movement of the vocal tract. In a narrower sense, it may refer to the dynamic movement of the vocal tract, chiefly the lingual movement, and the consequent sound production, while excluding the resonance effect. (Isshiki, 1989, p. 5)

Since there is an association with poor articulation and hypernasality, exercises which improve articulation can help to reduce excessive nasality. Such exercises would be used to increase the flexibility and activity of the articulators. Appropriate exercises would be those combining a variety of open and closed vowels with consonants formed with the lips and tongue. These might be five-note patterns either up or down on syllables such as [do] [bi] [do] [bi] [da] or [la] [pi] [ta] [pi] [lu].

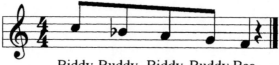

Biddy Buddy Biddy Buddy Bee

Lop -py Top -py Lop-py Top-py   La

The first of these examples is particularly effective for reinforcing a sense of hyponasality, especially when contrasted with "minnie-money-minnie-money-me" on the same descending five-note pattern shown in the following section.

The physical structures concerned with resonance are also concerned with articulation (Shanks, 1983, p. 40). Eisenson and Ogilvie state that nasal speakers are frequently also the ones lacking in precision and clearness in their overall articulation (1983, p. 358), and Prater and Swift found that speakers with frequent articulation errors are perceived by listeners as being more hypernasal than those with fewer misarticulations (1984, p. 236). Therefore, improving a client's articulation often reduces actual and/or perceived hypernasality. Prater and Swift work for improved articulation in hypernasal speakers (1984, p. 236), and Eisenson and Ogilvie find that increasing the activity of the lips and tongue provides a reflexive increase in soft palate activity so that nasality is improved as well as general articulation (1983, p. 358). Murphy found exercises that increased flexibility of articulators and improved articulation of individual speech sounds effective in working with a 22-year-old male with mixed nasality (1964, pp. 56-57).

Hyponasality
    Some degree of hyponasality is considered desirable by many singers and voice teachers. Unless he or she is experiencing a temporary condition caused by nasal congestion, hyponasality is considered a resonance disorder in a singer only if the singer glides over the [m]'s and/or [n]'s in words, sometimes replacing them with [b] or [d]. Such a singer may also exhibit hypofunctional behavior in other parts of the vocal tract. Reduction of constriction and relaxation of other muscles of the vocal tract will usually reduce the hyponasality so that the singer can pronounce the [m] and [n] while maintaining the desired tone focus for his or her type of production.
    Exercises made up of [m]'s and [n]'s will help increase nasal resonance. They can be made up of ascending and/or descending scalewise passages.

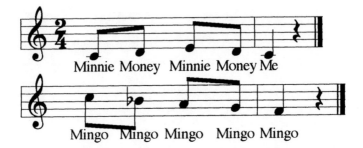

Minnie Money Minnie Money Me

Mingo Mingo Mingo Mingo Mingo

These exercises reflect suggestions made by several therapists to increase nasal resonance. Williamson (1944, p. 478) recommends use of [m], [n] and [ŋ] in combination with vowels to develop some assimilative nasality in the hyponasal speaking voice. Polow and Kaplan (1979, p. 102) and Eisenson and Ogilvie (1983, p. 358) use a hum on [m] or [n] for the same purpose. Polow and Kaplan then have the client add a vowel sound to the [m] or [n]. This is repeated with other vowel sounds to achieve the proper balance of nasopharyngeal resonance (p. 102).

Chapter 5

Ethics

The subject of ethics is largely ignored in voice pedagogy texts, even though at some point every studio teacher must deal with ethical questions such as when to discourage a less than talented student or when to call it quits with an unproductive or uncooperative student. In fact, every time a teacher makes a conscious decision to change or not change a student's technique, that teacher makes an ethical decision.

> To be specific, no voice teacher wants to "ruin" a voice -- or voices. One of the best ways to avoid this danger is to employ knowledge about human physiology and the internal/external acoustics associated with singing and speaking in ways that help the student avoid stressing their mechanism. (Hollein, 1985, p. 282)

Most states have licensing requirements for speech and voice therapists, and ASHA, the American Speech-Language-Hearing Association, has an extensive Code of Ethics by which its members must abide to retain their membership. But voice teachers are not licensed. The Code of Ethics of the National Association of Teachers of Singing (NATS) contains admonitions against proselytizing students and criticizing colleagues. It remains silent on other areas of ethics, partly because, in the past, such areas were considered matters of personal or artistic tastes. In 1992 NATS and ASHA together issued a statement endorsing licensing of voice therapists, outlining the role and training needed for voice teachers to participate in rehabilitating singers who have sustained laryngeal damage and admonishing voice teachers who are not licensed as voice therapists against practicing or claiming to practice voice therapy.

Case Studies

The three examples which follow have been selected for inclusion in this chapter because each requires a studio teacher to make an ethical decision beyond what type of technique to teach.

Case 1: Mark
The part-time teacher at the small, church-affiliated liberal arts
college has taken this one-year position to supplement her in-
come while she is finishing an advanced degree. Her past
teaching experience includes seven years in a similar college
in a different part of the country and two years as a graduate
assistant. She has a strong background in voice therapy and
some experience working with damaged voices. On her first
day of teaching she is told that Mark, the one music major
among her five assigned students, is planning to do a non-re-
quired senior recital for which he would have a hearing in
seven weeks, that Mark has polyps and that Mark must sing
literature he has already learned because he does not learn music easily. Mark must have credit for two more semesters of
voice lessons to graduate with his class the following May. A
conversation with Mark's laryngologist and subsequent letter
from his office confirm that the student does have bilateral vocal cord polyps. The laryngologist recommends voice therapy
for Mark's speaking habits and states that he can continue to
sing so long as he is careful. Mark is informed of the laryngologist's recommendations. Happily, he makes his own decision shortly before the hearing to cancel it and the recital.

Case 2: Cathy
Cathy is a sophomore majoring in special education in a private women's college located in a rural area. She takes voice
lessons because she is in the school choral ensemble where she
sings second alto. She is a heavy smoker who seems to have a
constant cold and who speaks on a flat low pitch, often trailing
the ends of her sentences into a whisper. Her singing voice is
breathy, and she is unable to sustain more than a few measures
on one breath. Cathy's lessons are inconsistent: one week the
voice appears a little freer and she produces a breathy but acceptable tone. The next week she sounds strained, and she
stretches for notes still on the staff. Her teacher searches for
an upper register while vocalizing Cathy in the upper middle
range and working to reduce constriction. Because of her history of upper respiratory infections and the sound of her
speaking voice as well as her singing, the teacher is concerned
about an underlying medical problem. She urges Cathy to see
a doctor, preferably a laryngologist. However, the college
where Cathy is enrolled has no doctor. She will have to see a
private practitioner and pay a regular fee, and Cathy is a schol-
arship student from a large, single-parent family. She
promises to see a doctor while she is home at Thanksgiving
break and then again at Christmas break. She does neither.
The teacher recognizes that Cathy is abusing her voice by
speaking and singing below her natural range and suggests
Cathy should seek therapy for her speaking voice. Such ser-

vices are available at a university located in a larger community a few miles away, to which transportation is available, and are free of charge to all area students. Cathy repeatedly promises to call and set an appointment for an evaluation with a therapist but never does. She has to continue voice lessons during the second semester to remain in the choral group, something both she and her director maintain is absolutely essential. In May she is still promising to follow up on referrals.

Case 3: Hillary
Hillary is a forty-five year-old woman who has returned to school at the local, non-residential college to pursue studies in theater. She has signed up for voice lessons as an elective. Her teacher has ten years' experience as a college voice teacher. Hillary speaks and sings in the tenor range. Although the teacher tries to work on finding a "top" to the voice and suggests Hillary might want to try raising the pitch of her speaking voice, Hillary is resistant to his efforts and suggestions. She cites several older, popular actresses who speak and sing in the male range and seems to prefer to find songs that fall comfortably within her limited range while ignoring the teacher's efforts to improve the voice. The teacher decides to let Hillary sing whatever and wherever she wants but gives her a grade of C for the quarter to discourage her from future study. The college has enrollment problems, and studio teachers are not allowed to reject students.

Given the choice, few teachers would willingly accept Mark, even with written permission for study from the laryngologist and with assurances that the recital hearing, and possibly the recital itself, could be postponed and/or canceled. Likewise, many teachers would require Cathy to visit a laryngologist before accepting her as a student. But most administrators do not look favorably upon a teacher who rejects students for whatever reasons. Teachers in most small, and some large, music departments are assigned their students. Many of these departments face constant enrollment problems and will go to extreme lengths to keep students. Part-time or junior faculty usually get the "less talented" voices, the ones more likely to come into the studio with a history of vocal misuse and/or abuse. Today's young teachers may be better educated to deal with these problems, but their lack of experience also puts them in a vulnerable position.

If there is any question about the condition of a student's vocal tract it should be examined by a doctor, preferably a laryngologist. If the laryngologist approves of continued voice study, this approval must be in writing to protect the teacher and the school the student attends from possible legal action. If a vocal pathology

exists, it is up to the teacher and the laryngologist to decide if continued study is in the student's best interest. Today most laryngologists do not prescribe voice rest, and more and more voice teachers have the anatomic and pedagogic background to decide if they
are capable and willing to work with the student in cooperation
with his or her laryngologist and/or voice therapist. At the **very
least** a questionable student should be evaluated by a qualified
speech-voice pathologist who is certified by the American Speech-
Language-Hearing Association. Most voice therapists require a laryngeal examination by a doctor before they will begin treatment,
and some require it before doing an assessment.

Most students are agreeable to see at least the college physician. If the student must continue lessons but refuses a medical examination, or if care is beyond the student's financial resources, the
teacher faces a difficult decision: should he or she terminate the
lessons for his or her own professional safety, or should he or she
continue to teach the student on the theory that someone will and it
might as well be an informed someone?

Each teacher must weigh the factors involved when
considering students he or she feels are not acceptable. Ideally, the
teacher should not be forced to accept a student if there are salient
reasons behind the decision. However, in many cases the teacher
must weigh reduction of pay or even possible loss of their job as
one of the factors when rejecting students. In other cases there is
simply no choice but to attempt to teach whoever is assigned,
hopefully without inflicting more damage and perhaps affecting
some improvement.

While Mark and Cathy may be unusual examples, the problems
encountered with Hillary are all too common. The decision to dis-
continue efforts to improve Hillary's voice may seem a bit rash,
but it is very difficult to teach a student who likes the way he or
she sings better than what the teacher is trying to teach. Even the
most competent and committed teacher wonders at times why he or
she exerts the effort to help students who appear to ignore
everything the teacher is trying to teach them. Fortunately, most
teachers do not give up but make the best of the situation. Some
suggest another studio for those who are stubborn about resisting
their instruction or with whom they make no progress.

The studio teacher must also help students deal with situations
which may be potentially abusive to the voice. One such example
is incorrect classification of voices for choral singing. While the
studio teacher is concerned with the long-term goals of establishing
good vocal technique and practices that maintain vocal health, the
choral director is concerned with the immediate sound of the
group. It is possible for these positions to be in conflict. Thus, a

student who, after a few weeks of private voice study, discovers a completely new way of singing and with it a new voice classification, may not be allowed to change to a different section of the choir. Sopranos may be asked to sing second alto in their chest voices because they produce a particular color that the director wants in that section, or baritones who can reach a few notes in the tenor range may be used to fill out a weak section.

Opera or theater directors may also cast students in roles that are unsuitable for them. A studio teacher can only warn the student of the pitfalls of singing Wagner at age twenty or of belting out songs on the musical theater stage until the upper voice is all but gone. Ultimately the decision on how to use the voice will rest with the student.

Unfortunately, the student may lack the experience, expertise or foresight to realize the damage extended use of the voice in an incorrect manner can inflict on that organ. He or she may also enjoy the ego gratification of participating in the group. Or maybe, like Hillary, the student **likes** the method of voice production used in such situations better than the elusive technique the teacher is trying to build.

The teacher should speak directly with these students about their goals and tastes and how they relate to the technique the teacher is attempting to teach. It is also essential for the studio teacher to establish and try to maintain communication with choral, opera and musical theater directors. Allowing the relationship to deteriorate into an adversarial one too often puts the student in a difficult position of having to choose.

Additionally, the teacher should keep a realistic outlook on the manner in which the individual student will be using his or her voice in the future. Many will never sing alone in public after leaving college. For them the choral experience is particularly important. Others will use their knowledge of the voice primarily in the public school classroom or in front of a church or community choral group. Teaching them good habits of voice production will help raise the standards of voice usage for future choral singers. Consistently teaching all students to understand and use their voices correctly is the greatest lesson the studio teacher can give them. The more aware a student is of his or her own voice and how best to achieve its potential, the more likely that student is to make choices that will positively affect his or her future vocal health.

Popular, café and country singers also make their way to the studio, often after a vocal breakdown has cost them performing time or caused them to visit a laryngologist who recommended training with a traditional voice teacher. Many of these singers, like Hillary, prefer to use one register almost exclusively. While the teacher may not be able to mold such students technically in the usual manner, accepting them for study does obligate him or her to teach them as much as possible about maintaining vocal health. Such students will be adapting everything they are taught to their own style, so they must be taught more than rote exercises. They must be given a general understanding of the basics required to preserve vocal health and of the concepts behind what they must do to maintain their own instrument. These will often include finding and vocalizing in the other register. Virtually every singer can be taught at least some techniques which will improve his or her vocal health without destroying individual style.

And what of the singer who finds himself or herself with vocal damage? Hopefully that singer will use the experience to examine his or her vocal production to find the causes of the problem. If the problem is with use of the voice during speech, a voice therapist is a must. It is best if the singer works with a clinician who special-izes in working with singers and other professional voice users and is accustomed to the stresses of these professions and the close identity singers have with their voices. If the problem is the singing technique, the singer is best-advised to find a teacher with a reputation for producing singers with good vocal health who know what they are doing. And most of all the singer **must** moni-tor future efforts with the dictum "If it feels bad, it is wrong."

Chapter 6

The Singer Outside the Studio

Even the most careful program of training cannot assure the singer of good vocal health if there are factors in his or her life which adversely affect that health. The singer's instrument is part of the singer's body, and, as such, is affected by all the outside influences on that body. It is used virtually every waking hour for speaking and for other bodily functions such as protecting the airway during swallowing. And, as a part of the body, the voice is a member of a living organism and is as subject to tissue changes as its other parts.

The Speaking Voice

When we consider how many hours a day the voice is used for speech, it is easy to understand why misusing it can have such a devastating effect on the singer's larynx and, consequently, on his or her singing. Singers are often unaware of the pitch level and range they should use when speaking and of the effect misuse of the speaking voice can have upon their singing. Such misuse is revealed by "weakness and subsequent trouble of the singing voice" and by "hoarseness, laryngitis, tired voice, sore throats, voice breaks, pain in the throat, throat clearing, coughing" and other symptoms (Cooper, 1970, p. 7). Teachers may find the students who chronically misuse their voices when speaking are the ones who make little or no progress and always seem to have more than normal amounts of congestion in their throats.

Use of the wrong speaking pitch. The range of fundamental frequencies used by speakers varies from about 60 Hz. to about 500 Hz. The average fundamental frequency used by men is about 120 Hz.; for women it is about 225 Hz.; and for children it is about 265 Hz. (Fry, 1979, p. 68). The *optimum pitch* is the pitch at which an individual's voice functions most efficiently to provide the best quality, variation in volume and ease of production. Eisenson and Ogilvie state this is usually "one-fourth to one-third above the lowest" level of pitches available to that person (1983, p. 350). They find that for most persons the most effective speaking range is between the optimum pitch and a point about one-third below the

highest available pitch (p. 351). Ludlow, Conner and Coulter found
that vocal function is best in the upper 50% of the speaking range in
normal speakers (1984, p. 166).

Batza states that "except for a very few cases of falsetto voice
patients with excessively high pitch levels are almost nonexistent in
the writer's experience" (1977, p. 15). Batza, Bryce (1974, p. 73),
Cooper (1973, p. 187; 1977, p. 24), Fisher and Logeman (1970,
pp. 277-278) and Landes (1977, p. 123-124) all consider speaking
at an unnaturally low pitch a cause in the development of dysphonias. Cooper found that 441 or 91% of 486 functionally mysphonic
patients and 432 or 92% of 470 patients with organic dysphonias
were habitually using *basal pitch* (the lowest tone available for
speaking) or near basal pitch ranges for speaking (1973, p. 18).
Shelton provides the example of a politician who "insisted on using
a low-pitched voice to convey an authoritative image, despite the fact
that he ended his speaking day with a painful throat" and "even
though his larynx was chronically inflamed" (1985, p. 275).

Case considers a too-low speaking pitch both a cause and a
symptom. While some people may try to compensate for nodules
by speaking higher, most speak too low. "This low-pitched characteristic should be considered as both an etiological and a by-product
or factor" (1984, pp. 103-104).

Boone does not see pitch range as an absolute. "Few clinicians
would hold today to the belief that there is an absolute pitch level
that both normal and pathological voices should have" (1984, p.
146). He indicates that changes in pitch are affected by other therapy procedures as well as by therapy directed at pitch change.

Murry sees little or no correlation between voice abuse and
speaking at a pitch which is too low (1982b, p. 495). He too
prefers to work on other components of voice which will allow laryngeal and strap muscles to relax, thus causing the pitch to change
as a result of the change in tension. He does suggest that the therapist should work to reinforce usage of the new pitch through auditory feedback (1982b, pp. 495-496).

Wilner and Sataloff agree that muscular tension is often the
cause of speaking at the wrong pitch. They prefer to work on
achieving correct breathing techniques, relaxed phonation and
proper resonance rather than trying to change the person's pitch.
Once these components of speaking are improved, the musculature
will function normally and the speaker will use the correct range of
pitches (Wilner and Sataloff, 1987, pp. 316-317).

Koufman and Blalock use the term "laryngeal tension fatigue
syndrome" to describe a voice disorder characterized by "chronic
intermittent dysphonia and vocal fatigue" (1988, p. 493). Over the
five-year period from July 1, 1981 to July 1, 1986 they treated 67

adult professional voice users with dysphonia caused by musculoskeletal tension disorder which involved the larynx and/or its supporting structures. They determined that tension fatigue syndrome (TFS) in professional voice users is different from that in nonprofessional voice users. Whereas, the nonprofessional voice users showed limited available pitch range and obvious muscle tension, the vocal fatigue experienced by the professional voice users was caused by use of a too-low pitch and inadequate breath support for the speaking voice. Both groups demonstrated poor breath usage (Koufman and Blalock, 1988, pp. 497-498). They found that as a group professional voice users pitch their speaking voices quite low (1988, p. 493).

A singer who would never allow the sung tone to be placed incorrectly may speak with a low tonal focus. The focus of the speaking voice should be similar to that of the singer's sung tones in the same pitch range. This can be forward, up in the head or forward and up. Any voice placement above the line of the chin is healthy. The voice most people experience upon first awakening in the morning has both low pitch and a low tonal focus. Cooper calls this "morning voice" and recommends use of the "um-hum" slide (1973, p. 82) described in Chapter 4 to raise the pitch and tone focus of the morning voice. Because of the low pitch and placement of the morning voice the speaker must exert more effort to be heard and understood. Continuing to use that low pitch and tone focus throughout the day can lead to voice problems caused by the pharyngeal and laryngeal tensions characteristic of that voice (Cooper, 1973, p. 21).

Vocal sound is made louder by increasing airflow from the lungs and increasing vocal fold resistance to that airflow. Together these factors cause an increase in subglottal pressure (Case, 1984, p. 26). If there is an increase in airflow without the necessary glottal resistance the sound will be breathier rather than louder. If enough glottal resistance is maintained, subglottal air pressure will build up to a point where it can blow the cords apart. The resultant sound wave will excite the air in the vocal tract with high energy and will be perceived as loud. To sustain the loud sound, the high air flow and high glottal resistance must be maintained (Case, 1984, p. 28). This tighter closure must also be maintained for a greater part of the vibratory cycle than at normal, less intense volume levels. Maintaining the strong glottal resistances for a longer time period is potentially damaging to the cords (Bryce, 1974, p. 72).

Vocal fatigue. Sataloff defines vocal fatigue as the "inability to sing for extended periods without change in vocal quality" (1987a, p. 94). Symptoms of vocal fatigue include hoarseness, diminished range, change of quality, register breaks and what he describes as "other uncontrolled aberrations" (pp. 94-95). Sataloff believes that well-trained singers should be able to sing for several hours without developing vocal fatigue and that those experiencing such fatigue may be misusing abdominal and neck muscles or trying to sing too loudly for too long a period of time. He also indicates that vocal fatigue may be a sign of overall body fatigue or of general illness (pp. 94-95).

Programs of Vocal Hygiene
    Several authors provide programs of vocal hygiene (viz. Boone, 1980, p. 36; Cooper, 1973, p. 128; Feudo & Zubick, 1988, pp. 214-215; and Wilson, 1977, p. 262). All of these programs are designed to eliminate voice abuse. Some programs, like Cooper's and Wilson's, are designed to assist voice therapy patients in recovering from laryngeal damage and to prevent its future recurrence or the onset of other voice problems. Other programs like Feudo and Zubick's and Boone's are designed to provide optimal vocal health and voice usage for professional voice users.

1. Identify vocal abuse and misuse (shouting, throat clearing, laughing, etc.)
2. Reduce or eliminate the identified abuse and misuse.
3. Develop an easy glottal attack.
4. Use a speaking pitch level that is where you should be. Avoid speaking at extreme pitch levels.
5. Keep your speaking voice at the lower end of your loudness range.
6. Take an easy relaxed breath when speaking.
7. Reduce vocal demand as much as possible. Speak or sing less.
8. While listening, keep your teeth separated with a slight lip opening.
9. Avoid talking in loud settings (disco[s], airplanes, cars, boats, etc.)
10. Avoid smoking and excessive use of alcohol.
11. Avoid odd sounds with your voice, such as imitating engines, funny voices, etc.
12. Keep the membranes of your mouth and throat as moist as possible.
    (Boone, 1980, p. 36)

    All of the programs cited above caution against talking over loud music, machinery, motor vehicles or other environmental noises.

Cooper and Wilson also caution their patients against shouting over loud conversation at parties or other gatherings and against shouting, yelling and cheering. Boone, Feudo and Zubick, and Wilson suggest the use of an easy onset of phonation. Boone, Cooper, and Feudo and Zubick suggest using pitch and loudness levels which are appropriate to the individual, elimination of smoking and minimizing usage of alcohol. Boone, Cooper and Wilson advise against making funny noises with the voice. Boone and Feudo and Zubick both suggest increasing moisture in the mucosa through humidification of air and increasing the intake of liquids.

Excessive coughing and throat clearing can be damaging to any larynx. Both require an abrupt and forceful adduction of the vocal cords and increase the friction between the cords by drying them (Landes, 1977, p. 124). The cough is "a sudden expulsion of air against tightly closed cords that shakes foreign matter out with the expelling air" (Brodnitz, 1961, p. 42). Case states that, while neither coughing nor excessive throat clearing by themselves will cause nodules, both do act as irritants to laryngeal tissues and can be an additional factor in the development of pathology in a larynx already weakened by other forms of abuse (1984, p. 109). Coughing and throat clearing can linger as habits well after the bout of bronchitis or sinus drainage which caused them in the first place has passed. McFarlane believes that frequent throat clearing and/or coughing which does not immediately improve the voice is potentially harmful. He suggests replacing them with "'sniff then swallow'" and the "'silent cough'" (1988, p. 427). Case suggests replacing throat clearing with a "small blast of air" followed by a quick swallow (1984, p. 109).

The mucosa of the respiratory tract is kept moist by both external and internal means. Breathing air with adequate humidification and drinking water both improve the mucous flow. This helps with drainage. Humidification of the air is essential in locations which have extended periods of cold temperatures that require constant heat in homes and other buildings which, in turn, causes interior humidity levels to drop, sometimes to desert range. This is compounded by the fact that most locations with extremely low temperatures also have low humidity. Although many people find cold-water humidification easier and more comfortable, steam is equally effective in raising inside humidity. Excessive use of air conditioning, particularly in very dry climates, may also dry inside air excessively and require added humidification.

Drinking water also helps to keep the respiratory tract lubricated. Vaughan and Gould suggest at least 80 ounces (10, 8-ounce glasses) daily and remind us that drinks containing alcohol and caffeine, both diuretics, do not increase fluid intake (1988, p. 206).

Popular singers are particularly vulnerable to voice problems because of the environment in which they must work and because many are untrained. They often perform in smoke-filled clubs for four or more hours nightly. Most must project over a variety of amplified guitars, electronic keyboards and drums for 20-30-minute sets. (Those in piano bars have considerably less competition.) Although the singer is also amplified, placement of the speakers is crucial if the singer is to hear his or her own voice in the cacophony of amplified sounds. During breaks they may further abuse an already stressed voice by talking with customers and friends (Mowrer & Case, 1982, cited in Prater & Swift, 1984, p. 76).

Warming Up and Warming Down

Warming up. Unless impaired by illness or injury, the voice is always "there" and ready to talk. But singing is more than extended speech. Just as the muscles of the legs which walk and stand upon command must be stretched and flexed before a run, so must the muscles of the voice be warmed up before we sing. Most singers also work out technical problems through vocal exercises done during the warm-up period. Tone quality, balance of registers and placement are all determined by the vocalises and the order in which they are done. At the end of the first lesson the teacher should carefully instruct new students, especially beginners, on the order in which vocalises should be done and on the appropriate vowels to use. The student must understand that the vowels are selected carefully and are not interchangeable. This list should be updated in subsequent lessons until an overall pattern is established. As the student's voice develops the teacher may suggest changes in the exercises or the order in which they are executed.

With more advanced students, particularly those who have studied previously, the teacher and student can work together to determine a warm-up routine. Although some students may want and need a completely new start, some can integrate old warm-ups with new ones. In either case, it is important for the teacher to be diplomatic. If the student has been using a pattern that the new teacher feels is harmful to his or her technique, the new teacher should explain to the student what this exercise does and why it is not appropriate for the student at this time.

Warming down. Most singers have learned to warm up effectively, but few are aware of the benefits of warming down. During performance or hard practice the muscles of the larynx work intensely. The singer will find the voice less fatigued and more easily warmed up the next time if he or she does some quiet slides or scales following the performance or practice. These exercises should be done in the upper middle of the student's voice and can involve things as simple as a descending five- or eight-note scale on a quiet hum or ah. Warming down is particularly important for rock singers whose voice usage may sometimes approach screaming or with concert or opera singers who must sing loudly enough to be heard over a full orchestra.

Singing with a Cold or Allergies
To the average person a cold or upper respiratory infection (URI) is a minor annoyance. To a singer it is a disaster. The stuffy nose, blocked sinuses and post-nasal drip increase laryngeal irritation and may cause coughing. Blocked eustachian tubes may impair hearing, and the whole thing causes changes in what the singer feels. Moore states in clinical terms what happens to the voice during a cold or sinus infection.

> Inflammations of the nasal or laryngeal mucosa exert their deleterious effects on the voice, primarily through the swelling or drying of the surface membranes or combinations of these factors. Dilation of the minute blood vessels, associated with related edema, causes an engorgement of the mucosa and reduces the size of the resonator and modifies both the compliance and mass of the vocal folds. These changes tend to lower vocal pitch and alter nasal resonance, as when a head cold is present. Conversely, drying of the surfaces tends to increase the viscosity of the mucous and to cause crusting in both the nose and larynx. The conditions create discomfort, coughing and impairment of vibration. (Moore, 1971a, p. 99)

With a cold or allergies, the altered state of the mucosa of the vocal tract makes it more vulnerable to injury (Sataloff, 1981, p. 256; 1987a, p. 98). In addition, the singer may compromise technique to try to overcome the perceived voice and resonance changes. Arnold indicates vocal polyps may follow an acute respiratory infection. If the singer inflicts more trauma by trying to overcome the temporary hoarseness caused by the URI, a laryngeal hematoma may develop which, if the irritation continues, becomes a polyp (1962, p. 208).

Kaufman and Blalock indicate that they often see professional voice users weeks or even months after their recovery from an upper respiratory infection or viral laryngitis. They believe that compensating for such illnesses by altering elements of voice production affected by the illness, such as "pitch, breath support or muscle tension -- tips the balance in patients already predisposed to vocal fatigue" (1988, p. 498). They feel that these patients had functional voice problems (voice usage practices) before the illness which predisposed them to these compensatory habits. This feeling is reinforced by the fact that remedial voice therapy provides almost immediate improvement with these patients (p. 498).

However, Sataloff indicates that a singer with a cold can perform provided certain precautions are taken. He recommends resting the voice at all times other than necessary warm-up and performance, some antihistamine therapy and plenty of liquids and external hydration if the climate warrants it (1981, pp. 263-264; 1987c, p. 286).

The experienced singer who relies primarily on how the voice feels and does not attempt to compensate for the diminished resonance, clarity and range caused by a cold or other URI will probably fare better than the one who depends somewhat on auditory feedback. Not to be overlooked is the effect of congestion on both conductive and external hearing. Even if the singer can hear a whisper across a crowded room (which is doubtful!), blocked eustachian tubes may alter the way the singer hears his or her own voice. While experienced singers may be able to sing in a nearly normal fashion, the same singers may inflict vocal damage by speaking louder and more forcibly than usual in order to "be heard." Again, the singer who is kinesthetically aware when singing may not have the same awareness about speaking.

Allergies can cause many of the same symptoms as a head cold, but they can also cause additional problems. Swelling of the mucous membranes can change the shape of the resonators and reduce their flexibility. In addition to the stuffy nose and runny eyes normally associated with it, allergy can affect the larynx directly with edema and erythema. Tucker reports that this edema, which may be sudden, is normally mild and creates only hoarseness and irritation (1987, p. 229).

Allergens such as bee stings and certain foods which cause systemic reactions can cause enough laryngeal swelling to obstruct the airway and compromise breathing (Tucker, 1987, p. 229). *Urticaria* or giant hives can develop over the lips, tongue, soft palate and/or pharynx (Frazier, 1974, p. 20). Frazier reports that such reactions are a serious but, fortunately, rare result of gastrointestinal allergy. More common reactions are hoarseness and loss of voice. "One doctor reports the case of a woman who lost her voice for months at a time. Removal of milk, eggs and wheat from her diet restored her ability to talk normally" (Frazier, 1974, pp. 20-21).

Laryngeal swelling can be caused by factors other than allergy (Tucker, 1987, p. 229). *Angioedema* can be the result of an allergic reaction or an hereditary autoimmune reaction (Quincke's disease). In the case of the latter, swelling of all or parts of the body may be severe enough for the sufferer to own different sizes of clothes, or laryngeal edema may be the only symptom. The singer who experiences even mild changes in the voice during these episodes may have concurrent laryngeal and upper airway responses. Anyone experiencing such recurrent swelling would be well-advised to seek medical advice. As with any medical question directly involving the larynx, the singer is fortunate if he or she can find a laryngologist in the geographical area who enjoys and has experience working with singers. A doctor who understands that singing is far more than a way of earning a living will be most helpful in such cases.

Bronchial constriction as a response to allergies and to asthma can also seriously impair the singer's performance (Lawrence, 1987, p. 322). Recurrent croup with its consequent coughing can result from asthma (Pennoyer & Sheffer, 1988, pp. 285-286). Treatment for asthma through inhalant therapy can also cause chemical irritation to the larynx and vocal tract. Reactions to steroid inhalers include dysphonias and candidal infection (Pennoyer & Sheffer, 1988, pp. 285-286).

The singer's breathing may also be impaired by reactions to food allergies in the intestinal tract. These reactions can include swelling, constipation, cramping, increased flatulence and diarrhea. The first three make abdominal and costo-abdominal breathing difficult and, in some cases, painful. The singer may use abdominal tension to prevent the onset of the other symptoms. Anything which causes abdominal discomfort may compromise a singer's breathing and must be seen as detrimental to his or her singing.

Of course, the ideal solution for the allergy sufferer is to remove him or herself from all contact with the offending allergen(s). This may be possible in the case of foods once the culprit is identified. Although testing for food hypersensitivity is not always definitive and must be conducted with extreme care because of the possibility of systemic reactions, such tests do serve to identify a starting point (King, 1990, p. 116). By keeping a detailed diary of foods eaten, including ingredients of casseroles, sauces, baked goods, etc. if necessary, the patient and doctor can isolate and eliminate the offending foods.

Testing for inhalant and contact allergens is much safer and more efficient. Once the allergens are identified, the patient undergoes a series of weekly injections of a serum made up of minute quantities of the substances to which he or she is allergic. By gradually increasing the quantity of these antigens, the patient is "desensitized" to them. Spiegal, Sataloff, Cohn, and Hawkshaw consider this treatment particularly advisable for singers with multiple allergies.

Such treatment provides relief from symptoms without the side effects of oral drugs or nasal sprays (1988, p. 46). While desensitization shots may not be effective in every case, they have freed many from a life of runny noses; itchy backs, feet, eyes and throats; and antihistamine dependence.

Medications
Decongestants and antihistamines.
At some point every singer will be tempted to take or will take an over-the-counter preparation to relieve the symptoms of a cold, sinus headache or allergic rhinitis. All antihistamines dry the mucous tissues of the larynx as well as those of the nose and throat (Harrison & Tucker, 1987, p. 156; Lawrence, 1987, p. 318; Mowrer & Case, 1982, p. 204). They also cause a marked decrease in secretions of the mucous membranes (Vaughan & Gould, 1988, p. 209). Lubrication of the vocal tract is best served by generous quantities of thin secretions. The reduction and thickening of these secretions by antihistamines may cause a dry cough (Sataloff, 1987c, p. 287) and can adversely affect the quality of sound and increase the vulnerability of the larynx to abuse (Mowrer & Case, 1982, p. 204). Post-nasal drip is particularly annoying to the singer because it can irritate the throat and increase the amount of mucous on the cords. However, removing the excessive mucous can sometimes do more harm than good. "We should perhaps think of pharyngeal and laryngeal mucous more as a friend than as an enemy" (Boone, 1980, p. 42).

Decongestants combined with anti-inflammatory agents (ibuprofen, aspirin) can reduce swelling in an injured larynx and restore normal voice. This may cause additional damage to an already injured larynx (Vaughan & Strong, 1984, p. 707). In addition, excessive use of decongestants sometimes causes "rebound congestion" (Martin, 1985, p. 196; 1988, p. 341). Martin indicates that the patient can cause a spiraling effect by increasing the use of decongestants to counteract this rebound congestion. "The nasal mucous membranes of these patients show characteristic lesions that are due to the long-term reduction of blood flow to the tissues; in severe cases the mucous membranes may become necrotic and perforation of the nasal septum may occur exactly as occurs in the chronic cocaine 'snorter'" (1988, p. 341).

One side effect of antihistamines is sedation of the central nervous system (Vaughan & Strong, 1984, p. 707). Antihistamines usually carry warnings about drowsiness and cautions against operating machinery, an indication of the effects they have on coordination. Such effects will surely mar the fine muscle control required by the singer.

Pseudophedrine, marketed under the brand name of Sudafed and several "house brands," seems to have less detrimental effects. It "produces smooth muscle relaxation and arteriolar contraction and is thus an effective bronchial dilator and mucous membrane decongestant" (Vaughan & Gould, 1988, p. 208). Taken alone in simple form (it is also marketed in combination with other drugs) it does not produce the drying effect of other over-the-counter preparations.

Nose drops and sprays may appear to be less dangerous because they are directed to a specific area. The same rebound congestion can develop if they are used frequently or regularly over a long period of time (Proctor, 1980b, pp. 156-157). Most carry warnings that they may become habit forming. Normal breathing can be restored by stopping their use.

Lozenges and local anesthetics used on the throat. While lozenges, cough drops and throat sprays can provide temporary relief from sore throats and that little tickle that stimulates a cough, choosing the right one is important. Pain exists as a warning that something is not right and to inhibit actions that will cause further damage. Thus, the singer should avoid lozenges, sprays and cough drops containing topical anesthetics. These products also impair laryngeal control and input (Lawrence, 1987, p. 321; Martin, 1988, p. 340). Vaughan and Gould suggest non-medicated isotonic lozenges (1988, p. 210).

Aspirin and analgesics. Even the common aspirin effects the voice. It inhibits coagulation of the blood which increases the possibility of submucous hemorrhage (Brodnitz, 1962, p. 450; Sataloff, 1981, p. 265; 1987c, p. 288; Vaughan & Gould, 1988, p. 207). All analgesics mask pain and thus can reduce feedback mechanisms. If the analgesic is for headache or discomfort outside the larynx, Sataloff recommends postponing treatment until rehearsal or performance is over (1981, p. 265; 1987c, p. 288). If laryngeal pain is severe enough to require analgesic treatment, the singer should not be singing (Sataloff, 1981, p. 265; 1987c, p. 288).

Aspirin or other analgesics are often found along with decongestants in compounds to treat colds or sinus discomfort. Many times these products are taken when the larynx is already vulnerable. Acetaminophen, marketed under brand names Tylenol, Tempra and Liquiprin, has no anti-inflammatory capabilities and does not adversely affect the larynx (Vaughan & Gould, 1988, p. 208).

Steroids. The body's two adrenal glands are located one above each kidney. Each has an outer layer called the adrenal cortex and an inner layer called the adrenal medulla. The main adrenal hormones are known as steroids, indicating they are chemically related to a family of chemicals called sterols.

> Corticosteroids control carbohydrate and protein
> metabolism, lipid (fat) metabolism, electrolyte
> (mineral) and water balance, sodium and potassium
> balance, and numerous other functions in the cardio-
> vascular, skeletal and central nervous system. Corti-
> costeroids and the ACTH (adrenocorticotropine hor-
> mone) from the pituitary gland that stimulates the
> adrenals to synthesize the corticosteroids also func-
> tion to modify the course of a variety of diseases and
> therefore have immunity functions. (Gilman,
> Goodman & Gilman, 1980, cited in Case, 1984, pp.
> 54-55)

Because high doses of glucocorticoids inhibit inflammation and
other responses to infections and allergies, they can be used effectively as nasal sprays or in injection form to treat allergy (Masset &
Sutherland, 1975, p. 123). The use of steroids in the treatment of
laryngeal inflammation and swelling is extremely controversial.
Questions about the safety and long-term effects of such treatments
were raised as early as the 1979 Symposium Care of the Professional Voice at the Julliard School. Barry Wyke, M.D., director of
the neurological unit of the Royal College of Surgeons of England,
responded to a question about the use of steroids to enable singers
with swollen cords to perform. He cited evidence from the fields of
rheumatology and orthopedics which indicates that exposing
cartilages to steroids over a long period of time will cause degeneration and eventually microsis (erosion) (Phonatory mechanisms panel, 1980, pp. 76-77).

Part of the problem with treating laryngeal inflammation and
swelling with steroids is that they constitute what Case calls
"palliative therapy" and do not affect the etiology of the symptoms
(1984, p. 55). Proctor warns about the risk of injury to inflamed laryngeal tissues which have been treated with drugs, including
steroids, decongestants and antihistamines, to reduce swelling. He
suggests that, while such emergency measures may be used safely
once, long-term usage may result in "gradually increasing injury to
the tissue of the vocal folds. Sometimes the professional who at-
tributes his weakening voice to age may actually be suffering the results of such hazardous management of episodes of acute laryngitis
over the years" (1980b, p. 136).

Vaughan and Gould indicate that an additional side effect of
steroid treatment for laryngeal disorders may be inhibition of the
warm-up process. In such cases the voice remains thin and weak,
and the performer must exert a great deal of effort to achieve his or
her normal sound (1988, p. 209). They also warn about the use of

steroid compounds topically. These are considered safe because they are not thought to be absorbed systematically. Vaughan and Gould indicate that prolonged use of these drugs in a laryngeal spray has a 10% incidence of development of laryngeal candida infection. Withdrawal effects have also been noted following prolonged use (1988, p. 209). Martin warns that topical use of corticosteroids may cause steroid-induced myopathy (muscle disease) leading to dysphonia for a significant number of those who use them on a regular basis (1988, p. 343).

Without question steroid treatment can allow a singer with swollen cords to perform. However, evidence is strong that repeated use can be dangerous. The singer who has been given a throat spray containing steroids will find that, used conservatively, it can work wonders. It should, however, be respected and its use monitored by a laryngologist who deals with concert and opera singers. It is not aspirin!

When Not to Sing
Whereas most people consider illness adequate reason for missing work, singers and other performers often seek to rise above it because "The show must go on." The singer's decision to cancel a performance is a difficult one which may be complicated by concerns about finances and maintaining a reputation of reliability. Attitudes of managers, promoters, conductors and stage directors who are interested primarily in the immediate performance can place additional pressure on the singer. However, as Vaughan and Gould state, the main concern in the decision of whether or not a singer is well enough to sing should be the singer's long-term vocal health. This must take precedence over immediate concerns of managers, promoters, conductors, etc. (1988, p. 204).

"Acutely ill voice patients should not go to work" (Schechter & Coleman, 1984, p. 136). Schechter and Coleman offer one exception to this dictum: the performer who has a cold or an upper respiratory infection but whose voice remains clear of hoarseness (p. 136). Vaughan and Gould list three conditions which they consider "absolute contraindications to performing" (1988, p. 205). These include submucosal hemorrhage of the larynx, exudative or ulcerative laryngitis and debilitating illness of any kind. They indicate that vocal rest is essential to resolving cases of submucosal hemorrhage. Without it further bleeding may take place and may cause more serious conditions such as polyps. Sataloff expands this to "hemorrhage in the vocal fold and mucosal disruption" (1981, p. 263; 1985, p. 313; 1987c, p. 285) and states that permanent disruption of the vibratory function of the vocal folds can be the result of ignoring such advice. He also indicates that the use of aspirin by premenstrual women is the main cause of vocal fold hemorrhage among trained singers (1987c, p. 285).

The exudative or ulcerative forms of laryngitis are infections and usually result in total loss of voice. Less virulent forms of laryngitis also present a problem for the singer. Even singers who normally sing with good technique may compensate when they try to sing with impaired vocal function. They may make adjustments elsewhere in the vocal tract with hopes of producing a stronger and more secure voice (Sataloff, 1987b, p. 198). Such adjustments may include increased breath pressure and modifications of resonance, tongue position, and placement. These adjustments may increase strain on an already irritated larynx.

Vaughan and Gould state that they include debilitating illness "only for completeness. Common sense tells even the most determined artist that he or she cannot perform with 'double pneumonia,' etc." (1988, p. 205).

Surgery and the Professional Voice User
The singer should give special consideration to any procedure, surgical or otherwise, which requires general anesthetic and thus endotracheal intubation. If the procedure is deemed necessary, the anesthesiologist should be informed beforehand that the patient is a singer so as to use special care inserting the tube (Proctor, 1980b, p. 131; Sataloff, 1981, p. 260; 1985, p. 306; 187a, pp. 101-102). To avoid irritation, Sataloff recommends the use of a plastic tube rather than one made of rubber (1981, p. 260; 1985, p. 306; 1987a, pp. 101-102).

Tonsillectomy. The tonsils are located in the pharynx at the base of the pillars of fauces. If the singer has not had the tonsils removed during childhood or adolescence, there may come a time when removing them seems advisable. Removing them changes the shape of the pharynx, and scarring associated with their removal may cause changes in muscle function in the pharynx. Choosing a time for the surgery is particularly important since it usually takes 3-6 months for the singer to regain pre-operative voice use (Sataloff, 1981, p. 260; 1985, p. 306; 1987a, pp. 101-102). It is, of course, vital that the surgeon is skilled and aware of the importance of not harming surrounding pharyngeal tissues while removing the tonsils completely (Proctor, 1980b, p. 131).

Laryngeal surgery. Few things strike fear in a singer like the suggestion of laryngeal surgery. Harrison and Tucker (1987, pp. 156-157), Tucker (1987, p. 217 side note) and Schechter and Coleman (1984, p. 135) all recommend surgery for voice disorders in singers only as a last possible resort. Harrison and Tucker use laser surgery only when normal vocal function cannot be restored with other means (1987, p. 157). Tucker will not remove benign lesions surgically in professional voice users unless they are "totally unable to perform" (1987, p. 217 side note). If laryngeal surgery must be performed, care must be given to monitor voice use during the recovery period, particularly in the time immediately following the surgery. Some laryngologists now work with voice therapists and voice teachers who are trained in techniques to use with singers to facilitate their recovery and gradually return the larynx to healthy function. It is particularly important that speaking and singing time be limited immediately following the surgery and that the voice be restored slowly and with the guidance of trained professionals.

Irritating Substances
Different persons respond to different substances in differing degrees and ways. However, there are certain agents which can be considered potentially irritating to the general population. Irritating substances include airborne dusts, powders, pollens, fumes, smoke (Moore, 1971a, p. 79), smog (Cooper, 1973), stomach acidity (Landes, 1977; Lawrence, 1983) and excessive dryness (Boone, 1980; Moore, 1971a; Punt, 1967). Airborne dusts, powders, pollens and fumes fall in the category of allergies, which was discussed earlier in this chapter. The effects of stomach acid on the larynx is discussed in Chapter 7 and excessive dryness was discussed in the beginning of this chapter.

Alcohol. Singers' folklore contains colorful stories about the operatic soprano who hid small glasses of whisky in the scenery for quick swallows during the show or the tenor who always drank a particular combination with spirits before going on-stage so as to "lubricate" his larynx. While these stories are entertaining, such practices may not be in the best interests of vocal health given the following facts.

Alcohol dilates the capillaries of the vocal cords which increases the production of mucous and makes them more susceptible to vocal abuse (Arnold, 1962; Brodnitz, 1961; Sataloff, 1987a, p. 100). It can also cause excessive dryness of the interior of the larynx (Prater and Swift, 1984, p. 76). Occasional over-indulgence harms muscular coordination as well as the covering of the throat and vocal cords, but recovery is usually rapid. Repeated use can become habitual and does permanent harm to the vocal mechanism (Brodnitz, 1961, p. 97; and Punt, 1967). Boone finds occasional use of alcohol to have no harmful effects. He warns against its heavy use because the increased vascularization of the vocal folds produces more irritation and increases in the mass of the vocal cords, which leads to dysphonia (1980, p. 41). Proctor considers consumption of alcohol in moderation harmless, but he cautions that it should not be taken before a performance (1980b, p. 132). Sataloff states that, while some singers may experience no effects from a glass of wine or other small amount of alcohol taken before a performance, others may have mild allergies to wine or beer (1987a, p. 100).

Alcohol is also a central nervous system depressant. Both Martin (1988, pp. 339-340) and Lawrence (1987, p. 321) indicate that its action on the central nervous system may adversely affect vocal performance by altering control of fine muscle coordination. Martin indicates that alcohol, barbiturates and minor tranquilizers effect the voice "in large doses, slowing and slurring of speech. Smaller doses could be expected to have an impact on the control of pitch, timbre, volume, etc." (1988, p. 340).

Tobacco. The link between smoking and cancer and heart and lung disease is now well documented and well publicized. While these problems may be the result of smoking over a long period of time, effects on the vocal tract are manifest much sooner. "Tobacco smoke is often an allergen but it always is an irritant to respiratory tract tissues. Nicotine constricts the peripheral blood vessels, reducing blood flow" (Case, 1984, p. 111).

Smoke acts as a drying agent in the airway and an irritant to the larynx (Boone, 1983, p. 207). Smoking over a period of time lowers the pitch of the voice, possibly because it thickens the vocal cords or because relaxation of the user causes vocal misuse (Baker, 1962, p. 704; Case, 1984, pp. 111-112; Cooper, 1973, p. 26).

Heavy smoking affects the vocal cords in two ways: Reineke's edema or polypoid hypertrophy, and chronic hyperplastic laryngitis. These particular forms of laryngitis and edema (see Chapter 7) are directly attributable to smoking. Reineke's edema is a "chronic edematous lesion" (Perkins, 1985, p. 90) over the length of the membranous portion of both vocal cords. It occurs most often between the ages of 40 and 70 and slightly more often in women than in men (Kleinsasser, 1979, p. 119).

Men, on the other hand, more often develop chronic hyperplastic laryngitis, usually between the ages of 30 and 65 (Kleinsasser, 1979, p. 110). Although nearly all his patients were heavy smokers, Kleinsasser notes there may also be a correlation between other noxious agents and this condition. "Occupational hazards such as dust, heat, excessive use of the voice to overcome noise, and chronic inflammation in the nose, sinus and bronchi may be important in the pathogenesis" (Kleinsasser, 1979, pp. 110-111).

Chronic hyperplastic laryngitis begins with thickening of the squamous epithelium over the anterior third of the vocal cords. As the disease progresses this thickening extends over the entire length of the cords. With exacerbation of the inflammatory process, the connective tissues of the submucosal layers thicken. Finally, the surfaces of the vocal cords become irregular as the cords become thicker and lose their sharp contours. Movement of the mucosa is restricted. Eventually ulcers may form in the epithelium. If the ulcers are very deep, the cords may appear double. Red gelatinous swellings may form in the laryngeal ventricle or a sticky secretion may cover the cords or the internal surface of the larynx (Kleinsasser, 1979, p. 111).

This condition is treated by removal of the epithelium. If the anterior commissure is involved, it is done one cord at a time with four to eight weeks' time required for re-epithelization of the cords (Kleinsasser, 1979, p. 118).

Although it should seem obvious by now that smoking **anything** will affect the vocal tract, marijuana seems to be particularly drying to the mouth and throat. In addition, users report some difficulties with pitch changes and "raspiness in the voice" (Case, 1984, p. 112).

Cocaine. Cocaine can be injected under the skin, into the muscles or into a vein. It can be "snorted" up the nose, taken orally, rectally or vaginally or smoked (Cregler & Mark, 1986, p. 1495). The potential for long-term physical and psychological affects and life-threatening crises of even one-time excessive use of cocaine are so staggering it hardly seems necessary to include it here. However, it does exert some rather specific and immediate effects on the larynx and vocal tract. Perez-Reyes and associates paid six healthy male subjects to smoke 50 mg. of free-based cocaine. They found deposits of the drug in the mucosa of the respiratory tract **before** it penetrated the lungs. The result was anesthesia of the mouth and pharynx which the subjects reported as a "feeling of numbness that was sometimes distressing" (Perez-Reyes, et al., 1982, p. 464). Such numbness is associated with decreased sensations through the vocal tract which may result in less control of the voice and increased voice abuse and/or misuse (Sataloff, 1981, p. 259; 1987a, p. 101). Sataloff writes of the irritating effect of cocaine on the nasal mucosa and indicates that it also causes vasoconstriction (1981, p. 259; 1987a, p. 101). Schweitzer indicates free-base smoking of cocaine also causes "hoarseness, chronic cough, shortness of breath, chronic sore throat, and more severe pulmonary complications such as pulmonary insufficiency and tracheobronchial rupture" (1986, p. 209). "Snorting" cocaine will destroy the mucous membranes of the nose and sinuses and may lead to necrosis (destruction) of the septum cartilage (Schweitzer, 1986, p. 209). Cocaine is also mood-altering and causes euphoria and an increase in motor activity (Rang and Dale, 1987, p. 574).

Hormones and the Female Voice

From the fourth month after conception throughout her life estrogen is vital in a woman's body. It is responsible for the development of female characteristics in the fetus; it molds the young girl into a woman and it shapes much of her physical and emotional life thereafter. Both men and women produce hormones of each sex; it is the balance between the male and female hormones that is crucial. An upset in that balance before birth endows either sex with characteristics of the other: at puberty the child may fail to mature sexually while secondary sexual characteristics such as the boy's facial hair and the deepening voice do not appear (Cooper, 1975).

Change in the level of the adult female's estrogen influences her monthly menstrual cycle, her skin tones, her arterial elasticity and often her moods. Long accepted in Europe, it is now becoming accepted in the United States that hormone changes in a woman's body, either natural or artificially imposed, also affect her voice.

Abramson, Essman and Steinberg indicate the epithelium of the larynx contains binding sites for estrogenic compounds which are comparable to binding sites found in other tissues such as normal breasts (1985, p. 293). Abitbol et al. indicate that "The stratified squamous epithelium undergoes modification in structure and function depending on the hormonal stimulation it receives, affecting functions such as biomechanical and muscular stimulation" (1989, p. 161). While increased estrogen causes the superficial layer to thicken, higher levels of progesterone stimulate development of the intermediate level. In addition, changes in the balance between estrogen and progesterone stimulation cause water retention, vasodilation (Abitbol et al., 1989, p. 161) and vocal fold edema (Abitbol et al., 1989, p. 161; Harrison & Tucker, 1987, p. 155). Thus, hormonal changes of the menstrual cycle, pregnancy, birth control pills, menopause and anabolic steroids will directly affect the voice.

Premenstrual syndrome. During the last decade the medical community has acknowledged that the wide range of chemical changes in a woman's body are responsible for the emotional and physical fluctuations she experiences throughout her monthly cycle. Studies and research on the effects of hormones on the female voice, especially immediately before and during the menstrual period, have proliferated. The causes of these voice changes are decreased levels of estrogen and progesterone and an increase in an anti-diuretic hormone which causes fluid retention in the tissues of the larynx and throughout the body (Sataloff, 1981, p. 264; 1987c, p. 287). Sataloff (1981) and Lawrence (1987, p. 320), both laryngologists treating professional voice users, indicate that water thus retained is not affected by common diuretics. Such "protein-bound water" is, however, directly affected by corticosteroids and by topical or systemic decongestants which reduce the size of submucosal vascular structures. Both classes of drugs may, however, produce a "rebound" phenomenon with increased swelling occurring following discontinuation of their use (Lawrence, 1987, pp. 320-321). Symptoms of the effects of premenstrual hormone changes on the voice include loss of high notes (Abitbol, 1988, p. 263; Darby, 1981, p. 23; and Sataloff, 1987a, p. 99), loss of low notes (Abitbol, 1988, p. 263), vocal fatigue (Abitbol, 1988, p. 263; Sataloff, 1987a, p. 99), hoarseness (Prater & Swift, 1984, p. 77; Sataloff, 1987a, p. 99), reduced vocal fold approximation and consequent reduction in vocal efficiency associated with vocal fold edema (Abitbol, 1988, p. 263; Darby, 1981, p. 23; Sataloff, 1987a, p. 99) and resonance changes.

Gould and Lawrence cite premenstrual edema as a cause of increased swelling in polyps. They recommend endocrine therapy along with voice therapy as an alternative to surgery in some cases (1984, p. 5). Numerous studies indicate there may be a link between submucosal hemorrhages in the larynx and premenstrual hormone changes. Abitbol observed 10 women and two men with unilateral hemorrhages. All were professional voice users: singers or voice teachers. Nine of the women had premenstrual syndrome characterized by vocal dysfunction. Two also complained of "cyclic rhinitis with pharyngitis" (1988, p. 263). Symptoms appeared the two or three days preceding and the first one or two days during menstruation. Only three of the 12 healed without some type of therapy and medical treatment. Nine required surgery (Abitbol, 1988, p. 263).

Lin, Stein and Gould examined 44 cases of vocal cord hemorrhage over a period of six years. Thirty of these were women, and eight of these 30 had some type of estrogen imbalance.

> One patient had discontinued the use of her oral contraceptive pills, developed irregular menses, and beginning 3 months later, had three episodes of hemorrhage spaced 1 month apart that occurred during singing. Upon resuming estrogen therapy, the recurrent vocal cord hemorrhages stopped. Four patients had single episodes of vocal cord hemorrhages while singing during their menstrual period. Another patient with an irregular menstrual cycle had three episodes of vocal cord hemorrhage while singing during her menstrual period. One patient was receiving postoperative estrogen therapy subsequent to a bilateral oophorectomy [removal of an ovary] and had recurrent hemorrhages when she missed her es-

trogen replacement pills. One patient had a vocal cord hemorrhage while singing 2 days after a voluntary interruption of pregnancy. (Lin, Stern & Gould, 1991, p. 75)

These researchers felt that their observations and those of other researchers indicate a correlation between estrogen imbalance and vocal cord hemorrhages in female singers (Lin, Stein & Gould, 1991, p. 76).

Abramson, Steinberg, Gould, Bianco, Kennedy and Stock studied the responses of over 120 trained singers to a detailed questionnaire on their perceived vocal quality just before and during menses. They distinguished between respondents with regular periods, those who were menopausal and those who had been pregnant at any time. The researchers concluded that the critical factor in voice changes during menstruation is the constant changes in the levels of estrogen rather than the actual estrogen levels. They felt that physiological changes in the larynx and pharynx which resulted from constantly fluctuating estrogen levels would present more difficult adjustments for the singer than either the high level of estrogen caused by pregnancy or the low level which follows menopause (1985, p. 412).

In addition to fluctuating hormones, the woman may experience abdominal congestion and distention during the premenstrual period and abdominal cramping during the actual menstruation. Either of these factors can compromise breathing and support. As Sataloff indicates, a singer whose breathing is significantly impaired in this manner should not sing (1987a, p. 100).

Pregnancy.   While the menstrual cycle causes fluctuation in hormone levels, pregnancy causes an elevated level of estrogen over a substantial period of time. This high estrogen level may cause non-inflammatory laryngeal edema similar to that of premenstrual women. It usually resolves once the pregnancy is over (Brodnitz, 1971; Damsté, 1987, p. 139; Damsté & Lerman, 1975; Friedmann & Ferlito, 1988, p. 37). The voice quality may be rough and the pitch lowered (Brodnitz, 1971; Damsté, 1987, p. 137; Damsté & Lerman, 1975). The condition may become more serious if the woman is predisposed to voice problems. In such cases the ventricular bands and aryepiglottic folds may also swell, and hemorrhage and loss of epithelium are possible. Severe swelling can lead to aphonia and compromise of the airway affecting stridor and shortness of breath (Damsté, 1987, p. 137).

The abdominal distention of pregnancy may interfere with the singer's breathing. Sataloff's warning for the singer whose breath-

ing is compromised in this manner to avoid singing until such distention is no longer a factor is again applicable (1987a, p. 100)

Through their research on the effects of hormones on the female
voice, Abramson and colleagues also assessed the effects of pregnancy on the voice. Most of the singers who had been pregnant
considered their singing improved during pregnancy. Sixty-two
percent of them reported that their voice quality remained unchanged
during the first trimester; 16% reported an improved quality, and
22% reported a decline in voice quality. The latter group gave
morning sickness as the reason for the decline. Forty percent said
their singing remained stable in the second trimester; 45% found it
improved; and 15% said it declined. While 47% said their singing
improved during the final trimester of pregnancy, the rest were
equally divided into 26% who said it remained stable and 26% who
said it declined. The researchers surmised from the responses that
the elevated estrogen levels of pregnancy benefit the quality of a
woman's voice (Abramson et al., 1985, p. 411).

Oral contraceptives. Early studies showed that progesterone
alone would prevent ovulation in women as well as in test animals.
However, progesterone taken orally by humans created problems
including low potency level. By the mid-1950s scientists were able
to synthesize progesterone in substances known as "gestagens."
When the gestagens were administered alone, bleeding between
periods varied from spotty to profuse. To overcome this an orally
active estrogen was added (Wood, 1969, pp. 138-140).

The balance between the hormones in "the pill" has changed
radically since its development and still varies depending on the
specific pill prescribed. In 1971 Brodnitz stated that pure estrogen
would not affect the female voice (p. 187). In 1972 LeBaron indicated that high estrogen levels caused retention of salt and water in
body tissues. Progesterone stimulates breast development at puberty and maintains the lining of the uterus during pregnancy. It
does not seem to affect the body otherwise (p. 121).

In 1975 Massett and Sutherland recommended use of oral contraceptives containing proportionally more progesterone. And in
1984 Gould and Lawrence provided a totally different outlook.

> "Pills" usually contain a mixture of the two female
> hormones: an estrogen and a progestin. Progestins,
> owing to their very close biochemical similarity to
> testosterone can see a virilizing effect which may be
> manifested by a loss of the top one or more tones.
> (Gould & Lawrence, 1984, p. 5)

In 1987 Lawrence repeated the warning that birth-control pills with high progesterone content could cause significant changes in the voice. He indicated the pill today is much improved over those of the past (1987, p. 321).

> Birth control pills, with relatively high progesterone content, are most likely to produce androgen-like changes in the voice. The earlier versions of these pills contained a fairly high dosage of steroids and were initially heavily weighted with progesterone. With time for gynecologic experience and awareness, the tendency in the newer medications is toward a relatively lower content of ovarian steroids. (Lawrence, 1987, p. 321)

Although there is disagreement on the reasons for the changes, it is apparent that oral contraceptives do affect the female voice. The changes are not permanent; when the medication is discontinued and the body returns to normal, the voice also returns to its previous state.

Menopause. During menopause the level of estrogen in a woman's body drops radically. This drop causes changes in her body chemistry which in turn cause changes in the body's elastic and collagenous fibers (Damsté, 1987, p. 136). Such changes affect the structure of the voice directly. Abramson, Essman and Steinberg's survey indicates that post-menopausal women reported the low (23%) and middle (38%) ranges were primarily affected by hormonal changes. "Less than 10% of the women in menopause reported a change in the upper middle or high range" (1985, p. 411). Damsté states that careful use of the voice can enable the woman to compensate for the effects of hormone changes. Practicing her middle register daily in a mezza-voce will prevent the chest or low register from becoming too prominent (1987, p. 136).

Abramson, Essman and Steinberg found that nearly one-third of the women they contacted said that "'everything about their singing was better'" (1985, p. 411). Only one-third had difficulty with attack and with sustained singing in the lower and middle registers. The other one-third considered their voice had stabilized (1985, p. 411).

Radical drops in estrogen can cause unpleasant symptoms such as night sweats and hot flashes. Estrogen replacement therapy is frequently administered to relieve these symptoms and to prevent long-term problems such as reduction of bone mass. Sometimes women are given medications which combine estrogen with testosterone. Damsté indicates that such medications always affect the voice, although the time before the effects become noticeable varies according to the woman's sensitivity to androgens. Such medications may cause thickening of the cords and lowering of the pitch of the voice (1987, p. 136). While Martin indicates that the amount of testosterone in these medications is low enough so the risk of side effects should be minimal, he also states there are no studies on the effects of such medications (1988, p. 343). The reader is referred to the following section for more information on the use and effects of anabolic steroids.

Anabolic steroids. The adrenal cortex manufactures male (androgens) and female (estrogen) hormones in both men and women; it is the balance between the two which determines sex (Masset & Sutherland, 1975). The balance in the female can be affected by the administration of hormone therapy or by conditions such as polycystic ovaries (Darby, 1981, p. 23), ovarian tumors (Darby; Sataloff, 1981, p. 258; 1987a, p. 99) or adrenal tumors (Sataloff). Anabolic steroids are synthetic derivatives of testosterone (*Physicians' Desk Reference*, 1991, p. 2356). They may be used to stimulate growth of muscle mass (Martin, 1988, p. 342) and to treat fibrocystic breast disease (Martin, 1988, p. 342), metastasized ovarian cancer (Damsté, 1987, p. 136), and severe endometriosis and the accompanying dysmenorrhea (Lawrence, 1987, p. 321). Anabolic steroids are also in some chemotherapies for breast cancer (Lawrence, 1987, p. 321). As described in the previous section, testosterone is sometimes administered as therapy for symptoms of menopause. Outside the United States it is sometimes prescribed for debilitating fatigue with no apparent etiology and may appear in so-called "tonics" available in other countries (Martin, 1988, p. 342).

The *1994 Physicians' Desk Reference* (PDR) lists two anabolic steroids: Teslac and Winstral Tablets. The section on "Precautions" for Winstral contains a general warning about anabolic steroids which includes female virilization. The first sign of virilization listed is "deepening of the voice" (p. 2122). "To prevent irreversible change, drug therapy must be discontinued, or the dosage significantly reduced when mild viralism is first detected. Some virilizing changes in women are irreversible even after prompt discontinuance of therapy and are not prevented by concomitant use of estrogen" (p. 2122). Winstral is prescribed for hereditary angioedema (p. 2122). Teslac is testolactone rather than testosterone and, as such, does not have the same virilizing effects. Teslac is prescribed for breast cancer (p. 672).

The PDR lists three combinations of androgens and estrogens which are prescribed for "moderate to severe *vasomotor* symptoms associated with menopause in patients not improved by estrogen

alone" (pp. 2305, 2600). The androgen and estrogen components
are discussed separately for each of these drugs. The PDR also lists
five androgens, all with warnings about potential side effects. Four
of these androgens are used to treat advanced breast cancer (pp.
1059, 2349), and one is used to treat aplastic anemia (p. 1048).
It should be noted that the use of these drugs is, in some cases,
for life-threatening conditions. This discussion is in no way meant
to discredit their use or the doctor's selection of them in such situations. In other cases, however, such as for treatment for symptoms
of menopause, the woman may wish to make her physician aware of
the fact that she is a singer, is **aware** of the potential side effects of
such drugs, and would like to explore other routes of treatment.

Increased androgen levels cause thickening of the vocal cords
and deepening of the voice. Such changes, called virilization of the
voice, are irreversible. Darby (1981, p. 23) indicates that even administration of estrogen may effect no change.

Damsté emphasizes the importance of recognizing early symptoms of virilization of the voice so that the drug can be stopped before virilization advances. Unfortunately, so long as her voice remains within a "normal" speaking range, the early changes may only
be apparent to the patient. As the virilization continues, the split between upper and lower registers will increase until the low or chest
register has a heavy quality like that of a man (Damsté, 1987, pp.
136-137).

In 1985 Martin described a synthetic androgen called Danazol as
an "'impeded' androgen, meaning that its structure has been
changed so that it does not fit well . . . with the receptor for testosterone" (1985, p. 198). He stated further, however, that literature
about the drug warns that it can cause voice changes. He cited an
incidence of about 10% for this side effect and indicated that it usually disappears when the drug's use is stopped (p. 198).

In 1988 the same author wrote about attempts to produce anabolic steroids capable of increasing development of muscle mass
without the effects of male sex hormones. "Although some separation of effect has been achieved, the separation is not absolute, and
voice changes in women or prepubertal males should be expected
when any of these agents are used, especially in high doses or for
long periods of time" (Martin, 1988, p. 342).

Although this information may be outdated with the development
of new drugs, it does indicate two things. First, attempts are being
made to produce drugs which will offer the same therapeutic treatments as anabolic steroids without the virilizing side effects.
Second, early trials of such drugs may or may not provide information which is definitive enough for the professional voice user.

Hypothyroidism

Some systemic illnesses are diagnosed when the sufferer goes
for help with voice problems. Other patients may live with and treat
chronic disorders for years with no noticeable affect on the voice or
their singing. While it is inappropriate in this type of book to discuss the effects of all systemic diseases and imbalances on the
larynx, *hypothyroidism* is included here because it can cause very
definite laryngeal symptoms.

The thyroid gland located in the neck produces thyroid hormone
which regulates the body's metabolic rate. Hypothyroidism is an
inadequate production of thyroid hormone which causes a low
metabolic rate. The person's voice may be hoarse and pitched excessively low because of thickened or edematous vocal folds
(Aronson, 1985, p. 6; Shemen, 1988, p. 225), weak and slow
(Shemen, 1988, p. 225). Some will have difficulty with high notes
(Shemen, p. 225), and in some cases articulation may be slurred
(Shemen, p. 225) or difficult (Damsté, 1987, p. 137). Hypothyroidism can cause *Reineke's edema* (see Chapter 7) in which the
area between the vocalis muscle and the epithelium fills with fluid.
This can be distinguished from other polypoid changes by the fact
that the entire length of the membrane is affected equally rather than
one particular portion showing marked swelling (Tucker, 1987, p.
215). Hypothyroidism and its accompanying voice symptoms are
controlled by administration of synthetic thyroid hormone under
medical supervision.

Exercise

Regular exercise provides definite benefits in overall conditioning and endurance which impacts singing directly and positively.
Certain types of exercise also have a direct negative effect on the
larynx and are best avoided by the singer.

The val salva maneuver forces air out of vocal cords that are
tightly held together (Clayman, 1989, p. 10037). It occurs during
activities which involve strenuous pressure of the muscles of the
upper torso, including weight lifting and other body-building activities. Lifting or carrying heavy objects requires tightly adducted
folds to keep air trapped in the chest. This trapped air keeps the rib
cage expanded and increases muscular efficiency for lifting and
pushing. Any vocalization produced while engaging in these activities will have to be forceful enough to overcome the hyperadducted
vocal folds and will sound strained because of the extreme amount
of laryngeal resistance (Prater & Swift, 1984, p. 75). Repeated
phonation with this glottal pressure will affect the cords adversely.
The danger of damage to normal vocal cords because of hyperfunctional closure is great, particularly if the person "grunts and groans"

while exercising. To experience the effect of such activities the reader should try phonating on an [a] vowel while standing and thrusting his or her closed fists downward from chest level.

> Daily exercise and lifting involve glottal closure under pressure in order to contain air in the lungs to stabilize the chest cavity so skeletal muscles can function efficiently. Each push-up, pull-up, lifting of weights, hard tennis serve or volley or jumping activity involves hard closure of the glottis. (Mowrer and Case, 1982, p. 200; Case, 1984, p. 109)

Large and Patton modified weight lifting to eliminate the val salva reflex by having the individual inhale at the beginning of the movement and exhale soundlessly during the actual execution of the movement. They asked male singers with advanced training to modify their weight training this way, kept the weight used low and the repetition rate high. They compared the effects of this weight training to those of jogging over a twelve-week period. Both groups exercised thirty minutes a day on Monday, Wednesday and Friday. Results were mixed with joggers showing improved vital lung capacity but decreased forced expiratory volume and weight trainers showing slightly decreased vital capacity but little change in forced expiratory volume. All subjects showed increased vocal power in all registers over the twelve-week period, and all were able to sustain these more powerful sounds longer. All were able to sing softer and to sustain these soft tones longer (1981, pp. 27-31).

Obesity and Dieting
The days of the self-indulgent, overweight singer seem to be passing. Singers, like the rest of the population, are aware of the benefits of a healthy diet and a lifestyle which includes regular exercise and maintaining a healthy body weight. Spiegel, Sataloff, Cohn and Hawkshaw indicate that excess weight can alter respiratory function and obesity is a cause of reduced pulmonary function (1988, p. 49). However, the singer who decides to lose weight must do so carefully. Sudden and drastic weight loss with loss in vitality often affects singing adversely. The old adage that weight is best lost gradually over a period of time is particularly important for singers (Sataloff, 1981, p. 256).

Bulimia. The long-term ramifications of eating disorders are well-known by the general public. One of these, bulimia also has immediate consequences for the singer or professional voice user. The bulimic induces vomiting of the stomach's contents by stimulating the gag reflex of the pharynx with a finger or an instrument.

The contents of the stomach which are then brought up through the esophagus and pharynx and out of the mouth are often acidic.

Morrison and Morris surveyed 10 bulimic female patients selected at random regarding pharyngeal and laryngeal symptoms following vomiting. Of those studied five had hoarseness which lasted from a few minutes to a few hours. Three showed a lowered speaking pitch. Two admitted to a sore mouth or throat, and two stated that they were prone to throat infections when vomiting was persistent. Laryngeal examinations were normal in two of the subjects. Four showed telangiectasia ("red spots within the skin which are clusters of capillaries and which can blanch with pressure" [Seyfer & Jacob, 1993, p. 4]) with one of these exhibiting a tumor made up of blood vessels. One showed severe laryngeal scarring and development of a laryngeal web. Two showed polypoid changes in the mucosa. Two showed erythema in the posterior portion of the cords, and one exhibited mild vocal cord edema. The researchers felt the frequency of vomiting and the ease with which the process took place affected the laryngeal symptoms.

> Whereas other patients describe an obsession with repeated vomiting, up to 20 times per day, and the use of objects such as eyeglass temples to stimulate the vomiting reflex. It was our impressions that these patients with more frequent or vigorous vomiting had noticeable diffuse telangiectasia in all areas of the glottic larynx. (1990, p. 79)

Morrison and Morris also indicated that some of their patients made demands on their voices which could have been responsible for this type of change (1990, pp. 77-79)

Fatigue

The voice is a muscle controlled by other muscles and, like the muscles of the arms and legs, is subject to the effects of general body fatigue. Causes may be temporary such as "lack of sleep, physical exertion or sexual orgasm" (Cooper, 1973, p. 32) or long-term including illness or depression (Cooper, 1973, p. 32). When the body is fatigued, the singer must give special attention to maintaining a high tonal focus. Speaking pitch and tone focus become particularly important because both will fall. A careful warm-up period is crucial at this time. Sometimes the singer will find fatigue prevents him or her from creating unnecessary tensions, and he or she will actually sing more freely. Other times fatigue will seem to evaporate as the singer concentrates and begins to relax and enjoy the act of singing. In cases of extreme or prolonged fatigue, it may be best for the singer to limit practice and performances until the source of the exhaustion is discovered and treated.

Cheerleading

Few of us are surprised when the cheerleader is hoarse after the big game. Most are healthy young people who recover after only a brief rest. But cheerleading can cause long-term effects, particularly if the junior high or high school cheerleader becomes the college voice student.

Andrews and Shanks studied 102 female cheerleaders from 13-17 years old by taking vocal histories and analyzing frequency characteristics of the cheers they produced. Thirty-seven percent of this group reported a history of voice problems. When broken down by age groups, the percentages with histories of voice problems increased from 27% at age 14 with an average of two years' cheering experience to 45% at age 17 with an average of five years' cheering experience. This increase suggests the reported voice problems increase with age and years of cheerleading. Thirty-six percent of the 11 13-year-olds in the study reported voice problems. The researchers believe such a high rate of voice problems in this age group may be due to the larynx' susceptibility to trauma due to mutational development of puberty (Andrews & Shanks, 1983, p. 153).

Case studied high school and college cheerleaders across the 1978 football season. Each cheerleader was examined and evaluated by an otolaryngologist at the beginning of and periodically throughout the season. Recordings were made of each subject's voice at the time of each medical evaluation and were used for spectrographic and listener analysis. None of the nine students in the high school group showed laryngeal pathology in the initial medical examination. Like those in the Andrews and Shanks study, all were female. Following the initial examination all nine subjects participated in a one-week cheerleading camp. Laryngeal examination at that point showed four of the nine had early vocal nodules or laryngeal edema which the otolaryngologist considered the result of voice abuse. Even with some counseling from the therapist doing the study, two of the subjects showed vocal nodules at the end of the season. Listener and spectrographic analysis agreed with the medical findings (Case, 1984, p. 116).

Case cites the specific practices of cheerleaders which are abusive:

- cheering without good abdominal breath support
- cheering with an energy focus in the larynx

- cheering with excessive tension in the neck and larynx
- using hard and abrupt onset of voice (hard glottal attack or coup de glotte)
- cheering during colds, infections, or severe allergy attack
- cheering at an inappropriate pitch level (too high or too low)
- excessive individual cheering in addition to group yells (1984, p. 117)

Aging

Just as our knowledge of overall health allows the general population to live longer, so our increased knowledge of the voice allows singers to sing longer. Singers of the past who knew how to take care of their voices, including how to avoid youthful "burn-out," spent a large percentage of their adult lives performing. Today's singer who takes care of his or her voice and body may find the voice retains its beauty into the fifth decade of life or longer. Color, endurance, agility and, in some cases, range change as the voice matures and ages. These changes are caused by changes in the laryngeal tissue, the articulation of laryngeal joints, the elasticity of the lungs, the air supply, muscle tone, hormones and hearing.

Age-related changes are not seen in the epithelium of the larynx but are seen in the structure of all three levels of the lamina propria of the larynx. The top and bottom layers become thicker while the middle layer thins. The top layer becomes more edematous, and collagenous, and elastic fibers show increased density there. Both the size and the density of collagenous fibers increase in the deep layer. Fibrosis may be seen after age forty as collagenous fibers no longer run parallel to the vocal cord edge but in random directions. The intermediate layer, however, shows a **decrease** in the density of the elastic fibers because of atrophy. This decrease causes the contour of the intermediate level to deteriorate. All of the above changes are less marked in females than in males (Hirano & Kakita, 1985, pp. 13 & 17; Hirano & Kurita, 1986, pp. 22-23).

The cartilages of the larynx ossify with age, and the articulations of the laryngeal joints stiffen (Sataloff, 1981, p. 253). Changes in articulation of the cricoarytenoid joint are particularly important. This includes irregularities and changes in the surface contours of the cartilage at the point of articulation. These changes may affect the movement and precision of the cricoarytenoid joint which in turn affects the movements of the vocal folds.

These, in turn, may affect the precision of positioning the vocal folds during prephonatory adjustments
and/or the responsiveness of the joint to muscular
forces acting on it during frequency change, while
producing voiceless phenomena, pauses, and other
suprasegmental features. The degree of vocal fold
approximation can be affected by changes in the
CAJ. The size of the posterior glottal chink may increase in association with articular surface and joint
capsule changes. These may produce greater latitude
of movement at the joint and may allow the muscular
processes to assume a more lateral position in the
joint space. Such a result could increase the size of
the glottal chink and/or add instability to the vibration
in the posterior portion of the vocal folds, particularly near the vocal processes. Possible negative vocal effects of such changes may include decreased
amplitude of vibration and increased aperiodicity in
the source spectrum. (Kahane & Hammons, 1985,
p. 25)

In addition, the cricoarytenoid joint, because it is a synovial joint, is
subject to the same diseases as joints in other parts of the body
(Tucker, 1987, p. 219).

With increasing age, atrophy is seen in the muscles of the larynx
(Hirano & Kurita, 1986, p. 23; Sataloff, 1981, p. 253; 1987a, p.
94; and Tucker, 1987, p. 219) and abdomen (Sataloff, 1981, p.
253; 1987a, p. 94). Sataloff considers vocal cord atrophy the most
striking change (1981, p. 253).

Aging also brings about changes in the lungs and diaphragm.
After the individual's peak vital capacity is reached in the twenties, it
begins to decrease. With decreasing vital capacity comes a reduction
in the function of the diaphragm (Perkins & Kent, 1986, p. 46); the
thorax becomes less distensible (Sataloff, 1981, p. 253; 1987a, p.
94); the lungs lose some of their elasticity (Sataloff, 1987a, p. 94);
and residual volume increases (Perkins & Kent, 1986, p. 46).

In the last few years there have been several studies on the effects of aging on the voice. Only one of these used trained professional singers. That the results of the other studies are not entirely
applicable to singers and professional voice users is made apparent
by those found by Brown, Morris and Michael. Their first study
compared 50 white women divided into two groups aged 20-32 and
75-90. Results indicated that, for women, the standard deviation of
the fundamental frequency lowers with aging, resulting in a decrease
in available range, an increase in the variability of the fundamental

frequency while speaking, and a slowing of the rate of speech and/or articulation (1989, p. 117).

However, when these researchers did a similar study using 19 female singers 63-85 years old (mean age 72 years), 10% of whom were still performing singers, the data changed. All of these women had been trained and were professional singers, voice teachers, choir members and/or performers in singing groups. The standard deviation of fundamental frequency of this group was most closely related to the young group of the previous study by the same authors. The singers also exhibited the lowest jitter ratio (vocal fold perturbations, asynchrony) with the young adults of the previous study showing slightly higher values and the oldest nonsingers having the highest mean value. It should be noted that statistical analysis of this data indicated differences in the three groups to be insignificant. However, the aged singers took 13 seconds longer than the young group and five seconds longer than the older non-singers to read the same passage (Brown, Morris & Michel, 1990, p. 137). Brown, Morris and Michel attribute the slower reading to the physical effects of age. However, one must ask if the slower rate indicates vocal deterioration, impaired vision or increased patience for the task.

Ringel and Chadzko-Zajko did studies in which they divided subjects on the basis of physiological condition as well as age. They first studied 48 men in three age groups: 24-35, 45-55, and 65-75, with each group further divided into those in good and poor condition. They found that subjects who were in good physiological condition were able to produce phonation of maximum duration with larger ranges and less jitter and shimmer than those of the same age who were in poorer physical condition. These results were most apparent in the oldest group studied (1987, p. 33). When results of the same study were analyzed using only the subjects' chronological ages, shimmer was the only acoustic measure that showed significant variation between young and elderly subjects. They noted no age-related differences for fundamental frequency, phonatory ranges or jitter (1987, p. 33). When vowel spectral noise levels were evaluated in relation to the speaker's chronological age only, the results were not significantly related. However, there was a high correlation with physiological condition and vowel spectral noise levels (p. 33)

Ringel and Chadzko-Zajko did two similar follow-up studies. In the first study they extracted two groups with high and low fitness which were matched for age. Those in the high fitness group had a mean age of 65.7 years, and those in the low fitness group had a mean age of 65.2 years. Those in the fit group exhibited less vocal jitter and had higher ratios of spectral harmonics to noise

(1987, p. 35). The other follow-up study used 30 male subjects with a mean age of 61 years which were divided into two groups in good or poor condition. Again, the healthy subjects exhibited less vocal shimmer and jitter and had higher harmonics-to-noise ratios. This data suggested to the researchers that better physiological health means increased laryngeal control (1987, p. 35).

Other studies involving non-singers indicate voice changes that may take place with aging. Linville used 75 women divided into three groups: ages 25-35, 45-55 and 70-80 years. He found that the standard deviation of fundamental frequency is higher in older women's voices and that both the first and second formants decreased progressively as women age, with the first formant showing greater change (Linville, 1987, p. 45). Hinjo and Isshiki evaluated 20 men and 20 women aged 69-85 years and found the average fundamental frequency for these men on the vowel [a] was 162 Hz., considerably higher than that of younger men (120-130 Hz.). They found the fundamental frequency of older women varied between 165 Hz. for vowel phonation and 177 Hz. for speech, both lower than the fundamental frequency of young women, 260 Hz. The pitch perturbation of the older women was also outside the normal range of that of the young women, indicating hoarseness (Hinjo & Isshiki, 1980, p. 150). Visual examination showed yellow or gray discoloration of the vocal folds in 39% of the men and 47% of the women, with yellow found more frequently than gray. Edema was present in 74% of the women and 56% of the men. Vocal fold atrophy, judged by bowing of the cords, visibility of the ventricle or prominence of the vocal process, was seen in 67% of the men and 26% of the women. Glottal gap was seen in 58% of the women and 67% of the men. Vocal sulcus was present in 10% of each group (Hinjo & Isshiki, 1980, pp. 149-150).

Dentures. Improvements in preventative dentistry during the past decades have lessened the need for dentures considerably. For those who lose teeth for whatever reason, dentures are still a blessing. Unfortunately, the blessing can be mixed for a singer. Upper dentures that fit across the roof of the mouth lower the vault of the hard palate. The texture of the acrylic denture and the lowered palate affect articulation and mouth resonance. Denture wearers will often open the mouth more for resonance purposes or to make it easier to articulate. Others may try to keep loose-fitting dentures in place by restricting the mouth opening (Shanks, 1983, p. 40).

Morris and Brown compared peak oral air pressures in one group of white women aged 20-35 with two groups over 75, 15 of whom had dentures and 10 of whom had their own teeth. While they found no significant differences between the younger group and the older women with teeth, they did find greater overall peak pressures on voiceless consonants among those with dentures. They believe this is due to the fact that the dentures reduce the size of the oral cavity and thus cause a greater build-up of air pressure in the smaller space (1987, p. 40).

Two striking facts emerge from the studies on aging. The first is that overall physical condition directly impacts the condition of the voice at all ages, but especially after age 60. The second is that trained singers who continue to sing after age 60 are able to avoid many of the effects advancing age could exert on their voices. We can only assume that the women in the study giving rise to this conclusion cared for their voices in the ways indicated throughout this chapter so as to maintain beauty and clarity in the voice.

Chapter 7

When the Voice Is Sick: Therapy and Dysphonias

Therapy

Therapy is intervention to eliminate or lessen pain and to improve existing conditions. *Voice therapy* works to improve the production of voice. It has existed for some time as a subsection of other disciplines. Speech therapists are trained in voice along with other areas such as stuttering or cleft palate speech. Although there are certain aspects such as tongue position and resonance that are common to both speech and voice therapy, there are also many areas that are different. While speech therapy works on the formation of vowels and consonants, voice therapy works on the ways in which the vocal sound is produced and used. Voice teachers interested in working with singers with laryngeal damage have added to the evolution of voice therapy. Because most states now have stringent licensing requirements for voice therapists, they are now largely speech therapists who have specialized in voice.

Voice therapy may be used to correct problems as severe as the inability to communicate because of a total loss of voice (*aphonia*) or as cosmetic as reducing excessive nasality. The therapist determines the cause of the voice problem and works with the client to establish new habits of voice usage regardless of where the client fits into the spectrum of severity.

Laryngologists are medical doctors whose area of specialization is the larynx, its disorders and treatment through medication and/or surgery. An *otolaryngologist* is one whose specialty also includes the organs of hearing. Some laryngologists have a special interest in singers and other professional voice users. They specialize in and understand the problems and capabilities unique to this group of people.

A *voice scientist* is a speech pathologist, engineer, psychologist, anatomist or voice pedagogue who uses scientific methods of research and measurement to study the physiological and aerodynamic capabilities of the larynx, vocal tract and respiratory tract. Voice scientists conduct controlled experiments or random sampling. They contribute valuable information to our understanding of the

126

voice and its components.

Many clients are referred to voice therapists by doctors they have consulted because of pain or because their voice just did not "sound right." The professional voice user may also be referred by a teacher or other professional associate or may be self-referred because of concern about the condition of the vocal cords or the possibility of damaging them while speaking or singing.

Therapy may also be diagnostic to obtain additional information for the client or another voice professional, such as a coach or teacher, who deals with the client. The physician may ask the voice therapist to do an evaluation on a patient, professional voice user or not, as part of the diagnostic process or as the primary treatment. Therapists are also involved with patients having laryngeal surgery to correct physiological changes brought on by abuse or misuse of the voice. Therapy is vital for these patients for retraining in phonation and/or lifestyle to prevent future recurrence of the damage. Therapy may be a necessity for re-acquiring normal vocal function lost because of physiological changes such as paralysis or stroke, for providing augmentation for structural losses such as partial laryngectomies, or to develop a method of compensation for permanent loss of vocal function following total laryngectomy (Harrison & Tucker, 1987, p. 141).

Before beginning voice therapy, the client should be examined by a laryngologist. Some state laws require such a visual examination before therapy can begin. This will determine the condition of the larynx and vocal tract and if the disorder is the result of illness or another physical problem requiring medical or surgical treatment. At the first appointment the voice therapist does an assessment of the new client. During this assessment the therapist attempts to discover the voice problem(s) and specific behavior or situations which cause or perpetuate that behavior. The therapist must learn the capabilities and limitations of the client's voice, contributing factors in the client's constitution and temperament and factors in the client's habits, environment or psychology which contribute to or sustain the voice problem (Damsté, 1987, p. 127). The clinician must then help the client understand the relationship between the client's current voice problems and those factors (Murry, 1982b, p. 497). Together the client and therapist work out a program of remediation which specifies the goals of therapy and the client's and therapist's responsibilities in it. The therapist is to direct the client towards improvement, but the client has to agree to do the work and make the changes required to reach the goal.

Instruments of Assessment

Various instruments are used by laryngologists, voice therapists and voice scientists to reveal the components of laryngeal and respiratory function in speaking and in singing and to quantify those components. Measurements made in the clinical setting are usually made for comparison of pre-treatment conditions with those during or following therapy or to compare groups of patients. Objective measurements of vocal function are usually made in the laboratory. In this way valuable information has been obtained to contribute to our understanding of the various aspects of voice and phonation (Harrison & Tucker, 1987, p. 140).

Following is a list of instruments of assessment and their place in the overall picture of vocal health and science. This author has taken the liberty of combining information contained in three tables in Mr. Boone's 1991 article.

Instrument	Function(s) Measured
Cinefleurograph	Resonance
Electromyograph	Phonatory, Respiratory
Fiber optic endoscope	Phonatory
Fundamental frequency indicator	Phonatory
Glottograph	Phonatory
Laryngeal mirror	Phonatory
Laryngoscope	Phonatory
Magnetometers	Respiratory
Manometers	Respiratory, Resonance
Nasoendoscope	Resonance
Nasometer	Resonance
Phonation function analyzer	Phonatory, Respiratory
Pneumotachometer	Respiratory, Resonance
Pressure transducers	Respiratory, Resonance
Spectrograph	Phonatory, Resonance
Spirometers	Respiratory
Stroboscope	Phonatory
Tonar II	Resonance
Video recorders	Phonatory
Visi-Pitch	Phonatory

(pp. 169-170)

Aerodynamic analysis.   Four parameters are usually measured in an aerodynamic analysis: subglottal pressure, supraglottal pressure, glottal impedance and volume velocity of the airflow at the glottis (Sataloff, 1987b, p. 195; Sataloff, Spiegel, Carroll, Darby & Rulnik, 1987, p. 310). The mean value of each of these measures is determined from the parameters. Measurements of airflow are made with a spirometer, pneumotachograph or hot-wire anometer. Such measures may be helpful during treatment of "vocal nodules, recurrent laryngeal nerve paralysis, spasmodic dysphonia and other conditions" (Sataloff, Spiegel, Carroll, Darby & Rulnik, 1987, p. 310).

Measurements of pitch. One of the easiest factors to measure is the vocal pitch of sustained vowel production. This can be done by three instruments: the stroboscope, the cathode ray oscilloscope and the sonogram. The stroboscope shows the pitch in Hz. on a meter; the cathode ray oscilloscope displays the sound wave from which the fundamental frequency can be calculated; and a sonogram is used for pitch calculation and other methods of pitch indication. Determining the vocal pitch in conversational speech is much more difficult. Instruments used for recording changing vocal pitch include a Glottal frequency analyzer, a Visi-Pitch, a Pitch-analyzer and a Fundamental frequency analyzer (Isshiki, 1989, p. 50). The Visi-Pitch provides a digital display of fundamental frequency, and two oscillographic traces track fundamental frequency and volume of the two together. Statistics available include average fundamental frequency, standard deviation from the average fundamental frequency, average volume in decibels, standard deviation from the average volume, pitch perturbation, maximum and minimum fundamental frequencies used and the total fundamental frequency range, percentage of voiced and unvoiced sounds and percentage of pause time. The two channels of display offer an opportunity for presenting a client with one channel as a pre-recorded model and the second for recording his imitations (Shelton, pp. 286-287). The Pitch-analyzer is microprocessor controlled and can obtain information about both fundamental frequency and intensity (Johnson, 1985, p. 148).

Muscle function. Electromyography (EMG) is used to indicate muscular activity. Electrodes inserted into the muscle pick up small electric signals, called action potentials, which are emitted by the muscle during muscular activity (Hirano, 1988, pp. 57-58). Electroglottography passes a weak high-frequency current between two electrodes placed on the skin of the neck above the juncture of the two wings of the thyroid cartilage. The opening and closing of the vocal cords varies this electrical current so the fundamental period of vibration of the glottis can be determined (Sataloff, Spiegel, Carroll, Darby & Rulnik, 1987, p. 308).

Examining the vocal cords. The stroboscopic camera is inserted into the pharynx through the mouth. Use of a topical anesthetic allows it to remain in the back of the throat from where it photographs the larynx. The light of the stroboscope allows an evaluation of the mucosal cover layer of the upper edge of the vocal cord, permitting detection of structural abnormalities, small masses, scars, and any other structural abnormalities that may cause asymmetry (Sataloff, 1987b, pp. 193-194; Sataloff, Spiegel, Carroll, Darby & Rulnik, 1987, p. 307). Characteristics which can be assessed include: "frequency, symmetry of bilateral movements, periodicity, glottal closure, amplitude, mucosal wave, the pressure of nonvibrating portions," and any other abnormalities which would be too minute for detection by normal light (Sataloff, Spiegel, Carroll, Darby & Rulnik, 1987, p. 308). The primary advantage of the stroboscope is the quality of the picture obtained. It is far clearer than other methods of laryngeal examination and provides an excellent picture of the mucosal wave. The disadvantage is that, with the size and placement of the stroboscope, the patient can only produce vowel sounds. Coupling the stroboscope with the video camera allows more careful study of the condition of the larynx after the examination is over. Video documentation can also be obtained with a flexible fiberscope or a rigid telescope (Isshiki, 1989, p. 52).

Diagnosis of laryngeal disease can also be done via laryngography, laryngotomography, xerolaryngography, computed tomography (CT) and magnetic resonance imaging (MRI). Xerolaryngography is particularly useful for diagnosing laryngeal trauma because of its ability to show the contour of the inner cavity of the larynx (Isshiki, 1989, p. 54). The rigid fiberoptic laryngoscope is inserted through the nose down to the level of the cords. In addition to evaluating the cords, it can be used to observe velopharyngeal closure and other aspects of the nasopharynx. Because it is extremely small the patient can produce regular speech while it is in place. It cannot be used to evaluate the mucosal wave.

In addition to the more sophisticated instruments, the stopwatch and a keyboard or pitch pipe are also of great value to the therapist. The keyboard and pitch pipe can be used to learn the pitch of the client's voice or to give the client a pitch to match when trying to change the speaking pitch. The stopwatch is a quick and easy way to measure phonation time. After taking a deep breath the client sustains the desired vowel sound for as long as possible on a comfortable pitch. The test should be repeated three times, and the greatest value used (Sataloff, Spiegel, Carroll, Darby & Rulnik, 1987, p. 308).

Although most assessment is done with the client in the room, objective analysis can also be done using recorded voice samples. Videotape from a stereo video recorder can be used to do recordings for computer analysis. Sound spectography documents the abnormalities and changes in vocal nodules or vocal-fold paralysis that are apparent to the ear of the listener but is not particularly good at validating more subtle alterations in voice quality (Sataloff, Spiegel, Carroll, Darby & Rulnik, 1987, p. 311).

Therapy Approaches
Cooper lists the five major approaches used by voice therapists in treating disturbed phonation or dysphonia as "surgery, palliative measures, psychological approaches, traditional vocal rehabilitation and modern vocal rehabilitation which incorporates vocal psychotherapy." Choice of the type of treatment used depends upon the origin and severity of the dysphonia and the philosophy and training of the treating physician and therapist (1973, p. 55). Surgical procedures include removal of nodules, polyps, contact ulcers, and other lesions on the vocal cords and stripping of the mucosa which covers the vocal cords. Palliatives include voice rest and various topical or systemic medications. The psychological approach presupposes that voice disorders lacking a physiological basis are symptoms of certain personality traits and/or problems and that no progress can be made on the improvement of those dysphonias until the underlying cause(s) is discovered and treated (for more information, see Cooper, 1973, pp. 63-66).

Voice Rest
Voice rest means total avoidance of any activity which causes the vocal cords to close or vibrate. Thus, clients for whom voice rest is a prescription must keep absolute silence and communicate only with a writing pad. In addition, they must also avoid "whispering, coughing, throat clearing, laughing, lifting or pushing heavy objects, and forceful effort during bowel movements" (Prater & Swift, 1984, p. 103).

There are two forms of whispering: the stage whisper and that which is used to tell secrets. The first requires a very firm vocal cord adduction with a small glottal opening through which a column of air is forced. The acoustic energy it carries makes it useful, but it requires the adduction which must be avoided to maintain voice rest (Landes, 1977, p. 135). The secretive whisper forces air through partially adducted vocal folds. As the air is forced through the narrow passage, it becomes turbulent and irregular. The noise or hiss of the whisper is the random motion of the air molecules above the larynx (Putnam & Shelton, 1985, p. 95). Although it avoids vocal cord adduction, secretive whispering is virtually useless because of this noise and its lack of carrying power.

Among laryngologist- and therapist-writers there is a prevailing opinion that voice rest should be required only when absolutely necessary. Cooper (1973, pp. 55-60) contains the most thorough discussion on the subject of voice rest. He finds it useful in only about one percent of his clients and relevant following surgery for "a week or two." He cautions that few actually follow the prescription for silence.

McFarlane and Sataloff recommend its use following serious vocal cord injury such as hemorrhage or injury to the mucosa to allow healing of the tissues (McFarlane, 1988, p. 426; Sataloff, 1985, p. 315, 1987c, p. 286). Boone, Kleinsasser, Myerson, Prater and Swift, and Reed suggest voice rest after surgery to allow tissues to heal (Boone, 1983, p. 178; Kleinsasser, 1979, p. 33; Myerson, 1964, p. 276; Prater & Swift, 1984, p. 101; Reed, 1983, p. 91). Boone, McFarlane, and Sataloff find it helps to clear acute laryngitis (Boone, 1983, p. 178; McFarlane, 1988, p. 426; Sataloff, 1985, p. 315). Moore and Teter employ it with their clients as a preliminary to therapy (Moore, 1971b, pp. 61-62; Teter, 1977, p. 405). McFarlane and Prater and Swift find it effective as an initial treatment for eliminating irritation and thus allowing lesions such as nodules and chronic laryngitis to regress (McFarlane, 1988, p. 426; Prater & Swift, 1984, p. 101). And Damsté considers it an effective way to rid the client of old habits of phonation before therapy (Damsté, 1987, p. 133). McFarlane also uses it when the dysphonia is a result of yelling or some other type of acute abuse and will likely go away with rest (1988, p. 426).

The major problems with voice rest as noted by those favoring it are that it may cause weakness of the vocal muscles if it is maintained for long, and it does not remove the cause of the dysphonia. Therefore, most prefer to limit voice rest to three to seven days (Boone, 1983, p. 178).

Sataloff recommends what he calls "relative voice rest." This requires speaking "softly, as infrequently as possible, at a slightly higher pitch than usual," and using abdominal support (1987c, p. 286). Harrison and Tucker also use what they call "Modified Voice Use" immediately following laryngeal surgery and as one of the steps in resolving disorders resulting from vocal abuse. The client is taught to modify the amount, intensity and stress of voice usage. Chronic voice abusers are taught to use similar modifications permanently (1987, p. 142).

Traditional Voice Therapy
Direct approaches. Traditional voice therapy using what Cooper calls the "direct approach," concentrates on the areas of "respiration, phonation or resonance" (Boone, 1983, p. 72) or "pitch, tone focus, quality, volume, breath support and rate" (Cooper, 1973, p. 66). Some therapists prefer to work on problem areas separately; others see breath control, relaxation, and vocal exercises as too interdependent to be approached separately (Damsté & Lerman, 1975, p. 64). The traditional approach is closely related to the mechanistic school of teaching singers in which the teacher works on the various aspects of singing such as breath control, reg-

istration or placement and explains to the student as precisely as possible what to do and how to do it.

Indirect methods. Rather than working on altering the client's pitch, method of attack and so forth, the therapist using the indirect approach gives the client exercises which will affect the changes for him or her (Cooper, 1973, pp. 68-70). One example of this type of approach is Froeschel's chewing therapy which is discussed in Chapter 3. Included in this category would also be what McFarlane and Lavorato call *redirection*. Rather than focusing on the component of voice being treated, such as breathing, the therapist focuses on physical characteristics of that aspect that can be controlled. Thus, a client who has been unsuccessful in working on breath support may do very well if told to push the abdomen forward toward the therapist's hand and then phonate. They find this technique particularly useful with clients who have failed with other more direct methods (1983, p. 33).

Likewise, imagery is an important component of voice therapy used to get a client to conceptualize something that will enhance the work he or she is doing. One example would be to ask a client to imagine an open stove pipe with air moving through the pipe and then to think of the throat as that pipe (McFarlane & Lavorato, 1983, pp. 33-34).

"Modern" Voice Therapy: Vocal Image

Some therapists rely less on exercises and more on changing the client's concepts of voice, particularly about his or her own voice. In this approach the focus is on the concept of a new voice and its image. Murry states that "therapy can be effective even when no specific exercises are used to control vocal parameters that appear to be abnormal." (1982b, p. 489). Haskell defines vocal self-perception as "the physical and psychological experience of one's own voice." It reflects the individual's sense of identification through the voice and acts as a monitor of the physical aspects of voice production (1987, p. 172). Haskell also speaks of the "vocal set" which he defines as "an habituated pattern of vocal communication, whether in speech or in singing" (p. 173). This vocal set may or may not be appropriate for the person or the situation, and it may or may not present what the individual intends.

After establishing the proper pitch and tone focus, Cooper spends a great deal of time on what he calls *vocal psychotherapy*, especially *vocal image*. In this he offers the client not only practice in proper vocal usage but also a new vocal identity, thus eliminating vocal misuse and abuse (1973, p. 11). Cooper's vocal psychotherapy also involves associate therapy, illustrative therapy and bibliotherapy (p. 71).

Some therapists have the client discover a new vocal model and then practice it until it becomes habitual. This model can be found either through exploring the client's own repertoire of phonation or by having the client imitate a model given by the therapist. Once the proper voice production is found, the therapist must reinforce it and offer helpful guidance so the client can recognize and eliminate faulty production (McFarlane & Lavorato, 1983, pp. 34-36; Murry, 1982b, p. 490; Van Riper & Irwin, 1958, p. 285). McFarlane and Lavorato use this technique because they find that people who speak in an abusive manner are often unaware of what a healthy, well-used voice sounds like (1983, p. 35) Murry points out specific qualities in the model voice which he encourages the client to hear in other speakers and to attempt to match with his or her own voice. This may be something as simple as reducing the loudness or changing the inflection. He sometimes incorporates specific exercises as a supplement. Murry also suggests that it may be worthwhile to provide recordings of voices which exhibit the types of behaviors the client is trying to correct as negative examples (1982b, p. 490).

McFarlane and Lavorato use a tape recorder to record the client's own production of "good model voice" as the client responds to "imagery, digital manipulation [of the larynx], or our vocal model" (pp. 35-36). They may also use the voice of a peer, a famous personality or someone who the client knows as the model voice. McFarlane and Lavorato also use a technique which they call *role identification*. As the name implies, role identification encourages the client to identify with a particular personality or role. A young girl who has been speaking in a very harsh, low-pitched voice might be told to imitate a pretty young lady who has been surprised with a nice gift. The parent accompanying the child would be involved in this identification and in role-playing sessions with the girl. The "role voice" might even be given a name such as Susie or Madeleine (1983, pp. 34-35).

The New Voice
Voice quality is affected by a variety of elements: the condition of the vocal folds and their freedom of movement, subglottal air pressure, periodicity of the glottal cycle and adjustments in the vocal tract above the vocal folds (Shelton, 1985, p. 271). Therapists work to achieve optimum function of all of these elements with minimum effort within the client's physiological capabilities.

McFarlane and Lavorato suggest working to ensure the new voice:

(1) Is hygienic -- produced without pathologic changes in the larynx; (2) has carrying power -- is

useful in normal speaking situations and demands; (3) is esthetic -- sounds good and is not distracting; (4) fits the patient -- with respect to age, sex, body size; and (5) is flexible -- can express the range of emotions and moods of the patient. (1983, pp. 36-37)

In their search for the client's best voice, therapists may try many different facilitating techniques. "That is, we try a particular therapy approach and see if it facilitates the production of a better voice. If it does, then we utilize it as therapy practice material. If it does not, we quickly abandon it" (Boone, 1983, p. 3). Good therapy avails itself of a variety of methods which must be suited to the client, the goals for which the therapist and client are working and many other factors.

Dysphonias

Types of Dysphonias

Therapists refer to disturbances in the sound of the voice as *dysphonias*. Most writers consider two general categories of dysphonias: organic and functional. *Organic dysphonias* are "those caused by anatomic or physiologic disease of the larynx itself, or by systemic illness indirectly influencing the larynx" (Harrison & Tucker, 1987, p. 139). They include both congenital and acquired structural defects such as cleft palate, laryngeal web and bowed vocal cords; neurological involvement such as vocal fold paralysis, Parkinson's disease, multiple sclerosis, and amytrophic lateral sclerosis; and partial and complete excision of the larynx (Cooper, 1973, pp. 5-6).

Functional dysphonias develop as a result of abuse and/or misuse within a normal laryngeal structure (Cooper, 1973, p. 5). They are sometimes called *psychogenic voice disorders* because they also include disorders which result from psychoneuroses and personality disorders (Harrison & Tucker, 1987, p. 139). The important distinction here is that the **structure** of the larynx and other parts of the vocal tract are normal and intact. Functional dysphonias include excessive nasality (without absent or paralyzed structures), exclusive use of falsetto by the adult male, and phonation with the ventricular bands. Harrison and Tucker include in this category voice disorders in which the severity of the dysphonia is far greater than the laryngeal damage would indicate. They suggest the etiology of these disorders as including "stress, emotional conflict, personality disorder or psychiatric illness" (1987, p. 148), and include voice disorders ranging from mild dysphonia to complete aphonia.

Cooper adds a third category of dysphonia which he calls *"functional misphonia,"* which he defines as "functional 'wrong voice.'" He uses this to describe voices that are "tired, hoarse, or weak . . . without organic or neurological involvement" (1973, p. 5). Harrison and Tucker define a *disordered voice* as "one that deviates from the expected in terms of quality, pitch, loudness, and/or flexibility. It may call attention to itself and may alter occupational and social performance" (1987, p. 139). Other general terms which may be used to describe functional misphonia include "chronic, nonspecific laryngitis (Baker), hyperkinetic and hypokinetic dysphonia (Arnold), phonasthenia (Flotow), hyperfunctional and hypofunctional dysphonia (Froeschels), executive dysphonia (Gardner) and aggravated voice (Tarnaud)" (Cooper, 1973, p. 5).

Because they represent structural changes, bowed vocal folds and benign growths on the vocal folds, such as nodules, polyps, contact ulcers, and cysts, are considered by some authors as organic dysphonias. (Cooper includes them in his discussion of organic dysphonias cited above.) Others consider them to be functional dysphonias. Here the problem is one of cause and effect. All authors agree that vocal cord lesions and bowed cords usually develop because of misuse and/or abuse, including faulty phonation; whereas the faulty phonation of organic dysphonias occurs as a response to structural defects or weaknesses. This is not to say that changes such as bowed cords and additive lesions do not contribute to the dysphonia.

Abuse and Misuse

Many therapists make a distinction between *vocal misuse* and *vocal abuse.*

> Vocal misuse is defined as the use of an incorrect pitch, tone focus, quality, volume, breath support and rate, either discretely or in combinations. By vocal abuse is meant the mistreatment of the vocal folds, as well as the laryngeal and pharyngeal musculature by shouting, screaming, or talking in competition with noise, i.e. talking above, under, around, or through the noise (Cooper, 1973, p. 8).

Shelton lists four categories of speaker abuse and misuse. The first two categories, "poor vocal skills" and "excessive shouting" parallel Cooper's definition. Shelton's third category includes coughs and throat clearing caused by "chronic respiratory conditions or air pollutant irritants" (1985, p. 275). It is important to remember that the cough which clears the airways of excess mucous or foreign

matter is actually a sudden expulsion of air against tightly closed
cords. The mucous or foreign matter is blown off the cords by the
expelled air (Brodnitz, 1961, p. 42). Shelton's fourth category is
nonorganic voice disorders (p. 275). Like Cooper, Shelton cautions
that speaking over noise for long periods of time leads to vocal abuse
(p. 276).

Hirano, Kurita, Matsuo and Nagata (1980, 1981) differentiate
between acute and chronic **reactions** to abuse and misuse of the
voice. Chronic reactions include nodules, polyps and contact ulcers.
Acute reactions occur following temporary abuse such as yelling at a
sports event (cited in Perkins, 1985, p. 91) Perkins describes acute
reactions.

> The superficial layer of the lamina propria be-
> comes edematous from leakage of serum and dilation
> of blood vessels. With increased stress, blood ves-
> sels rupture, resulting in sub-epithelial bleeding.
> Both of these acute conditions subside within a week
> or two of vocal rest and easy quiet phonation.
> (Perkins, 1985, p. 91)

In their studies of vocal cord stress and its relationship to vocal
cord pathology, Hirano and his colleagues (1980, 1981) confirmed
that subepithelial bleeding, nodules, contact granulomas, and polyps
are all due primarily to vocal abuse (cited in Perkins, 1985, pp. 89-
90). Johnson indicates that there may be additional factors of susceptibility which combine with the abuse and misuse to cause the
vocal symptoms and laryngeal pathologies.

> Susceptibility factors include histologic differences in
> basic cellular make up of the individual laryngeal
> mechanisms, the presence of an invading bacterial or
> viral organism, the physical conditioning history of
> the individual's laryngeal mechanism, and other such
> factors that could increase an individual's suscepti-
> bility to the development of laryngeal problems.
> (Johnson, 1985, p. 131)

Finally, Mossallam, Kotby, Ghaly, Nassar and Barakah conducted a seven-year study involving 106 patients with voice disorders with lesions requiring surgery. Patients studied included 60
males and 46 females ages 14-62. There were 44 cases with
polyps, 10 with nodules, seven with granulomas, 19 with cysts,
and 15 with polypoid degeneration. Analysis of patients' histories
showed two common factors. The most common factor was

138   The New Voice Pedagogy

abuse/misuse of the voice which occurred in 88% of the population studied. Smoking was the second most common factor which occurred in 34% of the population. The least common factor was infection, and allergy was not evident in patient histories (Mossallam, Kotby, Ghaly, Nassar & Barakah, 1986, p. 77)

Hyperfunction and Hypofunction

Emil Froeschels first used the terms *spastic* and *paretic hoarseness* to describe symptoms he saw in his therapy clients. He later changed them to *hyperfunction* and *hypofunction*. These expressions indicate too much (hyper) or too little (hypo) participation of muscles which produce the voice. Froeschels listed seven kinds of localized hyperfunctions including I) excessive breath pushed from below the cords, II) coup de glotte or hard attack, III) too violent contraction of pharyngeal constrictors leaving the observer with an "impression of slight self-strangulation," IV) retraction of the back and root of the tongue, V) cramp-like elevation of the soft palate, VI) stiffening the blade of the tongue and VII) a stiffening of the lips (Froeschels, 1940, pp. 139-140). Froeschels revised his list in 1943 omitting number I.

Hyperfunction is rarely localized (Brodnitz, 1961). The singer or speaker whose tongue is a knot in the back of the throat is putting extra strain on the cords and probably has a lowered palate as well. The muscles of the face and neck are connected, so tension in one is easily communicated to the other.

The degree of adduction required for phonation can be varied. Gauffin and Sundberg consider this a separate dimension of voice production and propose three possible types of phonation. Cords that are so loosely adducted that the glottis fails to close exhibit *breathy phonation*. The opposite extreme, *pressed phonation*, is characterized by firmly adducted cords, "high glottal resistance and a spectrum with dominant overtones" (Sundberg, 1985, p. 95). The ideal is the midground or *flow phonation*. Although the vocal cords are drawn together to close the glottis, glottal resistance is moderate and the tonal spectrum exhibits both a strong fundamental and strong overtones (p. 95).

In hyperfunctional or pressed phonation the cords are drawn together very tightly, and the closed portion of the vibratory cycle is increased. Thus it takes more pressure to blow the folds apart. The glottal attack, which is often part of this type of phonation, may cause the folds to meet with enough force to damage the vocal cords. If this type of phonation is continued, vocal fold tissue may thicken, and nodules may develop (Shelton, 1985, p. 274).

One cause of pressed phonation is continuing to speak or sing after most of the available air has been used up. Singers and speakers who use residual air must press the cords firmly together to compensate for the decreased airflow (Friedmann & Ferlito, 1988, p. 82).

Johnson considers any behavior(s) which creates "excessive muscular tension in the vocal tract" to be vocal hyperfunction (1985, p. 130). He cites three levels of vocal cord hyperfunction: respiratory, resonatory and phonatory (p. 4). Hyperfunction of a muscle eventually leads to hypofunction when that muscle fatigues to the point it can no longer contract. As one muscle becomes hyperfunctional, more effort must be exerted by other muscles which can subject them to fatigue, thus creating a "vicious spiral" (p. 13).

Hyperfunctional dysphonia. Yang and Mu use the term "*hyperfunctional dysphonia*" to describe excessive use of all laryngeal muscles. In addition to excessive tension in the vocal cords there is usually excess activity in the respiratory muscles, and the strain can frequently be seen in extended veins in the neck. Laryngoscopy may reveal reddened and thickened cords with hypertrophic ventricular bands. Most noticeable is an open posterior glottic chink between the arytenoid cartilages (1989, p. 338).

Hypokinetic/hyperkinetic dysphonia. Damsté uses the term "*hypokinetic dysphonia*" to describe a breathy voice caused by a too-open glottis. The opposite, "*hyperkinetic dysphonia*," produces a harsh, raspy voice from a too-firm glottal closure. If he is unable to distinguish the cause of the voice disorder as high thoracic breathing or from the location of the hyperkinesis (i.e., the glottis, ventrical or pharynx) he terms it "*dyskinesis*" (1987, p. 132).

Symptoms
Sensory. Most people seek help for their voices because of fatigue or pain associated with phonation and/or changes in the sound or range of the voice. Tucker lists "four *major symptoms* of infectious and inflammatory disorders of the larynx" as dysphonia, dyspnea, dysphagia, and pain (1987, p. 221). The first three are all difficulties or disturbances -- in phonating or producing voice, in breathing and in swallowing. Pain can vary from mild and occurring only after extended voice usage to constant and becoming extreme with swallowing.

Shumrick and Shumrick list hoarseness, the sensation of a lump or foreign body in the throat and sharp, stabbing pain as symptoms of voice abuse or gastric reflux (1988, p. 269). Cooper's description of the sensory symptoms of non-organic voice disorders written some eleven years earlier is somewhat more detailed.

> The sensory symptoms of functional dysphonias include non-productive throat clearing, coughing, pro-

gressive vocal fatigue following brief or extended
vocal use, acute or chronic irritation or pain in or
about larynx or pharynx; sternum pressure and/or
pain; neck muscle cording; swelling of veins and/or
arteries in the neck; throat stiffness; rapid vocal fatigue; feeling of a foreign substance or lump in the
throat; ear irritation or tickling; repeated sore
throats; a tickling, tearing soreness or burning sensation in the throat; scratchy or dry throat; tenderness of anterior and/or posterior strap muscles;
rumble in the chest; stinging sensation in soft palate;
a feeling that talking is an effort; a choking feeling;
tension and/or tightness in the throat; earache; back
neck tension; headache; mucous formation; tracheal
pressure; arytenoid tenderness; anterior or posterior
cervical pain; pain at the base of the tongue; and
chronic toothache without apparent cause. (Cooper,
1977, p. 7)

If it is not too severe the speaker or singer may notice the discomfort at first, ignore it and quickly become accustomed to it. This
is especially common in young singers who are still searching for
the sensations associated with correct singing.

Auditory. The most common auditory symptoms of voice disorders are hoarseness (Cooper, 1973; Schroeder, Krupp, Tierney
& McPhee, 1990, p. 144), changes in the quality of the voice,
change in pitches available for speaking, repeated loss of voice,
voice breaks or skips, and a voice which becomes lower and less
clear or harder to produce as the day progresses (Cooper, 1973).
For singers one could add to the symptoms listed above "holes" in
the voice, loss of some of the top notes (especially at soft volumes)
(Punt, 1967, p. 67), and an inability to sustain a phrase in one
breath. Additional damage can occur when the speaker or singer attempts to compensate for these changes to achieve normal voice.

There are two kinds of imbalance possible between the vocal
folds -- tension and mass. Isshiki states that such imbalances are

not great unless there is a glottal gap [emph-
asis added]. The voice thus produced would most
probably sound quite normal. If one vocal cord becomes more tense than the other, the tenser cord
opens and closes at a greater speed and waits for the
less tense vocal cord to come into contact; both
cords then start opening again at the same moment.
In short, tension imbalance between the two cords

causes only a phase lag, but neither hoarseness nor dyplophonia results. Two vocal cords imbalanced in tension vibrate at the same frequency. Almost the same applies to imbalance in mass; phase lag occurs with the lighter cord preceding the heavier, but there is no dysphonia. . . . (Isshiki, 1989, p. 29)

Perkins cites an "acoustic 'signature'" of individual vocal fold pathologies which affect "fundamental frequency, intensity or quality, singly or in combination" (1985, p. 82). These are the result of the changes in tension and mass described by Isshiki above. Changes in both vocal folds affect fundamental frequency; changes in one cord only cause asymmetric vibration of the cords. This in turn produces "breathiness, reduced intensity, pitch perturbation (*jitter*), and amplitude perturbation (*shimmer*)" (1985, p. 82).

Put more simply, "The larynx is on one hand, extremely sensitive so that the simplest manipulation will affect the quality of the sound it produces. On the other hand, it can compensate for the presence of large polyps and nodules" (Bryce, 1974, pp. 15-16). Such compensation, of course, may require extra effort on the part of the singer or speaker and may further damage the voice.

Visual.

The tissues of the larynx can respond to trauma in only a limited number of ways, regardless of whether the cause is infectious, allergic, toxic, thermal or physical. Edema, inflammation and exudation are the three main responses to acute injury, with hypertrophy or metaplasia of the mucous membrane and fibrosis of the deeper tissues of the larynx added in more chronic situations. Therefore, laryngeal symptoms of any inflammatory disorder will be essentially the same, differing only in degree, rapidity of onset, and the presence or absence of systemic findings peculiar to the specific cause. (Tucker, 1987, p. 221)

Laryngeal examination of patients with voice disorders usually reveals reddened cords that are swollen or thickened with increased mucous. Edema of the vocal cords, discussed later in this chapter, is caused by fluid retention under the epithelium. Kambic, Radsel, Zargi, and Acko indicate that, regardless of whether the outcome is nodules, polyps, or another pathology, the initial response of the vocal cords to trauma is edema.

> . . . Edema, containing variable amounts of muco-
> polysaccharides of the submucosal tissue is the fun-
> damental change found in all these processes. If the
> irritation is diffuse, Reineke's edema develops; if the
> irritation is localized, polyps develop; continued ex-
> udation of protein-rich exudate leads to fibrosis and
> nodule formation. (Kambic, Radsel, Zargi & Acko,
> 1981, p. 609)

The cords may also be bowed, and/or individual lesions such as
nodules or polyps may be present. Excessive mucous may be a response to irritation and may add increased weight on the cords,
sometimes impeding the smooth vibratory function. Swollen or
thickened vocal folds will produce lower pitches than healthy cords
(Punt, 1967, p. 74; Prater & Swift, 1984, p. 7). Any change in
mass or surface will also affect the way the cords meet or approximate. In his book *The Voice and Voice Therapy*, Boone includes an
excellent table which indicates the effects of various laryngeal disorders upon the mass and approximation of the vocal folds (1983, p.
46).

On the other hand, the larynx may appear visually normal. The
voice may sound or feel different before changes are evident during
visual examination of the larynx (Murry, 1982a, p. 477). This
would certainly be true for singers who are extremely sensitive to
any changes in their voices.

Hoarseness

Hoarseness is an auditory symptom that the normal vibratory
pattern of the larynx is being disturbed. Hoarseness usually describes a voice characterized by a lower than usual pitch, excessive
leakage of air and squeaks and breaks caused by alterations in vibratory characteristics of the folds. It is the coarse, scratchy sound of
the voice (Sataloff, 1981, p. 253) caused by upper respiratory
problems, allergies, vocal cord lesions, trauma or laryngitis.

Isshiki lists "3 key features of hoarseness: (a) *less periodicity* of
the vocal cord vibration; (b) *high frequency noise* components; and
(c) *reduced harmonic* components." He states that these are primarily the result of an imperfectly closed glottis (1989, p. 24).

Laryngeal fatigue. Sataloff defines fatigue of the voice as "the
inability to continue to sing for extended periods without change in
vocal quality" (1981, p. 253). Symptoms of fatigue include hoarseness, loss of range, change of timbre, sudden register shifts or other
loss of control (1981, p. 253).

Some speakers' voices are clear in the morning but become
hoarse as the day progresses. They may suffer from laryngeal fa-

tigue due to the increased effort required to compensate for poor approximation of the cords caused by small lesions (Bryce, 1974, p. 24).

Epithelial changes of hoarseness. Hoarseness is the result of changes in the mass or the approximation of the vocal cords. Changes in the mass may be due to inflammation or edema. Epithelial thickening usually means the speaker or singer must use more air to initiate sound. It also limits the range of intensity and tone available (Damsté, 1987, p. 134). Changes in the vibratory pattern are usually due to a mass such as a nodule or polyp (Bryce, 1974, p. 15), or they may reflect changes in the mobility of the mucosa which covers the cords. This mucosa loses its mobility "when it is *scarred, stretched* or *swollen*" (Isshiki, 1989, p. 7).

Yanagihara (1967) studied 30 cases of hoarseness, 10 slight, 10 moderate and 10 severe. His findings indicate the listener's perception of hoarseness increases or decreases as the range and energy of the noise components increase and decrease. The range and energy of the noise components are more evident in the vowels [a], [ɛ] and [i] than in the vowels [u] and [ɔ]" (pp. 532-533).

Laryngitis

Laryngitis is an inflammation of the larynx which usually involves the mucosa covering the cords (Boone, 1983, p. 47). Noninfectious laryngitis is the result of phonatory trauma such as yelling at a spectator sport (Boone, 1983, p. 47), excessive pre-performance rehearsing (Sataloff, 1981, p. 263; 1987, p. 285) or from external irritants such as allergy, excessive smoking or alcohol (Boone, 1983, p. 47; Sataloff, 1981, p. 263; 1987c, pp. 285-286). The inner edges of the folds become swollen and thickened. Sataloff feels that the presence of mucous stranding between the anterior and middle thirds of the cords may indicate voice abuse (1981, p. 263).

Friedmann and Ferlito indicate that the term laryngitis is often used by physicians to describe a wide variety of non-inflammatory conditions. They state that it has become a clinical convention to describe as laryngitis any laryngeal disturbance with a history of hoarseness that is not the result of paralysis of the vocal cords or cancer. (Friedmann & Ferlito, 1988, p. 29).

Acute infectious laryngitis is usually caused by influenza or the common cold (Michel & Weinstein, 1988, p. 238; Tucker, 1987, p. 228; Way, 1988, p. 810). Other factors include smoking, voice abuse, and lack of adequate humidification (Tucker, 1987, p. 228). Acute infectious laryngitis should be medically treated with systemic and topical measures. Hoarseness, cough and painful swallowing are often very noticeable. In some cases there will be minimal edema or redness of the true vocal cords (Way, 1988, p. 810). In other cases the cords may appear reddened, and infection and edema will be present in the entire larynx and the pharynx (Bryce, 1974, p. 24). Treatment of the underlying cold or flu accompanied by humidification, steam inhalation, voice rest and substantial fluid intake is usually effective (Tucker, 1987, p. 228).

Tucker indicates that the bacterial form of infectious laryngitis is usually found in patients with purulent rhinosinusitis. Diagnosis and treatment center around identification and management of the underlying infection (Tucker, 1987, p. 228).

If the singer or speaker attempts to use the larynx while he or she has laryngitis and to compensate for the impaired function, the irritated and inflamed mucosa does not get a chance to heal. Constant irritation can lead to other problems including the formation of polyps and nodules (Bryce, 1974, p. 25).

Chronic laryngitis. Any chronic inflammatory reaction of the laryngeal mucosa can be considered chronic laryngitis. The main auditory symptom is long-term hoarseness (Van den Broeck, 1987, p. 106). Causes include chronic allergies, inhalation of irritants such as cigarette smoke and voice abuse (Way, 1988, p. 811). Laryngeal examination reveals a variety of conditions which may change with the passage of time. The space beneath the epithelium of the cords (Reineke's space) may become fluid-filled; sometimes polyps develop (Way, 1988, p. 811) or granulomas are present. In other cases the inflammatory condition will be non-specific and may be characterized by a variety of conditions such as acanthosis, leukoplakia, keratosis or hyperkeratosis, all of which appear microscopically as a hyperplasia (overgrowth of cells) of the squamous epithelium and which differ only at the cellular level (Van den Broeck, 1987, p. 106).

Still other cases of chronic laryngitis may show no visible changes in the larynx at all. Proctor believes this type of chronic laryngitis is due to "repeated or chronic strain of the tissues of the vocal folds." Improper practices which cause such strain include use of excessively high subglottal pressures, poor resonance and poor use of the breath (1980b, p. 147).

Damsté indicates that removal of causative factors may allow reversal of all such chronic laryngeal conditions. He found that patients who stopped smoking and drinking and learned new voice habits experienced complete reversal of even severe forms of hyperplasia. He adds that "such a regimen is rarely practiced and most patients prefer surgery combined with voice correction" (Damsté, 1987, p. 134).

Aronson and Sataloff describe a condition called *laryngitis sicca.* It is characterized by "dysphonia, vocal fatigue and cough"

(Aronson, 1985, p. 61) and is caused by dry atmosphere, mouth breathing, antihistamine therapy and dehydration (Sataloff, 1981, p. 263; 1987c, p. 285). Aronson believes that cigarette smoking, air pollution, alcohol and vocal abuse contribute to the condition (1985, p. 61). Lack of moisture in the mucosa of the vocal tract results in irritation, coughing and mild inflammation (Sataloff, 1981, p. 263; 1987, p. 286). If this continues over a long period "persistent epithelial tissue changes occur in which the mucosal glands atrophy" (Aronson, 1985, p. 61).

Edema, Reineke's Edema

An edema is a swelling which is caused by retention of fluid. Because the mucosa is loosely attached to the vocal cord it can vibrate independently. Edema of the vocal cords occurs in the area between that mucosa and the muscular portion of vocal folds known as Reineke's space (see Chapter 1). The anterior commissure and the vocal processes of the arytenoids provide the front and back limits for the edema (Kleinsasser, 1986, p. 54; Michaels, 1984, p. 102; Shumrick & Shumrick, 1988, p. 272). The transition from squamous to respiratory epithelium provides the superior (upper) and inferior (lower) boundaries for the edema (Michaels, p. 102; Shumrick & Shumrick, p. 272). Medially (towards the center) it is bound by the mucosa itself and laterally by the vocal ligament (Shumrick & Shumrick, p. 272).

The vocal folds in general and Reineke's space in particular have poor lymphatic drainage. This allows blood products to accumulate there and edema, vocal cord polyps and vocal cord nodules to develop there (Michaels, 1944, p. 102; Mossallam, Kotby, Ghaly, Nassar & Barakah, 1986, p. 78; Shumrick & Shumrick, 1988, p. 272). These three conditions are thought to be various stages "in the process of exudation, organization and fibrosis occurring within Reineke's space" (Shumrick & Shumrick, 1988, p. 272). Drainage may become even worse as fluid accumulates in this area (Mossallam, Kotby, Ghaly, Nassar & Barakah, 1986, p. 78).

Vocal cord edema is normally bilateral (affecting both cords) and symmetrical. Although rare, it will occur in one fold to compensate for a glottis which will not close completely (Damsté & Lerman, 1975, p. 59).

The most noticeable symptoms of Reineke's edema are the lowered pitch, which is due to the added weight on the cords, and a "rough" voice, caused by changes in the contour of the cords. The prolonged mechanical abuse that leads to a fluid-filled Reineke's space may cause the epithelium to loosen and alter its vibratory pattern. If the epithelium is loosened it still functions as a protective sheet to prevent the lamina propria from shaking loose from vibra-

tion and air pressure. Extreme tension on the epithelium affects its
reaction to outer force. Then the vibratory pattern is only slightly affected by the properties of the lamina propria below (Hirano &
Kakita, 1985, p. 40). Therefore, while the tension created by
stretching and thinning the cords for high notes makes the epithelium more vulnerable to damage, it may also allow a normal vibratory pattern even with fluid in Reineke's space.

There are two types of pathologies possible in Reineke's edema,
the edematous and the fibrotic (Hirano & Kurita, 1986, p. 24). The
first is a temporary reaction to voice abuse, vocal trauma, infection,
allergy or hypothyroidism. The edema of a temporary reaction to
shouting, loud talking or singing will resolve with a short rest. That
of prolonged voice abuse or misuse resolves as the user is retrained
and the abuse or misuse is eliminated or reduced. Treating the underlying condition of the infection, allergy or hypothyroidism effectively reduces the resultant edema.

The fibrotic form of Reineke's edema is known by many names:
"*chronic polypoid chorditis, edematous fibroma, polypoid degeneration, polypoid laryngitis, diffuse vocal polyposis* and *diffuse polypoid thickening*" (Fritzell & Hertegard, 1986, p. 57). Many of
these names reflect the changes in the character of the mucosa which
are associated with this condition. This condition affects men and
women equally but is rarely seen in patients under the age of 30,
with most patients between 40 and 70 years old. Cigarette smoking
is usually indicated (Kleinsasser, 1986, p. 54; Tucker, 1987, p.
215) with other factors such as hypothyroidism and/or voice abuse
contributing (Sataloff, 1991, p. 274). Kleinsasser describes the appearance of the fluid in Reineke's space in these cases as "more gray
than yellow and the fluid thickening to a gluelike consistency"
(1986, p. 54). If the irritation is continued over a long period time,
changes may occur in the epithelium that resemble and perhaps anticipate the development of polyps (Tucker, 1987, p. 216). In extreme cases obstruction of the glottis can be so severe as to cause
stridor and choking attacks. Some patients even begin to speak with
the false cords (*dysphonia plica ventricularis*) because they are unable to phonate with the true cords (Kleinsasser, 1979, p. 20).
Whereas the slight edema of infection or abuse will resolve with
rest, time and retraining, resolution of the fibrotic type of edema is a
lengthy process. Often these patients prefer to have the affected mucosa removed which allows new, healthy mucosa to grow over the
stripped area (Damsté, 1987, p. 133).

Submucosal Hemorrhage

A break in a blood vessel(s) in the vocalis muscle is called a
submucosal hemorrhage. The most immediate effect is impairment

of all or part of the vocal range, depending upon the extent of the involvement of the vocal ligament. Because the cords are flaccid for production of low notes, low notes are sometimes all that is affected, and sometimes only one or two notes. If the vocal ligament is involved, vibration in the stretched position necessary for higher pitches may be impaired as well (Rubin, 1966, p. 24). The cause is acute vocal abuse: shouting, singing with excessive volume, or use of the voice when fatigued, affected by external irritants such as alcohol, or already impaired. The treatment is vocal rest until the hemorrhage is healed (Feder, 1983, p. 435).

Muscular Tension Dysphonia

Musculoskeletal tension dysphonia (MTD) describes voice disorders characterized by excessive tension in the extrinsic and intrinsic laryngeal muscles. It is usually a reaction to stress. Some therapists and laryngologists consider such a reaction the underlying cause of all functional voice disorders. MTD is used by some writers to describe a specific voice abnormality, the underlying cause of which is excessive tension of the laryngeal musculature, sometimes to the point of rigidity.

Auditory symptoms of MTD include a voice quality that is rough with evidence of strain and limited pitch and volume parameters (Harrison & Tucker, 1987, p. 150). Patients with MTD may also exhibit a breathy voice quality, particularly if the condition has been long-standing enough to produce vocal cord bowing. Harrison and Tucker also cite severe cases with "intermittent aphonia" (p. 150).

While Tucker limits diagnoses of MTD to those patients who do not have laryngeal lesions, Morrison classifies MTD patients into two major types. Type one show a posterior glottic chink but no visible change in the vocal folds. Muscle tension is excessive in the area above the hyoid bone and in other extrinsic muscles. Most patients in this group are female. In addition to the symptoms of type one, type two MTD patients exhibit additive lesions on the vocal folds. Morrison further divides type two patients into three groups. Those in group 2a are predominantly females. If a 2a patient is asked to sing an ascending and descending scale, her larynx will rise and fall with the pitch. These patients exhibit nodules and "almost polyps:" lesions which occur at the same location as nodules but which are more edematous and less firm then other nodules. Morrison observed that the more sessile (closely attached) nodules were seen in the presence of an excessively wide posterior glottal chink. In such cases the cords appear to meet at the point of the nodules, or the nodules appear at the point where the cords begin to close. Tension above the larynx is closely correlated. "The larger the chink the tighter the muscles are in the suprahyoid area -- be-

tween the hyoid and the mandible -- the tighter the tongue and
mandible seem to be held" (Morrison, 1985, p. 420).

Type 2b is made up of males in their upper teens and early 20's,
many of whom are would-be rock singers. Type 2c are mainly
older females who exhibit polypoid degeneration of the vocal cord
mucosa in varying degrees (Morrison, 1985, p. 400).

Harrison and Tucker treat MTD with counseling and voice therapy which includes direct laryngeal manipulation and easy onset of
voice (1987, p. 150). Koufman and Blalock teach patients relaxation and breathing techniques and help them select speaking pitches
that are in the middle of their range. They have also found that most
patients with MTD will speak normally with white-noise masking
(1988, p. 497).

The Breathy Voice: Bowed Cords/Glottal Chink

When the glottis is completely open, air flows out freely with
little or no glottal resistance to produce voice. The more closely the
folds approximate or close the clearer the voice will be. Thus, a partially closed glottis will produce a secretive whisper. For normal
voice the vocal folds approximate or close so that with every cycle
the edges meet evenly without touching.

A slightly breathy speaking voice is considered attractive and
seductive by some. However, when the air leakage is so excessive
that it limits the person's breath capacity to a few words or the voice
becomes too soft to be understood, breathiness becomes symptomatic. The causes of an excessively breathy voice may be 1) neu-
romuscular incoordination due to paralysis of one of the cords; 2)
laryngeal inflammations and swelling because of colds or allergies;
3) poor muscle tone or bowed vocal cords or 4) masses such as
nodules, polyps or carcinoma (Aronson, 1985, p. 289). Because
the paralyzed cord is unable to move from the position it is in when
it is frozen, the other cord must compensate by crossing the midline
to meet the frozen cord. The nearer the paralyzed cord is located to
the midline the better the glottal closure will be. Swelling and inflammation can alter the shape of the cords so that the edges do not
meet smoothly and air escapes. Aronson considers masses such as
polyps, nodules, webs (a congenital condition in which the glottis is
covered by a thick membrane which prevents closure) or carcinomas
the most common cause of a breathy voice (1985, p. 289). Masses
and obstruction on one or both of the cords may interfere with the
shape of the edges of the glottis and impede approximation or may
cause vibration between the cords to become asynchronous. In the
latter case, each cord is capable of moving to the midline, but they
no longer do it together. Therefore, the glottis remains partially
open at all times (Murry, 1982a). Breathiness is a symptom with

such varied etiologies that careful medical assessment must be carried out before any remediation is begun.

The result of prolonged hyperfunction is hypofunction; muscles weakened by excessive strain simply cannot continue to function normally (Brodnitz, 1962, p. 458). The first place this usually becomes evident is in the muscles of the larynx where the posterior portions of the vocal cords fail to close completely, leaving a "chink" often associated with a weak, breathy tone (Boone, 1983, p. 45). The muscular portions of the cords may bow if they become weakened by continued use of pressed phonation and forceful closure. In this case the arytenoid muscles will close the posterior, cartilaginous portion of the cords, but the muscular portion will not meet (Murry, 1982a, p. 486). The extra air escaping through this opening results in a breathy tone.

Stone asks hyperfunctional speakers to speak with breathy phonation. He believes that it is easier for the client to recognize a behavior at the opposite end of the spectrum from his or her own habits than the more subtle variations in between. Once the opposite pole has been perceived, the client can better appreciate subtle differences to modify behavior as directed by the clinician (Stone, 1984, p. 179). When a breathy tone is the result of vocal fold lesions, therapy consists of relaxation exercises designed to reduce the tensions which cause the rubbing together or forceful meeting of the cords that precipitated the lesion.

Bowing can also be caused by constantly blowing breath through the spoken or sung tone. Although the cords are physiologically and neurologically programmed to meet in the midline, constantly blowing out extra air keeps them from meeting. This causes the muscles to work harder to try to achieve closure until eventually they are unable to function and the cords bow. Therapists and voice teachers must teach these speakers and singers to initiate sound with a clean attack rather than an [h] and to control breath usage so as to avoid blowing air through the tone. Achieving a clean attack will usually control the flow of breath.

Since a normal larynx assumes an oval shape for production of falsetto, bowing of the cords and the oval shape it causes may result in excessive use of the falsetto mechanism (Arnold, 1964, pp. 430-431). In such cases the woman's upper register or the man's mixed head voice may sound all right in spite of the bowed cords. In addition, increased tension in muscles which regulate pitch (cricothyroid and to a certain extent thyroarytenoid muscles) means a higher pitch so that a hyperfunctional speaking voice will often be artificially high (Brodnitz, 1962, pp. 461-462).

Myasthenia Larynges

Every singer knows well the feeling of a tired voice resulting from oversinging or after resumption of singing following a rest of more than a few days. This muscular debility or weakness is called *myasthenia*. It may also occur with other functional disorders, such as nodules, secondary to disease or endocrine disorders; or as a result of deterioration of the muscles of the larynx associated with age (see Punt, 1967, p. 71).

Additive Lesions

Additive Lesions include any growth on or within the mucosa of the vocal folds. They include nodules, screamers' nodules, polyps, contact ulcers, cysts and varices of the vocal cord. The appearance and symptomology of some of these lesions are so similar that they are often labeled incorrectly. Most often confused are nodules and polyps. This is partly because both are usually bilateral and occur at the point at which contact between the cords is most easily made, the juncture of the anterior and middle thirds. In addition, pathologists and laryngologists often use the terms to mean different things. The laryngologist uses the term nodule to refer to "tiny, usually bilateral excrescences in the anterior portions of the vocal cords that are smaller than most polyps and that will have a different histologic appearance" (Tucker, 1987, p. 38). Histological findings will be fibrous tissue "under the surface of intact but somewhat thickened mucous membrane" (Tucker, p. 216).

The pathologist, on the other hand, uses the term nodule to denote lesions composed of "abundant vessels or moderately sized blood-filled spaces, prominent fibrin exudation, and perhaps some evidence of old hemorrhage" (Tucker, 1987, p. 38). Pathologists may also use the term vocal polyps to include vocal nodules (Tucker, p. 216).

All vocal cord lesions affect the function of the cords. Aronson indicates that one or more of the following pathological changes will affect the singer or speaker with these lesions.

1. Increase the mass or bulk of the vocal folds or immediately surrounding tissues.
2. Alter their shape.
3. Restrict their mobility.
4. Change their tension.
5. Modify the size or shape, or both, of the glottic, supraglottic, or infraglottic airway.
6. Prevent the vocal folds from approximating completely along their antero-posterior margins.

7. Result in excessive tightness of approximation.
(1985, p. 57)

Harrison and Tucker cite three symptoms of these changes: (1)
lowered pitch, (2) abnormal airflow through the tone due to incomplete closure and (3) greater force required to initiate and maintain
vocal sound because of increased tension in the vocal cords
(Harrison & Tucker, 1987, p. 137).

It can be surmised from this list that, in addition to being responses to abuse, these lesions can also alter significantly the manner in which the vocal cords function. While abuse may cause the
lesions initially, incorrect methods of compensation for the impaired
function they cause may lead to further irritation. Kleinsasser gives
the example of the cord opposite the unilateral polyp developing a
hollow into which the polyp will fit, thus allowing the glottis to
close tightly. Epithelial hyperplasia can also arise as a contact reaction on the cord opposite a polyp. Some patients with Reineke's
edema begin to phonate with the vestibular folds, and patients with
chronic hyperplastic laryngitis often strain. (Kleinsasser, 1979, pp.
33-34).

Vocal cord lesions are the result of abuse of the vocal folds. As
such, many can be reversed with voice therapy. Other larger, older
lesions may require surgical removal. Retraining in voice usage is
still required to assure that the speaker does not return to the old
habits that caused the lesions.

Nodules

Vocal nodules are fibrous growths of excrescences on the mucosa of the vocal folds. They are normally bilateral or paired and
occur opposite each other at the midpoint of the muscular part of the
cords. As Case points out, this is the point at which the cords come
together with the most force because it is the point at which the "excursion from midline" is the widest (1984, p. 100).

A great deal has been written about nodules. It all points to the
fact that they are a reaction by the mucosa of the cords to the trauma
of vocal abuse over time or vocal misuse (Cooper, 1973; Damsté &
Lerman, 1975; Greene, 1964; Moore, 1971a, 1971b; Polow &
Kaplan, 1979; Sataloff, 1991; Schroeder, Krupp, Tierney &
McPhee, 1990; Shelton, 1985; Tucker, 1987; & Way, 1988).
Nodules may vary in size from a pinpoint to a peppercorn and in
consistency from soft to hard and callous.

Case (1984) provides a list of causes of nodules as: "yelling and
screaming"; glottal attacks; abusive singing, professional or amateur; an aggressive personality; speaking over mechanical noise or
music or in night clubs; "coughing and excessive throat clearing";

grunting sounds made when exercising or lifting things; calling loudly for other people or pets; speaking or singing at inappropriate levels; speaking abusively or excessively when affected by colds, allergies or during the woman's menstrual period; smoking or speaking in a smoky environment; vocalizing excessively or when muscles are tense; speaking without breath support; hard abusive laughing; arguing; "vocalizing excessively while taking aspirin which can increase the potential of vocal fold blood vessels to hemorrhage"; cheerleading or cheering; making funny play noises such as animal or toy sounds (children); yelling while engaged in athletic activities such as coaching or quarterbacking in football and "reversing phonation" (pp. 104-105).

Kleinsasser claims that all of his patients with what he calls "Singer's Nodules" are women between the ages of 20 and 40.

> . . . Up to this day I have never seen true so-called singer's nodules in a man: All patients affected were women never younger than 20 and rarely older than 40 years of age. They were nearly all school teachers, nursery school teachers, or young mothers who tended to teach their children at the tops of their voices. A few were amateur singers in church choirs, several were professional pop singers -- but none of them had ever studied singing.
> (Kleinsasser, 1986, pp. 52-53)

Because of this he concludes that the fear many trained singers have of developing nodules is unfounded.

Sataloff indicates that swellings resembling vocal nodules may sometimes be found on the cords of professional singers who exhibit no symptoms.

> Caution must be exercised in diagnosing small nodules in patients who have been singing actively. Many singers develop bilateral, symmetrical, soft swellings at the junction of the anterior and middle thirds of their vocal cords following heavy voice use. There is no evidence to suggest that singers with such "physiologic swelling" are predisposed toward development of vocal nodules. At present, the condition is generally considered to be within normal limits. The physiologic swelling usually disappears with 24 to 48 hr [sic] of rest from heavy voice use.
> (Sataloff, 1991, pp. 267-268)

Symptoms. The presence of nodules is usually indicated by a breathy, harsh or hoarse voice, loud volume, pitch breaks (Harrison & Tucker, 1987, p. 149), intermittent aphonia and dyplophonia (Shelton, 1985, p. 274). In singers even a small nodule can interfere with the sound. Their presence along the glottal edges of the cords requires increased subglottal pressure to get the cords to approximate, particularly at higher pitches (Rubin & Lehrhoff, 1962, p. 155). Therefore, the singer may be unable to sing high notes at anything but a loud volume.

Like other mass lesions, nodules probably begin with the development of vocal cord edema, and possibly hemorrhage, as a response to the trauma of voice abuse or misuse. If the trauma is brief and is not repeated, the edema will resolve. If, however, the abuse or misuse is chronic, changes in the epithelium of the cords will persist. Laryngoscopy at this point may reveal what is often termed an "*incipient nodule*" (Tucker, 1987, p. 217). Histologically the changes involve edema, hypertrophy of the mucosa, and the formulation of granulation tissue. With repeated trauma, hemorrhage and inflammation become fibrosis, and a nodule is formed (Tucker, p. 217).

Nodules have clear-cut contours and do not penetrate the vocal fold beyond the margin. They do not involve blood vessel pathology, nor do they significantly alter the epithelium of the vocal cord beyond the area of the nodule itself. The epithelium at the base of the nodule and on its surface is normally thickened by an increase in layers, and the color changes to a lackluster shade of gray (Pogosov & Antoniv, 1987, pp. 91-92). Nodules are a kind of "epithelial callous" (Kleinsasser, 1986, p. 53) on the vocal cords. In many cases the portion of the cords in front of the nodules vibrate, but the space behind the nodule is left open to form a triangular posterior glottic chink (Kleinsasser, p. 53).

Treatment. Soft or "young" nodules will usually be re-absorbed with removal of the misuse, but older, more fibrous ones will probably require surgical removal. In either case, it is agreed that voice therapy must be initiated with the patient to prevent him or her from reverting to the abuse patterns which caused the nodules if their return is to be prevented (viz., e.g., Aronson, 1985, p. 345; Boone, 1983; Brodnitz, 1961; Greene, 1964, Harrison & Tucker, 1987, p. 149; Sataloff, 1991, pp. 268-269; Tucker, 1987, p. 217).

Treatment for singers with nodules should involve voice therapy, education in vocal hygiene and/or retraining of the singing voice to remove the abuse or misuse which has caused the nodules. Any kind of laryngeal surgery is risky for the professional singer. As Sataloff indicates, even the most careful surgery can permanently impair the voice.

Permanent destruction of voice quality is not a rare complication. Even following expert surgery, this may be caused by submucosal scarring, resulting in an adynamic segment along the vibratory margin of the vocal fold. . . . There is no reliable cure for this complication. Consequently, even large, apparently fibrotic nodules of long standing should be given a chance to resolve without surgery. In some cases, the nodules remain but become asymptomatic, with normal voice quality. (Sataloff, 1991, p. 269)

Screamers' nodules. Kleinsasser makes a distinction between nodules, or what he calls singer's nodules, and *screamers' nodules.* Screamers' nodules occur in children between the ages of three and ten who use the full volume of their voices constantly. Like adult nodules, screamers' nodules are bilateral and symmetrical. "They are long, smooth, spindle-shaped, poorly demarcated lesions about the center of the membranous part of the vocal cord. The epithelium over the nodule is somewhat hyperplastic and the nodule itself is soft and mobile" (Kleinsasser, 1979, p. 99).

Kleinsasser advises teaching the child to make fewer demands on the voice. Happily, screamers' nodules usually resolve spontaneously by puberty. They should only be removed if hoarseness increases or if the nodules become very large and the epithelium thickened (Kleinsasser, 1979, p. 99).

S/z indicator. Boone uses the s/z ratio as a screening measure for the presence of nodules in children. The time the child can prolong an [s] phoneme is compared to the duration of the [z] phoneme. Individuals with normal larynges are able to prolong both phonemes for about the same amount of time. Those with lesions such as nodules or polyps are able to prolong the [s] about the same length of time as normal subjects, but the duration of the [z] is significantly shorter. The s/z ratio is computed by dividing the maximum [z] time into the maximum [s] time (Boone, 1983, pp. 74-75). Comparing 28 subjects with nodules or polyps to 36 dysphonic subjects without laryngeal pathology and 86 subjects with no dysphonia, Eckel and Boone found that their patients with laryngeal pathologies demonstrated s/z ratios higher than 1.4 95% of the time. They interpreted this data to mean that vocal fold approximation was rendered less efficient by the presence of an additive lesion along the glottal margin (Eckel & Boone, 1981, p. 147).

Wilner and Sataloff suggest that this test may be invalid for professional singers (1987, p. 315).

Polyps
Whereas vocal nodules develop as a response to trauma to the glottal edges of the vocal cords, vocal cord polyps develop as a result of trauma at a deeper level. Vocal polyps may occur singly and unilaterally, singly and bilaterally, multiply and unilaterally or multiply and bilaterally. They may develop at any point on the vocal cord epithelium, but, like vocal nodules, they tend to occur where the cords meet with the greatest impact -- at the midpoint of the vocal ligament.
Tucker (1987, p. 39), Kleinsasser (1986, p. 52) and Michaels (1984, pp. 102-103) all consider voice abuse the most important factor in the development of vocal cord polyps. Damsté considers their cause unknown but states that

> some polyps may have originated from phonating with excessive subglottic air pressure and incompletely closed cords, so that the mucous membrane at the anterior commissure is sucked on and ballooned out. The accumulation of fluid in the subepithelial layer is later followed by the ingrowth of connective tissue, so that the polyp eventually becomes firm in consistency. (1987, p. 133)

Harrison and Tucker believe vocal polyps can arise from inflammation, allergy, immune problems and trauma, the latter meaning primarily voice abuse (1987, p. 149). Perkins states that polyps are formed after mechanical stress to deep layers of cord vibration ruptures blood vessels which hemorrhage (1985, p. 90).
Data indicates that polyps occur most often in middle age and more often in men than women. They do occasionally occur in childhood (Kleinsasser, 1986, p. 51; Perkins, 1985, p. 90). While Perkins indicates that smoking and drinking do not contribute to the development of polyps (1985, p. 90), Kleinsasser states that 80-90% of his patients were cigarette smokers who also abused their voices (1986, p. 51). Professor A. Fouricia, speech scientist of University College, London, describes the voice abuse that leads to polyps as resulting from violent impact during adduction following a build-up of excessive subglottal pressure. This practice is usually seen in people who shout or scream excessively. It results in the release of inflammatory blood products into Reineke's space (Michaels, 1984, p. 103).
At least some vocal polyps do appear to originate as hemorrhages on the vocal fold (Sataloff, 1991, p. 270). Blood accumulates under the epithelium in Reineke's space. If the swelling is generalized over the length of the cord, it is considered an edema. If

it is concentrated at one point and bulges out, it is a polyp.
Kleinsasser describes what takes place if the trauma continues.

> In the beginning a damage to the walls of the submu-
> cous capillaries of the vocal cords takes place and
> coiled or sinusoid vessels may appear. Depending
> on the extent of damage, an increased permeability of
> the vascular walls develops. Either a thin fluid per-
> meates or a compact fibrin insudation emerges. As a
> reaction the fissures between the fibers of the fibrin
> deposits are vascularized from the neighboring blood
> vessels and connective tissue. . . . Gaps in the en-
> dothelial lining of the newly formed vessels permit
> the further efflux and deposition of more blood
> constituents increasing the size of the polyp.
> (Kleinsasser, 1986, p. 52)

Polyps may be either *sessile* (directly attached to the vocal fold)
or *pedunculated* (attached by a stem or stalk). Pedunculated polyps
often hang below the surface of the cord and only affect voice quality when they blow up into the glottis. Large pedunculated polyps
can cause sudden and occasional hoarseness or loss of voice which
disappears just as abruptly as it appears as the polyp rises and falls
to and from the glottal opening (Tucker, 1987, p. 216). Since pedunculated polyps are not always in position to face the opposite
cord, they are less often bilateral (Friedmann & Ferlito, 1988, p.
78).

Symptoms. The pedunculated polyps described above usually
cause phonation to stop when they move on to the vibrating edge of
the vocal fold. At other times the voice appears normal. The voice
with massive vocal cord polyps is usually excessively low, partly
from the additional weight. In other cases of vocal cord polyps,
auditory symptoms will be similar to those associated with nodules
and other masses that occur on the vocal cords (Harrison & Tucker,
1987, p. 149). Thus, the voice may appear harsh, hoarse or breathy
and may have pitch breaks and fatigue easily.

Histologically polyps may vary from gelatinous to telangiectatic
with transitional and mixed varieties between. Kleinsasser describes
the gelatinous extreme as having a loose and edematous nucleus.
Collagenous fibers are sparse and are separated by blood vessels
with thick walls and, sometimes, cell-free, sinus-like spaces filled
with endothelial cells or with basophilic fluid (1986, p. 52). Hirano
and Kurita describe gelatinous polyps as having edema, collagenous
fibers and fibroblasts (1986, p. 24). Frenzel sees the structure of
gelatinous polyps as like that of the normal vocal cord mucosa ex-

cept for the accumulation of watery fluid (1984, p. 40). Hirano and Kurita describe telangiectatic polyps as epithelial hemorrhages with thrombus (a plug in a blood vessel often occurring at its base) and telangiectasia (dilated blood vessels and reddish appearance) (1986, p. 24).

The histological pattern of polyps seems to be dependent on the manner in which the initial trauma was assimilated by the tissues. An ingrowth of blood vessels leads to a polyp that is largely vascular (telangiectatic). A more fibrous lesion is produced by a proliferation of fibroblasts or by an ingrowth of fibrous tissue. The histology of the polyp is further affected by retention of the original edemic fluid (Friedmann & Ferlito, 1988, p. 82). Those which begin with a hemorrhage may also become more fibrous and hyalinized as they develop (Tucker, 1987, p. 39).

Transitional or mixed polyps are the most common. Kleinsasser describes them as "showing a reddish appearance and a nucleus of tortuous vessels embedded in a gelatinous surface covered by a thin layer of squamous epithelium" (1986, p. 51). Since mixed polyps are the most common, Frenzel concludes that both gelatinous and telangiectatic polyps have the same pathogenesis (1986, p. 49).

Treatment. Tucker suggests polyps should be treated like Reineke's edema with a trial period in which irritants such as alcohol and tobacco are removed and voice therapy is tried (1987, p. 216). Sataloff finds voice rest and a "few weeks of low-dose steroid therapy" will resolve some polyps, even large ones (1991, p. 270), but joins Damsté (1987, p. 133) and Harrison and Tucker (1987, p. 149) in advocating their surgical removal in the majority of cases. Damsté further indicates that polyps never resolve. Those still in an early stage which are more like localized edemas and are not yet organized by connective tissue can cure spontaneously by rupturing the epithelium of the cord which allows the contents to escape (Damsté, 1987, p. 133).

An interesting side note is provided by Kleinsasser who states that true polyps occur only on the vocal cords. "Neither will polyps or analogous or even similar lesions be found anywhere else in the human body" (1986, p. 51).

Cysts

Cysts can occur at any point in the larynx which has sero-mucous glands. These points include the laryngeal ventrical, the ventricular folds, the epiglottis and the vocal folds (Friedmann & Ferlito, 1988, p. 93). There seems to be general agreement that these are retention cysts which develop when glandular ducts become obstructed from trauma or inflammation. Mossallam, Kotby, Ghaly, Nassar and Barakah believe that cyst formation on the vocal

cords begins when microvocal trauma causes minute fragments of
the squamous epithelium to penetrate the lamina propria of the vocal
fold (1986, p. 78).

> According to this explanation these cysts may be
> a sort of implantation dermoid cyst produced by the
> microvocal traumata sending islets of stratified squa-
> mous epithelium into the lamina propria of the vocal
> fold. These islets may start the process of cyst for-
> mation. (Mossallam, Kotby, Ghaly, Nassar &
> Barakah, 1986, p. 78)

Vocal cord cysts are often misdiagnosed as nodules but, unlike
nodules, may be found on only one cord. Strobovideolaryngoscopy
will assist in diagnosis, sometimes by revealing that what was
thought to be a nodule is filled with fluid (Sataloff, 1991, p. 269).
Confusion with nodules is compounded by the fact that unilateral
cysts sometimes cause the opposing cord to swell or even form a
nodule from the trauma of impact. Sataloff indicates that cysts are
often found when one of what was thought to be bilateral nodules
resolves with therapy and the other does not. They are also found
when surgery is performed on what was thought to be nodules that
remain unresolved after voice therapy (1991, p. 269).
     Cysts do not resolve. Therefore, they must be removed surgi-
cally.

Contact Ulcers
     The vocalis muscle is underneath the front two-thirds of the vo-
cal cords. Under the back two-thirds are the vocal processes and
part of the body of the arytenoid cartilages. Because this posterior
third of the vocal cord is basically hard tissue covered only with a
tight mucoperichondrium, contact ulcers may develop there as a response to one or more of three factors: voice abuse, endotracheal
intubation associated with general anesthetic and gastroesophageal
reflux (GER). The posterior third of the vocal cord is also the area
that "undergoes the greatest excursion during opening and closing of
the glottis as well as the point at which any contaminated material
that may be cleared from the lungs by movement of the mucociliary
blanket leaves the larynx to be swallowed" (Tucker, 1987, pp. 217-
218)
     Contact ulcers are craters in the mucosa with granulated (grainy)
tissue around the edges and in the ulcer itself. Shumrick and
Shumrick describe them as "heaped-up accumulations of tissues
over the vocal processes of the arytenoids and interarytenoid area,
often with central depressions" (1988, p. 266). They also indicate

that the various names, "*contact ulcer, contact granuloma,* and *contact pachydermia*" are used to describe the various changes observed in the tissues (Shumrick & Shumrick, 1988, p. 266). Kleinsasser indicates that the contact ulcer "is always unilateral and has a two lipped form" (1986, p. 55). During phonation the two lips fit around the vocal process of the arytenoid cartilage on the opposite side. The epithelium on that side develops hyperplasia (abnormal cell growth) as a reaction to this contact (1986, p. 55). Pogosov and Antoniv, on the other hand, describe the contact ulcer as bilateral and compare it to a "hammer and an anvil," with the granuloma on the hammer side and the ulceration on the anvil side (1987, pp. 22 & 24). Meyer-Breitung and Burkhardt describe the contact ulcer as an "annular mucosal thickening on the inside of the vocal processes. . . with a central depression resembling an ulcer" (1988, pp. 172-173).

By manipulating excised human larynges with a thread, Hirano, Yoshida, Kurita, Kiyokawa, Sato and Tateiski (1985) simulated normal adduction and abduction. They discovered that the adductory process stretched the mucosa which covers the vocal processes because the vocal processes move more than the mucosa (p. 8). This stretching and consequent thinning of the mucosa makes it more vulnerable to damage from forceful adduction of the arytenoid cartilages, esophageal reflux and/or intubation.

Contact ulcers resulting from intubation associated with surgery differ somewhat from those caused by abuse. Shumrick and Shumrick indicate that post-intubation ulcers are usually bilateral, pedunculated and composed of "epithelialized granulation tissue." They are often rather large and will occasionally create respiratory problems (1988, p. 270). The introduction of the tube into the airway causes the initial trauma which is exacerbated by the rubbing up and down of the tube, particularly with prolonged intubation (Ward, Zweitman, Hanson & Berci, 1980, p. 263).

Symptoms. Unlike nodules and polyps, contact ulcers produce pain. The patient may experience musculoskeletal pain, dryness in the throat and pain on swallowing (Harrison & Tucker, 1987, p. 150) and speaking, and/or a foreign body sensation in the throat and consequent throat clearing (Pogosov & Antoniv, 1987, p. 93; Tucker, 1987, p. 218). Patients with gastric reflux may also experience heartburn (Harrison & Tucker, 1987, p. 150).

Vocal symptoms usually include excessively low pitch and low laryngeal position, a harsh quality and loud volume with low breath pressure and use of glottal fry (Harrison & Tucker, 1987, p. 150). Stroboscopic examination reveals only partial closure of the anterior two-thirds of the larynx with the forceful closure of the posterior third (Kleinsasser, 1986, p. 55).

Most patients with contact ulcers are middle-aged men (Harrison & Tucker, 1987, p. 149; Kleinsasser, 1986, p. 55; Pogosov & Antoniv, 1987, p. 24). Kleinsasser describes his patients as "introverted, rather depressive, tense, and tough appearing" (1986, p. 55). Harrison and Tucker see contact ulcers most often in men between 40 and 50 years of age who work in high pressure jobs, particularly in positions of authority which require excessive voice use (1987, pp. 149-150). In addition to these factors, Shumrick and Shumrick also cite work environments in which the patient must shout over loud noise, inhale noxious fumes, or lecture or control crowds. They do not consider smoking a factor (1988, p. 269). Pogosov and Antoniv find chronic lower respiratory inflammation, alcohol abuse, smoking and vocal abuse factors in the development of contact ulcers. Although allergy can be considered a predisposing factor, they do not consider it part of the etiology (1987, p. 93).

Habitual and constant throat clearing is both a symptom and cause of contact ulcers. It is often a response to the foreign body sensation associated with these lesions, or it may be a response to irritation of the larynx from either postnasal drip or gastric reflux (Ward, Zweitman, Hanson & Berci, 1980, p. 262). Tucker indicates that treatment of most contact ulcers must include both medical and voice therapy. Sataloff, however, finds that contact ulcers occur in young professional voice users with no other evidence of laryngeal injury and no history of intubation. He states that most vocal cord ulcers and granulomas are caused, or at least aggravated, by gastric reflux. Controlling the reflux usually allows these lesions to heal (Sataloff, 1991, p. 274). Because gastroesophageal reflux causes a variety of laryngeal problems, it is discussed separately in the following section.

Treatment. When voice abuse is part of the etiology of contact ulcer, voice therapy should be instituted. McFarlane has found reduction of the use of the glottal stroke sufficient to allow even large granulomas in the mucosa over the arytenoid cartilages to heal (1988, p. 430). Harrison and Tucker find work on several aspects of voice necessary to treat contact ulcers. They begin by reducing the intensity and amount of voice usage. This is followed by reduction in musculoskeletal tension, raising laryngeal position, eliminating vocal fry and harsh tone quality, and working on respiratory and glottal function and coordination. They also advise elimination of strenuous throat clearing and irritants such as alcohol and tobacco. Cases not responding to therapy and medication may require surgery (Harrison & Tucker, 1987, p. 150; Tucker, 1987, p. 218).

Gastroesophageal Reflux (GER)

In 1968 Cherry and Margulies reported finding "reflux peptic esophagitis" in three patients whose contact ulcers had not responded to accepted treatment.

> Three patients with persistent ulcers of the larynx refractory to the accepted treatment were studied using the cine esophagram pharyngography with an acid barium meal. All three patients showed reflux peptic esophagitis and when the esophageal motility disturbances occurred, showed reflux from the esophagus through the cricopharyngeus muscle into the pharynx.
>
> None of these patients volunteered symptoms of peptic esophagitis, but on careful questioning each patient had typical symptoms of reflux peptic esophagitis. (Cherry & Margulies, 1968, pp. 1937-1938)

Before this report, the accepted cause of contact ulcers was vocal abuse which wore away the mucosa covering the vocal processes of the arytenoids. This was the first report of the effect of gastroesophageal reflux on the larynx.

Laryngologists now know that gastroesophageal reflux is responsible for a variety of laryngeal problems, including contact ulcers. Koufman, Weiner, Wallace and Castel studied 32 patients with GER. They found one-half of these patients showed laryngeal redness, nine had redness only on the posterior aspects of the larynx and seven diffuse redness. Two patients also showed ulcers; two had granulomas; one had leukoplakia; eight had carcinoma and eight had subglottic stenosis. It is important to point out that, of the eight with carcinomas, only five were smokers (1988, p. 82). Lumpkin, Bishop and Katz found the following complaints in fourteen patients who had voice or laryngeal problems which were accompanied by dyspepsia.

Reddened mucosa over arytenoids   14
Contact ulcer   4
Aphthous ulcer   3
Diffuse erythema   3
Leukoplakia   1
Vocal fold hemorrhage   1
Nodules   1
Intubation granuloma   1
(1989, p. 352)

All 14 were evaluated by an otolaryngologist, a gastroenterologist and a speech pathologist and had pH monitoring to verify the presence of GER. Nine were professional singers.

Symptoms. Shumrick and Shumrick (1988, p. 270) report finding inflammation and mucosal thickening of the posterior false cords, the aryepiglottic folds and the posterior commissure of the larynx in addition to contact ulcers secondary to gastroesophageal reflux. Friedmann and Ferlito report "chronic, non-specific laryngitis characterized by redness, oedema and irritation of the posterior larynx and pharynx" resulting from hiatus hernia and "gastro-oesophageal-pharyngeal reflux" (1988, p. 32).

Kambric and Radsel examined forty-four patients with posterior chronic acid laryngitis including swollen and reddened mucosa covered with thick mucous. The most extreme cases exhibited varied granulomas, some with central ulceration. In all but two of the cases gastric hypersection with gastroesophageal reflux was clinically diagnosed (1984, p. 1238).

Bain, Harrington, Thomas and Schafer define gastroesophageal reflux (GER) as "escape of gastric duodenal contents into the esophagus without associated belching or vomiting" (1983, p. 175). Normally, the lower esophageal sphincter (LES) keeps the stomach contents from flowing back into the esophagus. Factors which lower LES pressure include the presence of a hiatal hernia, increased intra-abdominal pressure, smoking, certain enzyme secretions, pronounced weight gain and a nasogastric tube (Bain, Harrington, Thomas & Schafer, 1983, p. 175). Alcohol, caffeine and certain foods such as garlic, onions, spices (Bain, Harrington, Thomas & Schafer, 1983, p. 175) and seafood (Ward, Zweitman, Hanson & Berci, 1980, p. 264), especially eaten shortly before bedtime, appear to increase the reflux.

Tucker indicates that gastric esophageal reflux may cause contact ulcers directly or indirectly. Directly, the spill of acid across the posterior of the larynx erodes the mucosa. Indirectly, the arytenoid cartilages may grind together because of discomfort communicated to the recurrent laryngeal nerve from the vagus nerve when it is irritated by gastric reflux at the base of the esophagus (1987, p. 218). Lumpkin, Bishop and Katz state, and many others imply, that the inflammation and irritation of laryngeal tissues create a desire to clear the throat, and healing is affected when the throat clearing is eliminated (1989, p. 354). Of course, any type of voice abuse or misuse, such as loud talking or singing with poor technique, will exacerbate the effects of GER (Kambric & Radsel, 1984, p. 1238).

The most common digestive symptom of GER is heartburn. Other common symptoms include aspiration, nausea and vomiting and difficulty swallowing, especially solid foods (Bain, Harrington,

Thomas & Schafer, 1983, p. 177). Brewer, Gould and Hale list the
following symptoms associated with gastroesophageal reflux:

Lump in the throat	Heartburn
Epigastric pain	Water brash
Dysphagia	Crack or break in voice
Long vocal warm-up period	Reduced voice range
Choking spells at night	Frequent burping
Frequent throat clearing	Bad breath
Hiccoughing	Nausea
Vomiting	Sleep apnea.
(1984, p. 230)	

Koufman, Weiner, Wallace and Castel (1988, p. 79) indicate that
many patients, unfortunately often the ones with laryngeal manifestations, do not exhibit typical GER symptoms. Ward, Zweitman,
Hanson and Berci indicate that some patients with acid reflux
awaken during the night, drink water or take antacids and thereby
prevent the acid from irritating the laryngeal mucosa (1980, p. 269).
Others awaken suddenly in the night to a sour acid taste, coughing
and violent throat clearing. The next morning they feel the need to
clear the throat associated with the feeling of something foreign in it
(1980, p. 264).
     Spiegel, Sataloff, Cohn, & Hawkshaw describe methods of di-
agnosis of gastroesophageal reflux.

> Diagnosis is made by noting arytenoid and posterior
> glottic inflammation on laryngeal examination, re-
> flux during radiologic upper gastrointestinal study
> with esophageal manometric testing by
> esophagoscopy, and with 24-hour esophageal pH
> monitoring. Acid levels should be measured
> specifically during singing. (Spiegel, Sataloff, Cohn
> & Hawkshaw, 1988, p. 48)

Treatment. Treatment for gastroesophageal reflux may involve
antacids, changes in diet, and elimination of before-bed meals and
snacks. Because lying flat on one's back encourages the backward
flow of the reflux by placing the throat at the same level as the stomach, persons with gastroesophageal reflux may be told to raise the
head of their beds with bricks or by other means.

Other Lesions
Varices of the vocal cord. Kleinsasser describes vocal cord
varices as "a sort of blood blister which unlike a telangiectatic polyp

is compressible. Several dilated veins lead to and from the larynx"
(1979, p. 100). Varices usually occur singly and always on the free
edge or superior surface of the vocal folds. Kleinsasser found
varices more often in middle-aged women than in men and only in
patients who put great demands on their voices, including four
trained singers. Symptoms include dyplophonia at higher pitches
which, with continued voice use, progresses to hoarseness accompanied by laryngeal pressure and tension. Varices must be removed
surgically (Kleinsasser, 1979, p. 100)

Sulcus vocalis/sulcus glottideus.   Sulcus vocalis/Sulcus
glottideus is a lengthwise ridge along the superior surface of the
membranous portion of the vocal fold. It can be unilateral or bilateral (Sataloff, 1991, p. 277).   Symptoms are hoarseness
(Friedmann & Ferlito, 1988, p. 17;   Sataloff, 1991, p. 277),
breathiness and poor glottal function (Sataloff, 1991, p. 277).
Friedmann and Ferlito indicate that, when the bilateral sulcus is deep
enough, it may divide the cords enough to form a "double cord."
The resulting voice may have a hollow sound which they call "dys-
plastic dysphonia" (1988, pp. 17-18). Because the sulcus is accompanied by bowing of the edge of the vocal fold and increased
stiffness in the vibrating part of the vocal cord (Hirano, Tanaka,
Yoshida & Seichi, 1990, pp. 682 & 679), glottal closure is incomplete. Hirano, Tanaka, Yoshida and Seichi indicate that patients
with sulcus may also overadduct the ventricular folds (false cords)
in an attempt to compensate (1990, p. 679).

Dysphonia Plicae Ventricularis
Although rare, there are a few individuals with healthy, intact
true vocal cords who phonate with their ventricular folds or false
cords. The sound produced is harsh, raspy and pitched low and
sometimes has a strangled or groaning quality (Harrison & Tucker,
1987, p. 151). Dysphonia plicae ventricularis is most often seen in
people who are tense and aggressive and/or under prolonged pressure (Tucker, p. 218) and is then the result of severe musculoskeletal dysphonia. It is sometimes the result of hypertrophy (excessive
enlargement) of the false cords which prevents the true cords from
approximating fully (Tucker, 1987, p. 218). It may also be a compensation for vocal folds that will not meet properly because of lesions, often hidden from view other than by stroboscopy (Tucker,
1987, p. 218, side comment), or for those who have organic limitations, often paralysis, in the true cords (Harrison & Tucker, 1987,
p. 151). Treatment may include laser surgery to trim hypertrophic
cards, voice therapy or surgery to reverse or remove lesions such as
nodules or polyps or relaxation therapy to teach the client to produce

voice with less physical effort (Case, 1984, p. 317; Harrison & Tucker, 1987, p. 151).

Problems of Mutation

Both boys and girls go through voice change during puberty, with the male voice dropping as much as an octave and the female voice only a few notes. Most of the time this change takes place during the teens and then is over. Use of a falsetto by an adult male with a normally developed voice is considered a *mutational disorder*. Common mutational disorders include *incomplete mutation, mutation falsetto voice*, and *prolonged mutation* (Damsté, 1987, pp. 131-132).

Symptoms. Men with any of the three problems of mutation speak at a pitch that is higher than the normal male voice. Those with either mutational falsetto or prolonged mutation have a low register available. Those with mutational falsetto may exhibit the low register when they laugh or cough (Damsté, 1987, p. 132), while the man with prolonged mutation speaks mainly in falsetto, dropping into low register on occasional words or syllables. They display an inconsistency of timbre and pitch of which they may be unaware. Although such inconsistency is normal during voice change, if it extends over six months or does not decrease with time, it is considered prolonged mutation (Damsté, 1987, p. 132).

Incomplete mutation is the most frequently encountered problem of mutation (Brodnitz, 1983, p. 169). Men with it have no low or chest register available to them. The voice is high, lacks resonance, and fatigues easily (Brodnitz, 1983, p. 69; Damsté, 1987, p. 132). Often this poor voice quality began during the time when the voice was starting to change. In some cases the child continued to sing in falsetto, often in a boys' choir, after puberty began and thus delayed normal transition of the laryngeal tissues to the adult voice. It should be noted that persons with chronic respiratory diseases such as bronchitis or asthma may display a similar dysphonia because tense breathing prevents them from achieving a relaxed phonation (Damsté, 1987, p. 132).

Treatment. Both Damsté (1987, p. 132) and Brodnitz (1983, p. 70) use laryngeal manipulation and pressure on the thyroid cartilage to treat mutational falsetto. The treatment for incomplete mutation focuses on achieving more relaxed phonation. Because the structure of the muscles and connective tissues of the larynx must change, treatment for incomplete mutation may take some time (Damsté, 1987, p. 132).

When the voice is both high in pitch and breathy, it may represent an organic problem. Examination usually reveals a narrow glottal chink during phonation. Excessively stiff vocal cords which adduct with a narrow chink may be the result of "laryngeal trauma, radiation, chronic laryngitis, sulcus vocalis, vocal atrophy or systemic hormonal imbalance such as Werner's syndrome" (Isshiki, 1989, p. 132).

Isshiki believes that other cases of excessively high pitch may be due to organic conditions rather than or in addition to functional problems. He states that he has found the ala of the thyroid cartilage to be female in nature or the presence of scarring atrophy, either congenital or acquired, along the margin of the vocal cords. He has found these conditions while performing surgery on the larynx to lower the vocal pitch (1989, pp. 132-133).

While it might seem unnecessary to mention problems of mutation in a voice pedagogy book, there is some application. First, Damsté's findings with regards to the origin of incomplete mutation should caution anyone who is tempted to encourage a boy to continue to sing in falsetto, especially to the exclusion of the low register, after his voice has begun to change.

In a time of varied vocal styles, one occasionally encounters a male student who has sung only popular music or ballads using a falsetto with little or no low register. Usually this voice will bottom out around an octave below middle c. Training should be focused on relaxation of the throat and achieving a relaxed phonation. If the student is still unable to find the low register after he seems to have achieved relaxation and an appropriate time period has passed, examination by a laryngologist would seem to be in order. Of course, if the singer **likes** the voice the way it is and exhibits no other voice symptoms, he may prefer to leave things the way they are -- especially if he is achieving some professional recognition with the use of this voice.

Glossary of Terms

Abduct To open; used to describe the action of the vocal cords moving away from the midline.

Acute vocal abuse Sudden trauma to the vocal cords such as yelling.

Adduct To close; used to describe the action of the cords moving towards the midline.

Alveolar ridge Rim of gum behind the upper front teeth.

Anabolic steroids Drugs which are synthetic derivatives of the male hormone testosterone.

Anterior Front.

Aperiodic Exhibiting an irregular pattern of vibrations.

Aphonia Loss of voice.

Approximate To meet in the middle; used to describe a normal closure of the vocal cords.

Articulators Parts of the mouth used in the formation of speech sounds, e.g. tongue, lips, teeth, alveolar ridge, and hard and soft palate.

Aryepiglottic folds Mucous membranes on either side of the epiglottis which contain the arytenoideus muscle and help to close the airway during swallowing.

Arytenoid cartilages Two small, pyramid-shaped cartilages located on either side of the superior posterior aspect of the cricoid cartilage. The outermost base of each comprises the muscular process while the bases which are towards the inside of the cricoid ring are the vocal processes.

Arytenoid muscles There are two types: the **transverse aryte-**

noid muscles connect the muscular processes of the arytenoid cartilages, and the **oblique arytenoid muscles** cross the back of the cricoid cartilage diagonally to meet the aryepiglottic muscle. Both the oblique and transverse arytenoid muscles function to bring the arytenoid cartilages together, thus assisting in the closure of the vocal cords.

Aspirate   Characterized by release of air prior to phonation; the [h].

Assimilative nasality Carrying over nasal resonance from a nasal consonant to neighboring non-nasal sounds, especially vowels.

Associate therapy   Term used by Morton Cooper to describe carry-over of voice therapy to client's everyday life. Spouse or other "associate" is brought into therapy in the early stages and provides support throughout the therapy. This is especially useful in working with children.

Atrophy Muscular wasting.

Auditory feedback Monitoring speech or singing by ear.

Aural Related to hearing.

Basal pitch The lowest pitch available for speaking.

Bernoulli effect Suction which draws the vocal cords together due to the fact that air in motion has less density than air which is not in motion. See Vennard, 1967.

Bibliotherapy Method used by Morton Cooper in which the therapist gives the client reading material which relates to his or her voice disorder.

Bowed vocal cords Condition in which the edge of the vocal folds curve outward so that an opening between the folds exists even when they are in a closed position.

Breathy phonation Vocal tone produced with too little vocal cord closure.

Breathy tone Tone characterized by excessive leaking of air. Often weak and similar to a whisper.

Central nervous system Brain and spinal column.

Chronic vocal abuse Repeated or habitual abuse of the voice, i.e., cheerleading.

Clavicular breathing Method of breathing in which the upper chest, collarbones and shoulders are raised in an effort to expand the chest.

Cleft palate Congenital condition in which the palate or roof of the mouth fails to fuse during the prenatal period.

Congenital Present at birth.

Contact ulcers Lesions which occur at the posterior ends of the vocal folds or on the vocal processes themselves and which are thought to be the result of repeated forceful adduction of the arytenoid cartilages or of gastroesophageal reflux.

Conus elasticus Deep layer of lamina propria (cover of the vocal folds). This is the layer of dense connective tissue lying immediately above the vocalis muscle which is covered by the more elastic superficial layer of the lamina propria and the squamous epithelium.

Cordectomy Removal of vocal cords.

Cornu Horn-like projection or part of a cartilage. On the thyroid cartilage they extend both up (**Superior Cornu**) and down (**Inferior Cornu**) from the posterior aspect. The ends of the U of the hyoid bone are considered its **Greater Cornu**, and the projections on the superior aspect are the **Lesser Cornu**.

Crescendo Growing louder.

Cricoarytenoid muscles Paired muscles originating at the muscular process of the arytenoid cartilages. The posterior cricoarytenoids attach to the outer rim of the cricoid cartilages and act to close or adduct the cords. The lateral cricoarytenoids attach along the outer sides of the cricoid cartilages and act to abduct or open the cords.

Cricoid cartilage The topmost ring of the trachea and base of the larynx. It resembles a signet ring because the posterior aspect slopes gradually up to a higher point than the anterior aspect.

Cricothyroid muscles Muscles extending from outside center of the anterior of the cricoid cartilage to the inside of the sides of the thyroid cartilage. The **vertical** cricothyroid lengthens and stiffens the cords by pulling the front of the cricoid cartilage higher and closer to the thyroid cartilage. The **lateral** cricothyroid lengthens and tenses the cords by pulling the back of the cricoid cartilage back.

Cyst A sac filled with liquid.

Decrescendo Growing softer.

Diaphragm Dome-shaped muscle that separates the thoracic and abdominal cavities and assists in inspiration.

Diaphragmatic breathing System of breathing in which the diaphragm flattens downward and the abdomen protrudes to allow for maximum expansion of the lungs.

Dorsum Back.

Dyplophonia Phonation at two different pitch levels simultaneously; can be due to simultaneous vibration of true and false vocal cords or asynchronous vibrations of the true vocal folds.

Dysphonia Disturbed phonation.

Edema/oedema Swelling caused by accumulation of fluid in the tissues.

Elasticity Ability to stretch beyond original size and shape and to return to the original size and shape.

Erythema Red coloration caused by irritation and dilation of capillaries.

Epiglottis The "lid" of the larynx; cartilage rising anteriorly from the thyroid cartilage.

Etiology Medical or scientific cause of disease or malfunction.

Eustachian tube Tube connecting the middle ear with the throat.

Exhalation Expelling or releasing air from the lungs.

Extrinsic laryngeal musculature Muscles which surround and support the larynx and by which its relationship to the surrounding structures can be altered.

Falsetto Series of tones which are produced when the vocal bands are thinned and dampened so that only the anterior-most portion vibrates.

Fibrous Tissue composed of threadlike structures.

Flow phonation Vocal sound produced with optimum balance between vocal cord pressure and subglottic air pressure.

Formant Frequency of the vibrations of vocal tract resonators.

Frequency The number of cycles per second produced by a given pitch.

Functional voice disorder A voice disorder which is caused by incorrect usage rather than by disease or malformation in the vocal tract.

Fundamental frequency The sound produced by the vibrator before resonance is added; thus, the lowest tone of a resonated sound.

Glottal attack Initiating a vowel by forcing apart tightly adducted vocal folds with air pressure.

Glottal chink Opening between the vocal cords.

Glottal fry An extremely low-pitched sound produced by the vocal folds; so-called because the sound comes out in closely spaced pops, not unlike the sound of grease frying.

Glottal stop Initiation of sound by building up sub-glottic air pressure so the cords are forcefully blown apart as phonation begins.

Glottis Space between the vocal cords.

Granulation tissue Grainy or fleshy masses formed in wounds.

Granulomas Growths composed of granulation tissue.

Harmonic Vibration which is a multiple of the fundamental.

Hemangioma A tumor composed of blood vessels which forms on the vocal cords as the result of trauma.

Hematoma Sac filled with blood.

Hemi- Prefix meaning half.

Hemilaryngectomy Surgical removal of one side of the larynx.

Hoarseness Term used to describe the sound of vocal symptoms of disturbed phonation which is usually related to increased mass and incomplete closure of the vocal folds.

Hyoid Bone U-shaped bone at base of the tongue from which the larynx is suspended.

Hyperfunction Term used by Emil Froeschels to indicate over-contraction of the muscles of the larynx and the resonators.

Hypofunction Term used by Froeschels to indicate the condition in which the muscles of the larynx and resonators have inadequate muscle tonus because of previous excessive use.

Illustrative therapy Term used by Morton Cooper to describe the contact of the voice therapy client with previous clients who have successfully overcome similar voice problems.

Impedance Obstruction to airflow.

Incomplete closure Failure of the cords to adduct completely to the midline thus leaving an opening or "chink" through which air escapes.

Indirect laryngoscopy Examination of the vocal cords using a mirror placed near the soft palate. The cords are seen in a reverse image.

Infraglottic Below the level of the vocal cords.

Intensity Acoustic correlate of volume.

Intra-tracheal intubation Insertion of a tube into the larynx and windpipe to monitor and assist with a patient's breathing.

Jitter Irregular variations in fundamental frequency.

Keratosis Build up of "horny" tissue.

Lamina propria The portion of the mucosa of the vocal cords which lies between the vocalis muscle and the epithelium. It is divided into a superficial, intermediate and deep layers composed of gelatinous, elastic and fibrous tissue, respectively. The intermediate and deep layers comprise the vocal ligament, while the less opaque superficial layer, called Reineke's space, is where most pathologies occur.

Laryngeal mirror Small, hand-held mirror specially designed to be used to view the larynx through the mouth.

Laryngeal paralysis Loss of muscle power in the larynx due to loss of innervation, usually of the laryngeal nerve.

Laryngeal strap muscles Extrinsic laryngeal muscles, those which attach the larynx to other body structures.

Laryngeal ventricle The space between the true and false cords.

Laryngeal web Malformation in which the glottis is covered partially or completely by a thin membrane. Generally congenital, but sometimes the result of prolonged trauma such as bulemia.

Laryngologist A licensed member of the medical profession who specializes in the disorders and treatment of the larynx by medication and/or surgery. An **Otolaryngologist** is one whose specialty also includes the organs of hearing.

Laryngopharynx Lower throat; the area above the larynx.

Lateral Side.

Lesions Growths.

Leukoplakia Build up of mucous membrane characterized by white patches; may be a precancerous condition.

Lombard effect Tendency to increase volume of one's own voice to compensate for surrounding noise.

Low register Laryngeal adjustment in which vocal bands are thick, so called because it is used for low pitches.

Malocclusion Faulty positioning of the teeth or jaws so that the relationship between upper and lower jaws is out of line.

Mandible Lower jaw.

Mucosa Mucous membrane; lining the upper respiratory tract including all laryngeal surfaces.

Mucous Lubricating secretion which coats and protects body passages and cavities.

Myasthenia Muscular weakness.

Nasolaryngopharynx Upper throat and nose area.

Nasopharynx Area of pharynx above soft palate.

Nebulization A spray of fine mist.

Necrosis Death of tissue.

Nodule Build up of fibrous tissue at the edge of the vocal cord; resembles a callous.

Oedema See Edema.

Omohyoid muscle Extrinsic laryngeal muscle which runs down the side of the neck and connects hyoid bone to scapula.

Organic voice disorder Voice disorder caused by physical changes or illness.

Oropharynx Upper throat or rear of mouth.

Otolaryngologist See Laryngologist.

Papillomas Warty epithelial growths that occur, often in clusters, in the airways. They may be viral in origin and occur especially in young children.

Paretic hoarseness Term used by Emil Froeschels to denote muscular weakness secondary to excessive strain or hyperfunction. The voice is heard as rough or husky.

Periodic Occurring regularly; used to describe vibrations causing sound.

Pharyngeal wall Back wall of the oral cavity.

Pharynx Throat.

Phonation The production of sounds by vocal cords.

Pianissimo Very soft.

Pitch Level of sound or voice related to the musical scale.

Pitch break Sudden, uncontrolled change in pitch.

Polyps Lesions of the vocal cords which are filled with fibrous tissue and blood or fluid.

Pressed phonation Vocal sound produced with excessively tight vocal cord closure, often with inadequate breath flow.

Professional voice user Anyone whose profession depends upon the quality and endurance of his or her voice; includes singers, actors, lecturers, clergy, teachers, salespeople and others.

Psychogenic Functional problem originating with emotional or psychological factors.

Pulsated voice Laryngeal adjustments, usually at low pitches, which allow the sound to be emitted at such a slow rate of vibration that it is heard as rhythmic pulses. Sometimes called vocal fry.

Register Series of consecutive tones of like quality which are produced using same muscular coordination; from low to high they include fry, low or chest, upper or falsetto, and whistle or flute.

Register break Abrupt shift of muscular coordination in the larynx resulting in a sudden change in vocal tone quality

Resonance Addition of supplemental vibrations to enrich or intensify sound.

Resonators Bony portions and cavities of the neck and head which add vibrations to the fundamental sound produced by the vocal cords. Includes the mouth, nose and sub- and supra-glottic areas of the throat.

Respiration Process of inhaling and exhaling breath to sustain life.

Retracted/retroflex tongue Tongue position pulled back in the throat, often with its base thrust down.

Scapula Shoulder blade.

Septum Cartilage separating the two sides of the nose.

Soft palate Soft part of the roof of the mouth directly behind the hard palate, separates nasal passages from the mouth.

Speech pathologist A professional who holds at least a Master's Degree in Speech Pathology and Audiology and is certified by the American Speech-Language-Hearing Association. While many are trained in treatment of voice disorders, speech pathology itself is directed primarily at the manner in which vowels, consonants and words are formed.

Sternohyoid muscles Extrinsic laryngeal muscles which connect the hyoid bone to the sternum or breastbone.

Sternum Flat, vertical bone which forms the front of the chest and to which the upper ribs and clavicle or collarbone are attached.

Steroids Any chemical compound with the basic structure of sterol. Steroid has come to mean synthesized hormones which are functionally similar to those produced by the cortex of the adrenal gland.

Stridency A harsh, grating, usually high-pitched, voice quality.

Styloid process Pointed, downward extension of the temporal bone or lower side of the skull below the ear.

Stylopharyngeus muscles Extrinsic laryngeal muscles which connect the styloid process of the arytenoid cartilages to the rear of the thyroid cartilage.

Submucosal hemorrhage Rupture of blood vessels in the vocalis muscle.

Synovial joints Joints which are contained in a sac and lubricated by synovial fluid.

Temporomandibular joint The "hinge" of the jaw. The joint which connects the temporal bone or lower part of the skull with the mandible or lower jaw.

Tessitura Notes around which most of the melody lies. Pitches most often used in song or aria.

Thorax Part of the body between the neck and abdomen; enclosed by the ribs, sternum and spine.

Thyroarytenoid muscles Pair of intrinsic laryngeal muscles extending from the muscular processes of the arytenoid cartilages to the inside of the anterior aspect of the thyroid cartilages. The inner edges form the vocalis muscle. With their mucosal cover they form the main body of the vocal cords.

Thyrohyoid muscles Extrinsic laryngeal muscles which connect the sides of the thyroid cartilage to the hyoid bone.

Thyroid cartilage The top ring of the trachea and the largest of the cartilages making up the larynx; it encloses the front and sides of the larynx with two shield-like wings.

Thyroid notch Anterior protuberance formed by the thyroid cartilage where its two sides fuse; sometimes called the Adam's apple.

Timbre Quality or color of sound.

Topical Medication applied to the skin or mucosa.

Trachea Windpipe.

Unilateral One side.

Unvoiced Consonants produced without laryngeal vibration, e. g., [p] and [t].

Uvula Small fleshy protuberance from the posterior of the soft palate.

Upper register Laryngeal adjustments in which the vocal bands are thinned and stiffened; used for higher pitches.

V-notch Thyroid notch.

Velopharyngeal closure Closing off the nasal passages from the mouth and throat by raising the soft palate and by the anterior and lateral movements of the pharyngeal wall.

Velum Soft palate.

Ventricular dysphonia Vocal sound produced with the false cords instead of or in addition to the true cords.

Ventricular folds False vocal cords; bands of tissue located parallel to and above the true cords.

Virilization Masculinization of the female; specifically changes in the secondary sex characteristics because of changes in the woman's hormonal balance.

Viscera Internal organs located within body cavities, especially those in the abdomen.

Vocal cords The outer edge of the thyroarytenoid muscles; the thyroarytenoid ligaments.

Vocal folds Also known as vocal cords or vocal bands; the thyroarytenoid ligaments.

Voice Sound produced by vibration of the vocal cords and supplemented by resonance of the vocal tract.

Voice coach A professional who works with the singer or actor on text alone or, with the singer, as the text relates to the musical setting. The coach works primarily on pronunciation of the words and interpretation.

Voice scientist   A professional who uses scientific methods of research, controlled experiments and measurement to study the capabilities of the vocal tract acoustically, physiologically and aerodynamically. The voice scientist is usually trained as a speech pathologist, psychologist, anatomist, engineer or voice teacher.

Voice teacher   A professional whose interest and background are music-centered; the voice teacher trains the singer in vocal technique, languages and interpretation.

Voice therapist   A professional trained to diagnose and treat disorders of the voice by retraining. Must be certified by the American Speech-Language-Hearing Association. Most states now require licensing.

References

Abitbol, J. (1988). Vocal cord hemorrhages in voice professionals. *Journal of Voice* , **2**, 261-266.

Abitbol, J., de Brux, J., Millot, G., Maison, M. F., Mimoun, O. L., Paw, H., & Abitbol, B. (1989). Does a hormonal vocal cord cyst exist in women? Study of vocal premenstrual syndrome in voice performers by videostroboscopy-glottography and cytology on 38 women. *Journal of Voice*, **3**, 157-162.

Abramson, A. L., Essman, E., & Steinberg, B. (1984). Membrane receptors for 17-B-Estradiol in the human larynx. In V. L. Lawrence (Ed.), *Transcripts of the Twelfth Symposium Care of the Professional Voice. Part II: Vocal therapeutics, respiration, medical*, (pp. 292-294). New York: The Voice Foundation.

Abramson, A. L., Steinberg, B. M., Gould, W. J., Bianco, E., Kennedy, R., & Stock, R. (1985). Estrogen receptors in the human larynx: Clinical study of the singing voice. In V. L. Lawrence (Ed.), *Transcripts of the Thirteenth Symposium Care of the Professional Voice Part II* (pp. 409-413). New York: The Voice Foundation.

Adler, S. (1960). Clinical forum: Some techniques for treating the hypernasal voice. *Journal of Speech and Hearing Disorders*, **25**, 300-302.

Andrews, M., & Shank, K. H. (1983, July). Some observations concerning the cheering behavior of school-girl cheerleaders. *Language, Speech and Hearing Services in Schools*, **14**, 150-156.

Appelman, D. R. (1967). *The science of vocal pedagogy.* Bloomington: Indiana University Press.

Arnold, G. E. (1964). Clinical application of recent advances in laryngeal physiology. *Annals of Otology, Rhinology and Otolaryngology*, **73**, 426-442.

Aronson, A. E. (1985). *Clinical voice disorders: An interdisciplin-*

aryapproach (2nd ed.). New York: Thieme, Inc.

Bain, W. M., Harrington, J. W., Thomas L. E., & Schafer, S. D. (1983). Head and neck manifestations of gastroesophageal reflux. *Laryngoscope,* **9 3**, 175.

Baker, D., Jr. (1962). Laryngeal problems in singers. *Laryngoscope,* **7 2**, 902-908.

Barlow, W. (1973). *The Alexander Technique.* New York: Alfred A. Knopf.

Batza, E. M. (1977). Adventures in vocal rehabilitation. In M. Cooper & M. H. Cooper (Eds.), *Approaches to vocal rehabilitation* (pp. 3-21). Springfield, IL: Charles C. Thomas.

Bell, W. E. (1990). *Temporomandibular disorders: Classification, diagnosis, management* (3rd ed.). Chicago: Year Book Medical.

Bernthal, J. E., & Bankson, N. W. (1981). *Articulation disorders.* Englewood Cliffs, NJ: Prentice-Hall.

Bless, D. M. (1983). Treatment of functional voice disorders. In W. H. Perkins (Ed.), *Voice disorders* (pp. 21-30). New York: Thieme-Stratton.

Boone, D. R. (1980). Vocal hygiene: The optimal use of the larynx. *Journal of Research in Singing,* **4**, 35-43.

Boone, D. R. (1983). *The voice and voice therapy.* Englewood Cliffs, NJ: Prentice-Hall.

Boone, D. R. (1984). Some considerations of optimum pitch. In V. L. Lawrence (Ed.), *Transcripts of the Twelfth Symposium Care of the Professional Voice. Part I: Vocal therapeutics, respiration, medical* (pp. 143-147). New York: The Voice Foundation.

Boone, D. R. (1988). Respiratory training in voice therapy. *Journal of Voice,* **2**, 20-25.

Boone, D. R. (1991). Expanding perspectives in care of the speaking voice. *Journal of Voice,* **5**, 168-172.

Brewer, D. W., Gould, L., & Hale, D. E. (1984). Diaphragmatic hernia and the singer. In V. L. Lawrence (Ed.), *Transcripts of the*

Twelfth Symposium Care of the Professional Voice (pp. 229-232). New York: The Voice Foundation.

Brodnitz, F. S. (1961). *Vocal rehabilitation.* Rochester, MN: Whiting Press.

Brodnitz, F. S. (1962). Functional disorders of the voice. In N. Levin (Ed.), *Voice and speech disorders: Medical aspects* (pp. 453-481). Springfield, IL: Charles C. Thomas.

Brodnitz, F. S. (1971). Hormones and the human voice. *Bulletin New York Academy of Medicine,* **47**, 183-191.

Brodnitz, F. S. (1983). Treatment of post mutational voice disorders. In W. H. Perkins (Ed.) *Voice disorders* (pp. 69-73). New York: Thieme-Stratton.

Brown, W. S., Jr., Morris, R. J., & Michel, J. F. (1989). Vocal jitter in young adult and aged female voices. *Journal of Voice,* **3**, 113-119.

Brown, W. S., Jr., Morris, R. J., & Michel, J. F. (1990). Vocal jitter and fundamental frequency characteristics in aged, female professional singers. *Journal of Voice,* **4**, 135-141.

Bryce, D. P. (1974). *Differential diagnosis and treatment of hoarseness.* Springfield, IL: Charles C. Thomas.

Campbell, J. E. (1980, May/June). Rebuilding the damaged singing voice. *NATS Bulletin,* **23**, 20-27.

Case, J. L. (1984). *Clinical management of voice disorders.* Rockville, MD: Aspen Systems Corp.

Cherry, J., & Margulies, S. I. (1968). Contact ulcer of the larynx. *Laryngoscope,* **73**, 1937-1938.

Clayman, C. B. (Med. Ed.) (1989). *The American Medical Association encyclopedia of medicine.* New York: Random House.

Coleman, R. (1980, January). Objective measurements of the singer's voice as a "damage risk" indication. *Journal of Research in Singing,* **3**, 17-23.

Cooper, D. S. (1988). The laryngeal mucosa in voice production. *Ear, Nose and Throat Journal,* **67**, 332-351.

Cooper, M. (1970). Vocal suicide in singers. *NATS Bulletin,* **26**, (7) 10+.

Cooper, M. (1973). *Modern techniques of vocal rehabilitation.* Springfield, IL: Charles C. Thomas.

Cooper, M. (1977). Direct vocal rehabilitation. In M. Cooper & M. H. Cooper (Eds.), *Approaches to vocal rehabilitation* (pp. 22-41). Springfield, IL: Charles C. Thomas.

Cooper, M. (1983). Treatment of functional aphonia and dysphonia. In W. H. Perkins (Ed.), *Voice disorders* (pp. 75-79). New York: Thieme-Stratton.

Cooper, W. (1975). *Don't change.* New York: Stein and Day.

Cregler, L. L., & Mark, H. (1986). Special report: Medial complications of cocaine abuse. *New England Journal of Medicine,* **215**, 1495-1500.

Damsté, P. H. (1987). Disorders of the voice. In P. M. Still (Ed.), *Scott-Brown's otolaryngology* (5th ed., Vol. 5, pp. 119-143). London: Butterworth's.

Damsté, P. H., & Lerman, J. W. (1975). *An introduction to voice pathology.* Springfield, IL: Charles C. Thomas.

Daniloff, R., Schuckers, G., & Feth, L. (1980). *The physiology of speech and hearing: An introduction.* Englewood Cliffs, NJ: Prentice-Hall.

Darby, J. K. (1981). The interaction between speech and disease. In J. K. Darby, Jr. (Ed.), *Speech evaluation in medicine* (pp. 3-43). New York: Grune & Stratton.

Drudge, M. K. M., & Philips, B. J. (1976). Shaping behavior in voice therapy. *Journal of Speech and Hearing Disorders,* **41**, 398-411.

Eckel, F., & Boone, D. (May, 1981). The s/z ratio as an indicator of laryngeal pathology. *Journal of Speech and Hearing Disorders,* **46**, 147-149.

Eisenson, J., & Ogilvie, M. (1983). *Communication disorders in children* (5th ed.). New York: Macmillan Publishing.

Fairbanks, G. (1940). *Voice and articulation drill book.* New York: Harper & Row.

Feder, R. J. (1983). Varix of the vocal cord in the professional voice user. *Otolaryngology and Head and Neck Surgery,* **91**, 435-436.

Feudo, P., Jr., & Zubick, H. H. (1988). Strategies and outcomes of vocal rehabilitation. In M. P. Fried (Ed.), *The larynx: A multidisciplinary approach* (pp. 213-219). Boston: Little, Brown & Co.

Fields, V. A. (1947). *Training the singing voice.* New York: King's Crown Press.

Fisher, H. B. (1975). *Improving voice and articulation* (2nd ed.). Boston: Houghton Mifflin.

Fox, D. R., & Blechman, M. (1975). *Clinical management of voice disorders.* Lincoln, NE: Cliff Notes.

Frazier, C. A. (1974). *Coping with food allergy.* New York: Times Books.

Frenzel, H. (1986). Fine structure and immunohistological studies on polyps of human vocal folds. In J. A. Kirchner (Ed.), *Vocal fold histopathology: A symposium* (pp. 39-50). San Diego: College-Hill Press.

Fried, M. P., & Miller, S. M. (1988). Adult laryngeal anatomy. In Marvin P. Fried (Ed.), *The larynx: A multidisciplinary approach* (pp. 41-55). Boston: Little, Brown & Co.

Friedmann, I., & Ferlito, A. (1988). *Granulomas and neoplasms of the larynx.* Edinburgh: Churchill Livingstone.

Fritzell, B., & Hertegard, S. (1986). A retrospective study of treatment for vocal fold edema: A preliminary report. In J. A. Kirchner (Ed.), *Vocal fold histopathology: A symposium* (pp. 57-64). San Diego: College-Hill Press.

Froeschels, E. (1940). Laws in the appearance and development of vocal hyperfunction. *Journal of Speech Disorders,* **5**, 1-4.

(*Selected papers of Emil Froeschels.* Amsterdam: North-Holland Publishing, 1964.)

Froeschels, E. (1943). Hygiene of the voice. *Archives of Otolaryngology,* **38**, 122-130. (*Selected papers of Emil Froeschels.* Amsterdam: North-Holland Publishing, 1964.)

Fry, D. B. (1979). *The physics of speech.* London: Cambridge University Press.

Gelb, H. (1978). Temporomandibular joint disorders. In V. L. Lawrence (Ed.), *Transcripts of the Sixth Symposium Care of the Professional Voice, Julliard, 1977* (pp. 169-173). New York: The Voice Foundation.

Gilman, A. G., Goodman, L. S., & Gilman, A. (1980). *Goodman and Gilman's the pharmacologic basis of therapeutics* (6th ed.). New York: Macmillan.

Gould, W. J., & Lawrence, V. L. (1984). *Surgical care of voice disorders: Vol. 8 Disorders of human communication.* New York: Springer.

Gray, H., F. R. S. (1974). *Anatomy, descriptive and surgical* (1901 ed.). Philadelphia: Running Press.

Gray, S. G. (1983). Treatment of vocal abuse in adults. In W. H. Perkins (Ed.), *Voice disorders* (pp. 13-19). New York: Thieme-Stratton.

Greene, M. C. L. (1964). *The voice and its disorders.* New York: Macmillan.

Guyton, A. C. (1976). *Textbook of medical physiology* (5th ed.). Philadelphia: W. B. Saunders.

Harrison, M., & Tucker, H. M. (1987). Voice pathology. In H. M. Tucker, *The larynx* (pp. 135-162). New York: Thieme Medical.

Haskell, J. A. (1987). Vocal self-perception: The other side of the image. *Journal of Voice,* **1**, 172-179.

Hertegard, S., Gauffin, J., & Sundberg, J. (1990). Open and covered singing as studied by means of fiberoptics, inverse filtering and spectral analysis. *Journal of Voice*, **4**, 220-230.

Hinjo, I., & Isshiki, N. (1980). Laryngoscopic and voice characteristics of aged persons. *Archives of Otolaryngology*, **106**, 149-150.

Hirano, M. (1974). Morphological structure of the vocal cord as a vibrator and its variations. *FoliaPhoniatrica*, **26**, 89-94.

Hirano, M. (1981). The laryngeal examination. In J. K. Darby, Jr. (Ed.), *Speech evaluation in medicine* (pp. 47-75). New York: Grune & Stratton.

Hirano, M. (1985). Lecture: Anatomy of the larynx. In V. L. Lawrence (Ed.), *Transcripts of the Thirteenth Symposium: Care of the Professional Voice, Part II: Vocal therapeutics - medical* (pp. 329-346). New York: The Voice Foundation.

Hirano, M. (1988). Vocal mechanisms in singing: Laryngological and phoniatric aspects. *Journal of Voice*, **2**, 51-69.

Hirano, M., & Kakita, Yuki. (1985). Cover-body theory of vocal fold vibration. In R. G. Daniloff (Ed.), *Speech science: Recent advances* (pp. 1-47). San Diego: College-Hill Press.

Hirano, M., & Kurita, S. (1986). Histological structure of the vocal fold and its normal and pathological variations. In J. A. Kirchner (Ed.), *Vocal fold histopathology: A symposium* (pp. 17-24). San Diego: College-Hill Press.

Hirano, M., Kurita, S., Matseo, K., & Nagata, K.. (June, 1981). Vocal fold polyp and polypoid vocal fold (Reineke's edema). *Journal of Research in Singing*, **4**, 33-44.

Hirano, M., Tanaka, S., Yoshida, T., & Hihi, S. (1990). Sulcus vocalis: Functional aspects. *Anals of Otology, Rhinology and Laryngology*, **99**, 679-683.

Hirano, M., Yoshida, T., Kurita, S., Kiyokawa, K., Sato, K., & Tateiski, O. (1985). Anatomy and behavior of the vocal process. In T. Baer, C. Sasaki & K. S. Harris (Eds.), *Laryngeal function in phonation and respiration* (pp. 3-13). Boston: Little, Brown & Co.

Hixon, T. J., & Hoffman, C. (1979). Chest wall shape in singing. In B. Weinberg and V. L. Lawrence (Eds.), *Transcripts of the Seventh Symposium Care of the Professional Voice, Julliard, 1978* (pp. 9-10). New York: The Voice Foundation.

Hollein, H. (1974). On vocal registers. *Journal of Phonetics, 2*, 125-143.

Hollein, H. (1977). The registers and ranges. In M. Cooper & M. H. Cooper (Eds.), *Approaches to vocal rehabilitation* (pp. 76-121). Springfield, IL: Charles C. Thomas.

Hollein, H. (1985). That golden voice -- talent or training? In V. L. Lawrence (Ed.), *Transcripts of the Thirteenth Symposium Care of the Professional voice. Part I: Scientific papers* (pp. 279-289). New York: The Voice Foundation.

Hollein, H., Gould, W. J., & Johnson, B. (1974, August 25-29). A two-level concept of vocal registers. In E. Loebel (Ed.), *Proceedings XVIth International Congress of Logopedics and Phoniatrics* (pp. 188-194). Basil: S. Karger.

Isshiki, N. (1989). *Phonosurgery theory and practice.* Tokyo: Springer.

Johnson, T. S. (1985). Voice disorders: The measurement of clinical progress. In J. M. Costello (Ed.), *Speech disorders in adults: Recent advances* (pp. 3-12). San Diego: College-Hill Press.

Kahane, J. C., & Hammons, J. A. (1985). Developmental changes in the articular cartilage of the human cricoarytenoid joint. In T. Baer, C. Sasaki & K. S. Harris (Eds.), *Laryngeal function in phonation and respiration* (pp. 4-28). Boston: Little, Brown & Co.

Kambic, V., & Radsel, Z. (1984). Acid posterior laryngitis. *The Journal of Laryngology and Otology, 98*, 1237-1240.

Kambic, V., Radsel, Z., Zargi, M., & Acko, M. (1981). Vocal cord polyps: Incidence, histology and pathogenesis. *Journal of Otolaryngology and Otology, 95*, 609.

King, H. C. (1990). *An otolaryngologist's guide to allergy.* New York: Thieme Medical.

Kleinsasser, O. (1979). *Microlaryngoscopy and endolaryngeal microsurgery* (2nd ed.) (P. M. Still, Trans.). Baltimore: University Park Press.

Kleinsasser, O. (1986). Microlaryngoscopic and histologic appearance of polyps, nodules, cysts, Reineke's edema, and granulomas of the vocal cords. In J. A. Kirchner (Ed.), *Vocal fold histopathology a symposium* (pp. 51-55). San Diego: College-Hill Press.

Koufman, J. A., & Blalock, P. D. (1988). Vocal fatigue and dysphonia in the professional voice user: Bogart-Bacall syndrome. *Laryngoscope, 98*, 493-498.

Koufman, J. A., Wiener, G. J., Wallace, C. W., & Castel, D. O. (1988). Reflux laryngitis and its sequelae: The diagnostic role of ambulatory 24-hour pH monitoring. *Journal of Voice, 2*, 78-89.

Landes, B. A. (1977). Management of hyperfunctional dysphonia and vocal tension. In M. Cooper & M. H. Cooper (Eds.), *Approaches to vocal rehabilitation* (pp. 122-137). Springfield, IL: Charles C. Thomas.

Large, J., & Patton, R. (1981). The effects of weight training and aerobic exercise on singers. *Journal of Research in Singing, IV*, 23-32.

Lavorato, A. S., & McFarlane, S. C. (1983). Treatment of the professional voice. In W. H. Perkins (Ed.), *Voice disorders* (pp. 51-61). New York: Thieme-Stratton.

Lawrence, V. L. (1983, March/April). Laryngoscope: Do buzzards roost in your mouth at night? *NATS Bulletin, 39* (4), 19-20.

Lawrence, V. L. (1987). Common medications with laryngeal effects. *Ear, Nose and Throat Journal, 66*, 318-322.

Leanderson, R., & Sundberg, J. (1988). Breathing for singing. *Journal of Voice, 2*, 2-12.

LeBaron, R. (1972). *Hormones a delicate balance.* Indianapolis: The Bobbs-Merrill Co.

Lin, P. T., Stern, J. C., & Gould, W. J. (1991). Risk factors and management of vocal cord hemorrhages: An experience with 44 cases. *Journal of Voice, 5*, 74-77.

Linville, S. E. (1987). Acoustic-perceptual studies of aging voice in women. *Journal of Voice*, **1**, 44-48.

Lumpkin, S. M. M., Bishop, S. G., & Katz, P. (1989). Chronic dysphonia secondary to gastroesophageal reflux disease (GERD): Diagnosis using simultaneous dual-probe prolonged pH monitoring. *Journal of Voice*, **3**, 351-355.

Martin, F. G. (1985). Drugs and the voice -- Part II. In V. L. Lawrence (Ed.)., *Transcripts of the Thirteenth Symposium Care of the Professional Voice. Part I: Scientific papers* (pp. 191-201). New York: The Voice Foundation.

Martin, F. G. (1988). Drugs and vocal function, *Journal of Voice*, **2**, 338-344.

Massett, L., & Sutherland, E. W., III. (1975). *Everyman's guide to drugs and medicines.* Washington, D.C.: Robert B. Luce.

McClosky, D. B. (1959). *Your voice at its best.* Boston: Little, Brown & Co.

McClosky, D. B. (1977). General techniques and specific procedures for certain voice problems. In M. Cooper and M. H. Cooper (Eds.), *Approaches to vocal rehabilitation*, (pp. 138-152) Springfield, IL: Charles C. Thomas.

McFarlane, S. C. (1988). Treatment of benign laryngeal disorders with traditional methods and techniques of voice therapy. *Ear, Nose and Throat Journal*, **67**, 425-428, 430-432, 434-435.

McFarlane, S. C., & Lavorato, A. S. (1983). Treatment of psychogenic hyperfunctional voice disorders. In W. H. Perkins (Ed.) *Voice disorders* (pp. 31-37). New York: Thieme-Stratton.

Meyer-Breiting, E., & Burkhardt, A. (1988). *Tumors of the larynx.* Berlin: Springer.

Michaels, L. (1984). *Pathology of the larynx.* Heidelberg: Springer.

Michel, J. L., & Weinstein, L. (1988). Laryngeal infections. In Marvin P. Fried (Ed.), *The larynx: A multidisciplinary approach* (pp. 237-247). Boston: Little, Brown & Co.

Moore, G. P. (1971a). *Foundations of speech pathology series: Organic voice disorders.* Englewood Cliffs, NJ: Prentice-Hall.

Moore, G. P. (1971b). Voice disorders organically based. In L. E. Travis (Ed.), *Handbook of speech pathology and audiology* (pp. 535-569). New York: Meredith Corp.

Morris, R. J., & Brown, W. S., Jr. (1987). Age-related voice measures among adult women. *Journal of Voice,* **1**, 38-43.

Morrison, M. D. (1985). Muscle tension dysphonia. In V. L. Lawrence (Ed.), *Transcripts of the Thirteenth Symposium Care of the Professional Voice Part II* (pp. 419-421). New York: The Voice Foundation.

Morrison, M. D., & Morris, B. D. (1990). Dysphonia and bulemia: Vomiting laryngeal injury. *Journal of Voice,* **4** , 76-80.

Mossallam, I., Kotby, M. N., Ghaly, A. F., Nassar, A. M., & Barakah, M. A. (1986). Histopathological aspects of benign vocal fold lesions associated with dysphonia. In J. A. Kirchner (Ed.), *Vocal fold histopathology: A symposium* (pp. 65-80). San Diego: College-Hill Press.

Mowrer, D. E., & Case, J. L. (1982). *Clinical management of speech disorders.* Rockville, MD: Aspen Systems Corp.

Murphy, A. T. (1964). *Foundations of speech pathology: Functional voice disorders.* Englewood Cliffs, NJ: Prentice-Hall.

Murry, T. (1982a). Phonation: Assessment. In N. J. Lass, L. V. McReynolds & J. Northern (Eds.), *Speech, language and hearing: Pathologies of speech and language* (Vol. 2, pp. 477-488). Philadelphia: W. B. Saunders.

Murry, T. (1982b). Phonation: Remediation. In N. J. Lass, L. V. McReynolds & J. Northern (Eds.), *Speech, language and hearing: Pathologies of speech and language* (Vol. 2, pp. 489-498). Philadelphia: W. B. Saunders.

Myerson, M. C. (1964). *The human larynx.* Springfield, IL: Charles C. Thomas.

Negus, V. E. (1931). *The mechanism of the larynx.* St. Louis: The C. V. Mosby Co.

Pennoyer, D., & Sheffer, A. (1988). Immunologic disorders of the larynx. In M. P. Fried (Ed.), *The larynx: A multidiscipli-nary approach* (pp. 279-290). Boston: Little, Brown & Co.

Perez-Reyes, M., Di Guiseppi, S., Ondrusek, G., Jeffcoat, A. R., & Cook, C. E. (1982). Free-base cocaine smoking, *Clinical Pharmacology and Therapeutics*, **31**, 459-465.

Perkins, W. H. (1971). Vocal function: Assessment and therapy. In L. E. Travis (Ed.), *Handbook of speech pathology and audiology* (pp. 505-534). New York: Meridith Corp.

Perkins, W. H. (1977). Behavioral management of vocal abuse: A case of contact ulcers. In M. Cooper & M. H. Cooper (Eds.), *Approaches to vocal rehabilitation* (pp. 175-192). Springfield, IL: Charles C. Thomas.

Perkins, W. H. (1979). Mechanism of vocal abuse. In B. Weinberg & V. L. Lawrence (Eds.), *Transcripts of the Seventh Symposium Care of the Professional Voice, Julliard, 1978* (part 2, pp. 106-115). New York: The Voice Foundation.

Perkins, W. H. (1983). Optimal use of voice: Prevention of chronic vocal abuse. *Seminars in Speech and Language*, **4**, 273-286.

Perkins, W. H. (1985). Assessment and treatment of voice disorders: State of the art. In J. M. Costello (Ed.), *Speech disorders in adults: Recent advances* (pp. 79-112). San Diego: College-Hill Press.

Perkins, W. H., & Kent, R. D. (1986). *Functional anatomy of speech, language and hearing: A Primer.* San Diego: College-Hill Press.

Phonatory mechanisms panel discussion. (1980). In V. L. Lawrence (Ed.), *Transcripts of the Eighth Symposium Care of the Professional Voice, Julliard, 1979* (part 2, pp. 76-77). New York: The Voice Foundation.

Physicians' Desk Reference (45th ed.) (1991). Oradell, NJ: Edward R. Barnhardt.

Physicians' Desk Reference (48th ed.) (1994). Montvale, NJ: David W. Sifton

Pogosov, V. S., & Antoniv, V. F. (1987). *Microscopy and micro-surgery of the larynx and laryngopharynx*. (V. N. Bespalyi, Trans.). Madison, CT: International Universities Press.

Polow, N. G., & Kaplan, E. D. (1979). *Symptomatic voice therapy*. Tulsa, OK: Modern Education Corp.

Prater, R. J., & Swift, R. (1984). *Manual of voice therapy*. Boston: Little, Brown & Co.

Proctor, D. F. (1980a). Breath the power source for the voice. In V. L. Lawrence (Ed.), *Transcripts of the Eighth Symposium Care of the Professional Voice, Julliard, 1979* (part 2, pp. 14-18). New York: The Voice Foundation.

Proctor, D. F. (1980b). *Breathing, speech and song*. New York: Springer.

Punt, N. A. (1967). *The singer and actor's throat* (2nd rev. ed.). London: William Heinemann Medical Books.

Putnam, A. H. B., & Shelton, R. L. (1985). Speech production: Anatomy and physiology. In P. H. Skinner & R. L. Shelton (Eds.) *Speech, language and hearing: Normal processes and disorders* (2nd ed., pp. 82-121). New York: John Wiley & Sons.

Rang, H. P., & Dale, M. M. (1987). *Pharmacology*. Edinburgh: Churchill Livingstone.

Reed, C. G. (1983). Treatment of postsurgical laryngeal pathology. In W. H. Perkins (Ed.), *Voice disorders* (pp. 89-95). New York: Thieme Stratton.

Ringel, R. L., & Chadzko-Zajko, W. J. (1987). Vocal indices of biological age. *Journal of Voice*, **1**, 31-37.

Rubin, H. J. (1966, May). Role of the layrngologist in management of dysfunctions of the singing voice. *NATS Bulletin*, **2 2**, 22-27.

Rubin, H. J., & Lehrhoff, I. (1962). Pathogenesis and treatment of vocal nodules. *Journal of Speech and Hearing Disorders*, **2 7**, 150-161.

Sasaki, C. T. (1988). Laryngeal physiology: Normal and abnormal. In M. P. Fried (Ed.), *The larynx: A multidisciplinary approach* (pp. 57-68). Boston: Little, Brown & Co.

Sataloff, R. T. (1981). Professional singers: The science and art of clinical care. *American Journal of Otolaryngology, 2*, 251-266.

Sataloff, R. T. (1985). Evaluation and treatment of professional singers: An overview for laryngologists. In V. L. Lawrence (Ed.), *Transcripts of the Thirteenth Annual Symposium Care of the Professional Voice, Part II* (pp. 293-328). New York: The Voice Foundation.

Sataloff, R. T. (1987a). The professional voice: Part I. Anatomy, function, and general health. *Journal of Voice, 1*, 92-104.

Sataloff, R. T. (1987b). The professional voice: Part II. Physical examination. *Journal of Voice, 1*, 191-201.

Sataloff, R. T. (1987c). The professional voice: Part III. Common diagnoses and treatments. *Journal of Voice, 1*, 283-292.

Sataloff, R. T. (1991). Structural and neurological disorders and surgery of the voice. In R. T. Sataloff (Ed.), *Professional voice: The science and art of clinical care* (267-299). New York: Raven Press Ltd.

Sataloff, R. T., O'Connor, M. J., & Heuer, R.J. (1984). Rehabilitating a quadriplegic singer. In V. L. Lawrence (Ed.), *Transcripts of the Twelfth Symposium Care of the Professional Voice. Part II: Vocal therapeutics, respiration, medical* (pp. 233-236). New York: The Voice Foundation.

Sataloff, R. T., Spiegel, J. R., Carroll, L. M., Darby, K. S., & Rulnik, R. K. (1987). Objective measures of voice function. *Ear, Nose and Throat Journal, 66*, 307-312.

Sato, K., Hirano, M., Kurita, S., & Kiyokawa, K. (1990). Distribution of elastic cartilage in the arytenoids and its physiologic significance. *Annals of Otology, Rhinology and Laryngology, 99*, 363-368.

Saunders, W. H. (1964). *The larynx.* Summit, NJ: CIBA Pharmaceutical Co. (Reprinted from *Clinical Symposia, 16* [3], 67-99.)

Schechter, G. L., & Coleman, R. F. (1984, February). Care of the professional voice. *Otolaryngologic Clinics of North America*, **17**, 131-137.

Scherer, R. C., Titze, I. R., Raphael, B. N., Wood, R. P., Ramig, L. A., & Blager, F. B. (1985). Vocal fatigue in a trained and an untrained voice user. In T. Baer, C. Sasaki & K. S. Harris (Eds.), *Laryngeal function in phonation and respiration* (pp. 533-555). Boston: Little, Brown & Co.

Schneiderman, C. R. (1984). *Basic anatomy and physiology in speech and hearing*. San Diego: College-Hill Press.

Schroeder, S. A., Krupp, M. A., Tierney, L. M., Jr., & McPhee, S. J. (1990). *Current medical diagnosis and treatment 1990*. Norwalk, CT: Appleton & Lange.

Schweitzer, V. G. (1986, February). Osteolytic sinusitis and pneumomediastinum: Deceptive otolaryngologic complications of cocaine abuse. *Laryngoscope*, **96**, 206-210.

Seyfer, A. E., & Jacob, S. W. (1993). Surgery in the patient with scleroderma. *The Connector*, **22**, 4-5.

Shanks, J. C. (1983). Treatment of resonance disorders. In W. H. Perkins (Ed.) *Voice disorders* (pp. 39-49). New York: Thieme-Stratton.

Shanks, J. C., & Duguay, M. (1984). Voice remediation and the teaching of alaryngeal speech. In S. Dickson (Ed.), *Communication disorders remedial principles and practices* (2nd ed., pp. 240-287). Glenview, IL: Scott Foresman and Co.

Shapiro, S. L. (1973). Clinic of the month: On the management of professional voice disorders. *Eye, Ear, Nose and Throat Monthly*, **52**, 328-331.

Shelton, R. L. (1985). Disorders of phonation. In P. H. Skinner & R. L. Shelton (Eds.), *Speech, language and hearing: Normal processes and disorders* (2nd ed., pp. 268-304). New York: John Wiley & Sons.

Shemen, L. J. (1988). Diseases of the thyroid as they affect the larynx. In M. P. Fried (Ed.), *The larynx: A multidisciplinary approach* (pp. 223-233). Boston: Little, Brown & Co.

Shipp, T. (1979). Vertical laryngeal position in singers with jaw stabilized. In B. Weinberg & V. L. Lawrence (Eds.), *Transcripts of the Seventh Symposium Care of the Professional Voice, Julliard, 1978* (part I, pp. 44-47). New York: The Voice Foundation.

Shipp, T. (1987). Vertical laryngeal position: Research findings and application for singers. *Journal of Voice*, 1, 217-219.

Shipp, T., Sundberg, T., & Haglund, S. (1985). A model of frequency vibrato. In V. L. Lawrence (Ed.) *Transcripts of the Thirteenth Symposium Care of the Professional Voice. Part I: Scientific papers* (pp. 116-117). New York: The Voice Foundation.

Shumrick, K. A., & Shumrick, D. A. (1988). Inflammatory diseases of the larynx. In M. P. Fried (Ed.), *The larynx: A multidisciplinary approach* (pp. 249-278). Boston: Little, Brown & Co.

Spiegal, J. R., Sataloff, R. T., Cohn, J. R., & Hawkshaw, M. (1988). Respiratory function in singers: Medical assessment, diagnoses and treatments. *Journal of Voice*, 2, 40-50.

Stanley, D. (1957). *Your voice: Applied science of vocal art* (3rd ed.). New York: Pitman Publishing.

Stone, R. E., Jr. (1984). Application of intervention in functional dysphonia. In V. L. Lawrence (Ed.), *Transcripts of the Twelfth Symposium Care of the Professional Voice. Part II: Vocal Therapeutics, respiration, medical* (pp. 175-183). New York: The Voice Foundation.

Sundberg, J. (1985). Supralaryngeal contributions to vocal loudness and projection. In V. L. Lawrence (Ed.), *Transcripts of the Thirteenth Symposium Care of the Professional Voice. Part I: Scientific papers* (pp. 202-211). New York: The Voice Foundation.

Sundberg, J. (1990). What's so special about singers? *Journal of Voice*, 4, 107-119.

Tarasco, S. (1984). Correction of the phonorespiratory mechanism at the laryngologist's office. In V. L. Lawrence (Ed.), *Transcripts of the Twelfth Symposium Care of the Professional Voice. Part II: Vocal therapeutics, respiration, medical* (pp. 224-227). New York: The Voice Foundation.

Teter, D. L. (1977, October). Vocal nodules: Their cause and treatment. *Music Educators Journal*, **6 4**, 38-41.

Thurman, W. L. (1977). Restructuring voice concepts and production. In M. Cooper & M. H. Cooper (Eds.), *Approaches to vocal rehabilitation* (pp. 230-255). Springfield, IL: Charles C. Thomas.

Titze, I. (1988). A framework for the study of vocal registers. *Journal of Voice*, **2**, 183-194.

Tucker, H. M. (1987). *The larynx.* New York: Thieme Medical.

Van Deinse, J. B., Frateur, L., & Keizer, J. (1974). Problems of the singing voice. *Folia Phoniatrica*, **2 6**, 428-434.

Van den Berg, J. (1958). Myoelastic-aerodynamic theory of voice production. *Journal of Speech and Hearing Research*, **1**, 227-243.

Van den Broeck, P. (1987). Acute and chronic laryngitis, leucoplakia. In P. M. Still (Ed.), *Scott-Brown's otolaryngology* (5th ed., Vol. 5, pp. 99-118). London: Butterworth's.

Van Riper, C., & Irwin, J. V. (1958). *Voice and articulation.* Englewood Cliffs, NJ: Prentice-Hall.

Vaughan, C. W., & Gould, W. J. (1988). Management of vocal pathology in the voice professional. In M. P. Fried, (Ed.), *The larynx: A multidisciplinary approach* (pp. 203-212). Boston: Little, Brown & Co.

Vaughan, C. W., & Strong, M. S. (1984, November). Medical management of organic laryngeal disorders. *Otolaryngologic Clinics of North America*, **1 7**, 705-712.

Vennard, W. (1967). *Singing, the mechanism and the technic.* New York: Carl Fischer.

Von Leden, H., Chm. (1978). Medical care of the professional voice. Panel Discussion. In V. L. Lawrence (Ed.), *Transcripts of the Sixth Symposium Care of the Professional Voice, Julliard, 1977* (pp. 174-179). New York: The Voice Foundation.

Von Leden, H., & Moore, P. (1960). Contact ulcers of the larynx: Experimental observations. *Archives of Otolaryngology*, **7 2**, 746.

Walker, J. S. (1988). An investigation of the whistle register in the female voice. *Journal of Voice*, **2**, 140-150.

Ward, P. H., Zweitman, D., Hanson, D., & Berci, G. (1980). Contact ulcers and granulomas of the larynx: New insights into their etiology as a basis for more rational treatment. *Otolaryngology and Head Neck Surgery*, **88**, 262-269.

Way, L. W. (1988). *Current surgical diagnosis and treatment.* Norwalk, CT: Appleton & Lange.

Welch, G. F., Sergeant, D. C., & MacCurtain, F. (1988). Some physical characteristics of the male falsetto voice. *Journal of Voice*, **2**, 151-163.

Williamson, A. B. (1944). Diagnosis and treatment of eighty-four cases of nasality. *The Quarterly Journal of Speech*, **20**, 471-479.

Wilner, L. K., & Sataloff, R. T. (1987). Speech-language pathology and the professional voice. *Ear, Nose and Throat Journal*, **66**, 313-317.

Wilson, K. D. (1977). Voice problems of children and teenagers. In M. Cooper and M. H. Cooper (Eds.), *Approaches to vocal rehabilitation* (pp. 256-274). Springfield, IL: Charles C. Thomas.

Wood, C. (1969). *Birth control now and tomorrow.* London: Peter Davies.

Wyatt, G. L. (1977). The chewing method and the treatment of the speaking voice. In M. Cooper and M. H. Cooper (Eds.), *Approaches to vocal rehabilitation* (pp.274-298). Springfield, IL: Charles C. Thomas.

Wyke, B. (1980). Neurological aspects of phonatory control systems in the larynx: A review of current concepts. In V. L. Lawrence (Ed.), *Transcripts of the Eighth Symposium Care of the Professional Voice, Julliard, 1979* (part 2, pp. 42-53). New York: The Voice Foundation.

Yanagihara, N. (1967). Significance of harmonic change and noise components in hoarseness. *Journal of Speech and Hearing Research*, **10**, 531-541.

Yanagihara, N., Koike, Y., & Von Leden, H. (1966). Phonation and respiration. *FoliaPhoniatrica*, **1 8**, 323-340.

York, W. (1957, May 15). The F. M. Alexander technique in singing. *NATS Bulletin*, **1 3**, 28-29.

Index

Note: Names of authors appearing in the References have not been included.

vowel modification, 52
vowel spectral noise levels,
        123

wandering hum, 28, 37
wandering vowel, 37
warm-up, 49, 54, 73, 98, 100,
        104, 119, 163
warming down, 98-99
warming up, 98,
wave length, 57
weight lifting, 117-118
whisper, 46, 88, 100, 131,
        148, 168
whistle register, 61, 66, 175
windpipe, 1, 39, 172, 177
Winstral Tablets, 115

yawn-sigh, 35, 39
    technique, 43

About the Author

Marilee David attended Cornell College and received her Bachelor of Music and Master of Music degrees in voice from the University of Illinois at Urbana-Champaign. She received her Doctor of Music in voice performance from Indiana University at Bloomington. Dr. David lives and performs in Atlanta, Georgia, where she teaches voice at the Dunwoody School for the Arts. Her previous teaching experience includes Armstrong State College in Savannah, Georgia, St. Mary-of-the-Woods College in St. Mary-of-the-Woods, Indiana, Concordia College in Moorhead, Minnesota, and Central Missouri State College in Warrensburg. Her articles have appeared in the *Journal of Research in Singing* and the *NATS Journal*.